WITHDRAWN

BEYOND CHINA'S INDEPENDENT FOREIGN POLICY

BEYOND CHINA'S INDEPENDENT FOREIGN POLICY

Challenge for the U.S. and Its Asian Allies

Edited by
James C. Hsiung

**Published under the Auspices
of the Contemporary U.S.–Asia
Research Institute, Inc.
New York, N.Y.**

PRAEGER SPECIAL STUDIES • PRAEGER SCIENTIFIC

New York • Philadelphia • Eastbourne, UK
Toronto • Hong Kong • Tokyo • Sydney

Library of Congress Cataloging in Publication Data
Hsiung, James Chieh, 1935-
   Beyond China's independent foreign policy.

   "Published under the auspices of the Contemporary
U.S.-Asia Research Institute, Inc., New York, NY."
   Bibliography: p.
   Includes index.
   1. China—Foreign relations—1976-.   I. Title.
DS779.27.H75 1985   327.51   84-26306
ISBN 0-03-002578-8 (alk. paper)

Published in 1985 by Praeger Publishers
CBS Educational and Professional Publishing, a Division of CBS Inc.
521 Fifth Avenue, New York, NY 10175 USA

© 1985 by Praeger Publishers

All rights reserved

56789 052 987654321

Printed in the United States of America on acid-free paper

INTERNATIONAL OFFICES

Orders from outside the United States should be sent to the appropriate address listed below. Orders from areas not listed below should be placed through CBS International Publishing, 383 Madison Ave., New York, NY 10175 USA

Australia, New Zealand
Holt Saunders, Pty, Ltd., 9 Waltham St., Artarmon, N.S.W. 2064, Sydney, Australia

Canada
Holt, Rinehart & Winston of Canada, 55 Horner Ave., Toronto, Ontario, Canada M8Z 4X6

Europe, the Middle East, & Africa
Holt Saunders, Ltd., 1 St. Anne's Road, Eastbourne, East Sussex, England BN21 3UN

Japan
Holt Saunders, Ltd., Ichibancho Central Building, 22-1 Ichibancho, 3rd Floor, Chiyodaku, Tokyo, Japan

Hong Kong, Southeast Asia
Holt Saunders Asia, Ltd., 10 Fl, Intercontinental Plaza, 94 Granville Road, Tsim Sha Tsui East, Kowloon, Hong Kong

Manuscript submissions should be sent to the Editorial Director, Praeger Publishers, 521 Fifth Avenue, New York, NY 10175 USA

Preface

This volume embraces the premise that China's self-proclaimed "independent" foreign policy in the early 1980s is for real and is here to stay. That policy means carefully calibrating Beijing's good relations with the United States and also seriously seeking a normalization of relations with the Soviet Union. We raise the question: What is in store for us *beyond* China's independent foreign policy? The chapters that follow answer the question from a conceptual and theoretical perspective, as well as from a country or regional point of view (for example, the United States, Japan, Southeast Asia, which includes the ASEAN nations, Taiwan, and so on).

I wish to thank my fellow coauthors, who worked hard and finished on time, some going through more than one draft. To Peter Berton, who took on two early chapters and finished them despite personal hardships, I owe a special gratitude. I enjoyed working with this group of fine scholars and colleagues. In interpreting Beijing's present "independent" foreign policy, I also benefited enormously from insights provided by a few scholars from China, who shall remain anonymous.

Many individuals have helped me in the preparation of my own chapters and also in my work as editor of the entire volume; and yet, only a few can be singled out for acknowledgment. Among them are Rajini Balachandran, Patricia K. Lane, Lauren Lung, and Omer Karasapan, all of whom rendered valuable research assistance.

This book is sponsored by the Contemporary U.S.-Asia Research Institute, Inc., New York, N.Y., whose primary function is research on U.S.-Asian relations and intra-Asian relations. The views of the contributors, however, do not necessarily represent those of the Institute. Each wrote as a scholar and from his conscience. While each contributor is responsible for the contents of his chapter, I alone, of course, bear the responsibility for the overall design of the final product.

JCH

Contents

Preface		v
Introduction *James C. Hsiung*		1

Chapter

1	The Asian Strategic Balance and China *Peter Berton*	7
2	A Turn in Sino-Soviet Relations? *Peter Berton*	24
3	The Reagan Administration Turnaround on China *Stephen Uhalley, Jr.*	55
4	Implications of Changing Sino-Japanese Relations for the Future of the U.S.-Japan Nexus *George O. Totten*	71
5	Southeast Asia in the Sino-Soviet Tangle *Sheldon W. Simon*	80
6	The Taiwan Factor in U.S.-Beijing Relations *Winberg Chai and Shao-chuan Leng*	95
7	Sino-U.S.-Soviet Relations in a Triadic-Game Perspective *James C. Hsiung*	107
8	China's Foreign Policy: Domestic-International Linkages *Gavin Boyd*	132
9	Some Propositions on U.S. Credos about Sino-American Relations *Steve Chan*	152
10	Challenge of China's Independent Foreign Policy *James C. Hsiung*	166
Bibliography		190
Index		202
About the Editor and Contributors		213

Introduction

James C. Hsiung

When the People's Republic of China (PRC) broke with its former Soviet ally in the 1960s and eventually entered into a strategic partnership with the United States in the 1970s, it was hailed as the twentieth century's greatest turnaround. But, in the early 1980s, the PRC is consciously distancing itself from Washington and seeking a détente with Moscow. Premier Zhao Ziyang had to disappoint his guest Ronald Reagan during the President's 1984 visit, by reiterating China's genuine desire to "normalize" relations with the Soviet Union. Instead of endorsing his anti-Soviet crusade, as Reagan had hoped, the Chinese leader urged that the United States likewise end its deadlock with Moscow, for the sake of world peace. Premier Zhao repeated the same theme during his six-nation Western European swing a few weeks later, May 29-June 16, 1984.

The PRC's new stance is billed as its "independent foreign policy." In this volume, we attempt to explore the significance and implications of this new Chinese policy, especially its challenge for the United States and its Asian allies.

The PRC began its existence with a close alliance with the Soviet Union, signed in 1950. In less than 13 years, it broke its Party-to-Party relations with the CPSU (Communist Party of the Soviet Union) after a series of disputes dating from Khrushchev's de-Stalinization campaign in 1956 and a polemic war that peaked in 1963. Only perfunctory state-to-state relations were carried on since then. After much name calling and public linen washing and a hot border war (spring 1969), the PRC found itself in the company of the industrial West. Its strident verbal clashes with the Soviets were carried into the United Nations after the PRC's entry in October, 1971.

Following China's normalization of relations with Japan and the United States, the Sino-Soviet feud spilled over into other areas, such as

Indochina. The Kampuchea war, in which the Chinese-supported Khmer Resistance forces are fighting a Hanoi-installed regime, is sometimes called a "proxy" war fought because of the larger Sino-Soviet clash. The PRC's "pedagogical war" against Vietnam in February-March 1979—so called because the Chinese trooped in to "teach the Vietnamese a lesson"—was a function of heightened Sino-Soviet tensions, too.

The precipitating events were the signing of the Sino-Japan peace treaty in August, 1978, and Soviet entry into an alliance with Vietnam in November 1978. The latter was Moscow's response to what it considered to be a collusive China-Japan-U.S. entente. The entente, as it turned out, was more nominal than real. But the Soviet-Vietnamese alliance was real. Consequently, the Soviet Pacific Fleet, the largest of all Moscow's naval contingents, has gained the right to use Vietnam's Cam Ranh Bay. Vietnamese forces, bolstered by massive Soviet support, invaded and occupied Kampuchea in December 1978. Soviet aid, reportedly amounting to $5,000,000 a day, has helped prop up Hanoi's failing economy, weighted down by its operations against the Chinese-backed insurgents in Kampuchea.

The Kampuchea problem and the Soviet occupation of Afghanistan since the end of 1979 became two of the three outstanding issues that Beijing insists must be resolved if relations are to improve with Moscow. The third Chinese demand is pullout of Soviet troops along Chinese borders, estimated at 50 divisions.

The Chinese in April, 1979 notified Moscow that the Sino-Soviet alliance treaty would not be renewed on its thirtieth anniversary the following year. They nevertheless called for normalization of relations on the basis of the five principles of peaceful coexistence. Border talks, which had been on and off for 10 years, were resumed in September, 1979, but were soon disrupted by the Soviet invasion of Afghanistan at year's end.

On the Chinese side, the "thaw" was a long time in the coming. Back in December, 1979, an internal conference on Soviet literature was held in Northeast China (Manchuria), an area with extended periods of contacts with Russia in history. Despite the name of the conference, one of its findings was that the Soviets under the present regime were not "revisionists" but merely responding to changed circumstances that required creative adaptations of the Communist creed. The following spring, Wang Youping, former Ambassador to the Soviet Union, in a talk to the rank and file in the PRC Foreign Ministry, raised the question whether the Soviets were acting like "chauvinists" in East Europe. Thanks to Soviet assistance, Wang said, living standards in most East European countries were higher than in the Soviet Union itself. How could the Soviets, Wang asked rhetorically, be considered "chauvinistic" under the circumstances?

In the Chinese congratulatory message on the seventy-third anniversary of the October Revolution in 1981, Beijing responded favorably to an

Introduction 3

earlier Soviet message of felicitations, on China's October 1 National Day, which contained a suggestion for improving relations. In the spring of 1982, in a speech in Tashkent, President Brezhnev bent backwards to show conciliation to Beijing and made an earnest pitch for improving relations. Responding to the Soviet imprimatur, the 12th Congress of the Chinese Communist Party (CCP), meeting in September 1982, finalized a decision to press ahead with a normalization with the Soviet Union. That is part of the Chinese "independent" foreign policy mentioned above.

Important shifts have gradually but unmistakably taken place since 1982. Talks were resumed in October and since then have been held alternately in Beijing (October) and Moscow (March) each year. By the end of 1984, five rounds have been held at the Vice Foreign Minister level.

Although no breakthroughs are expected soon, contacts have been increasing on various fronts. There have been exchanges of visits by officials, scholars, and experts. Reversing its previous position, Beijing has dropped its insistence that Moscow show "deeds" before talks. It is now amenable to accept nonpolitical agreements before resolving political issues. Some functional agreements have been signed, covering cooperation in meteorological and environmental monitoring, exchanges of publications, and so forth. Under the latest trade agreement, bilateral trade for 1984 was increased to $1.2 billion.

A border trading port was opened at Huo City, Xinjiang, on November 17, 1983. There were reports that a new Soviet consulate would be opened in Shanghai, in return for a Chinese consultate to be established in the Soviet Union. As an unfailing sign of improved atmosphere, the Soviet-Chinese Friendship Association in Moscow adopted a resolution on January 25, 1984, calling on the Soviet government to push for better relations with China. A Chinese delegation visited the Soviet Union in early June, 1984, led by former Ambassador to Poland Wang Bingnan, who heads the Chinese People's Society for Friendship with Foreign Countries. It was received by a candidate member of the Politburo in Moscow. Significantly, the mission was not affected by the postponement of a visit to China scheduled for early May 1984 by First Deputy Premier Ivan Arkhipov, who would have been the highest ranking Soviet official to arrive since Premier Kosygin's stopover at the Beijing airport to meet with Premier Zhou Enlai in the fall of 1969.*

Any country's foreign policy is purportedly independent. But the word "independent" used by the Chinese for their own new policy has a certain ring to it. It conveys China's aims (1) to improve relations with its

---

*Arkhipov finally arrived on December 21, 1984. While in Beijing, he concluded four agreements on cooperation in trade, economic, and science and technology matters. Significantly, the arrangements resemble those which existed in the 1950's, at the height of the Sino-Soviet alliance.

Soviet neighbor, (2) to continue the good relations with the United States but to avoid getting too close to it, and (3) to find common cause with the Third World. Beijing puts a lot of weight on the epithet "independent," to dramatize its desire not to lose control over its foreign policy choices, and to shed the stigma of its erstwhile "stable marriage" with the United States, especially in the eyes of the Third World. The three parts of the new policy, which is designed to maximize China's foreign policy benefits and minimize its costs, are interrelated.

The current Chinese policy began to take shape from the end of 1981, although the desire to normalize relations with Moscow was first made known during the spring of 1979. The three components of the policy were codified at the 12th Party Congress in September 1982.

As we shall see in this volume, the Chinese are not abandoning their good ties with the United States, only to keep them below the level of any commitments that would upset Moscow. Nor do they expect another honeymoon with the Soviet Union. Nonetheless, they are committed to moving the stalemated Sino-Soviet relations off dead center. Their own security considerations are among the reasons calling for a genuine continuing dialogue with the Soviets. Certain "confidence-building" measures, such as advance notification on troop movements and observation of each other's military exercises, have been raised in the course of the confidential bilateral talks. But, for the Chinese, their security in the age of the bisuperpower nuclear arms race is not a bilateral matter, either in the Sino-U.S or Sino-Soviet sense. It would require (1) prior stability across the triad—hence, normalization in all three dyads is necessary—and (2) removing confrontation for a negotiated settlement in the U.S.-Soviet dyad. That, as we shall see, is the most significant rationale for China's current policy vis-à-vis the two superpowers.

From the standpoint of 1984, there is, to say the least, a reciprocal interest between Beijing and Moscow to continue their détente course. That is not likely to be disrupted by temporary deflections, such as the postponement of Arkhipov's visit. Shortly after the announced postponement, Premier Zhao Ziyang on May 15, 1984 assured the National People's Congress that the Chinese government "sincerely hopes for a normalization of Sino-Soviet relations and is willing to develop economic, technical, and cultural exchanges" with the Soviet Union. China would not give up improving relations with the Soviets "merely" because we oppose their hegemonism," he stressed.

China is once again wooing the Third World, with which it is ideologically and sentimentally in tune. Because China was too closely identified with the "American imperialists" during the 1970s, its influence suffered conspicuous decline for some time. At the 1979 nonaligned nations' conference in Havana, for example, when Fidel Castro of Cuba denounced China and the United States as the two "arch-enemies" of the Third World, no nation stood up in China's defense, other than Pakistan. To make amends with the Third World, therefore, also requires that the Chinese distance themselves somewhat from Washington. If the Third World can be counted solidly on its side, the PRC would have augmented its political capital in dealing with the two superpowers.

Hu Yaobang, the CCP's General Secretary, told the 12th Party Congress "our adherence to an independent foreign policy accords with the discharging of our lofty international duty to safeguard world peace and promote human progress." Deng Xiaoping, China's ultimate leader, put it more bluntly: "No foreign country can expect China to be its vassal or expect it to swallow any bitter fruit detrimental to its interests." The new emphasis on China's "independence" is evident.

All indications are that the Chinese independent foreign policy is for real and is going to continue. However, perceptions in the United States seem to lag behind the changing reality, especially among those who have stakes in the previous game plan to forge a common U.S.-PRC alliance against Moscow. It behooves us, therefore, to gain a clear understanding of the latest developments and their implications. In this volume, we do not see the latest realignments as necessarily bad for the United States. In fact, as we shall see, reduced tensions between any two players could be stabilizing for the entire Sino-U.S.-Soviet triad and have auspicious effects all around. Nevertheless, the new Chinese policy stance does pose a challenge for our own policy and requires some hard thinking.

One central question posed to each of the contributors to the present volume is: What lies beyond China's new independent foreign policy for your country or area of specialization? The first two chapters provide the background, the first one exploring the state of the East Asian strategic balance and examining China's changing relations with the two superpowers and Japan, and the second chapter zeroing in on the vicissitudes and evolution of Sino-Soviet relations. Both also discuss the role of the United States and how it shapes up in light of the related shifts. Chapter 3 looks at China itself and its new relations with Washington as the Sino-Soviet conflict is being attenuated. Chapter 4 through 6 look at the implications of China's new posture for Japan, Southeast Asia (including the ASEAN countries), and Taiwan.

The next three chapters attempt to grapple with more theoretical and conceptual dimensions. To varying degrees, they attempt to bring certain social-scientific insights to the study of China's relations with the two superpowers and other nations. Chapter 7 examines the dynamics of the Sino-U.S.-Soviet triad as a 3-person game, and suggests strategic-coalitional reasons why China wants to defuse its tensions with Moscow and put some limits on its good ties with the United States. Chapter 8 explores the linkage between China's domestic political process and its foreign policy realignments. Chapter 9 suggests some common problems ("credos") besetting Americans in their understanding of China's foreign policy. They in effect can explain why, despite the fact that the Sino-U.S. anti-Soviet league of the late 1970s is gradually changing or taking on a different shape, many Americans, including some experts, are yet to catch up with the new reality in their perception.

The concluding chapter, incorporating insights and findings of the preceding chapters, puts the question in perspective. Drawing certain lessons from the past, it takes note of the virtues of China's independent foreign policy and suggests a new policy for the United States to ponder.

The Asian Strategic Balance and China
—— 1 ——
Peter Berton

China, a regional Asian power, has the potential to become a global power. Although it is a very poor, underdeveloped country, China's population of over one billion (accounting for a quarter of all humanity) brings it into the top ten countries of the world in gross national product (GNP)—even with a low "Third World" per capita income. Just a modest rate of economic growth over the next few years is likely to make the Chinese economy the fifth largest in the world, after the United States, Japan, the Soviet Union, and West Germany. While the bulk of its economy is agricultural and rather primitive by modern standards, China was able to perform impressive technological feats, particularly in the development of nuclear weapons and missiles. China's military forces are equipped with outdated, if not obsolete, weapons, yet it is one of the very few nuclear powers, with an ever-increasing delivery capability. And while during the first two decades of its existence it was ostracized and isolated from most of the world community and from international organizations, the People's Republic of China is today one of the five veto-wielding permanent members of the Security Council of the United Nations.

It is because of these seemingly contradictory attributes that China is often characterized as a potential rather than an actual global power. Yet, China's breakout from the Soviet-Communist alliance system has given it the opportunity to play an independent role in the global strategic balance of power, a feat that neither Western Europe nor Japan has been willing or able to perform.

How and when did this happen? How did it affect the strategic balance at the regional level in Asia and in the global equation? To answer these questions one must first look at the evolution of the strategic balance in Asia since the end of World War II, particularly the relative weight of the United States and the Soviet Union and the alignment of other powers, including, after 1949, the People's Republic of China. I will then try to conceptualize the strategic balance and the Asian alignments, and offer some thoughts that might help the reader as he moves on to the chapters that follow.

The Evolution of the Asian Strategic Balance

The Pacific phase of the Second World War ended with a decisive Allied victory over the Japanese Empire, but only the United States was in a strong, if not dominant, position in that part of the world. In fact, while the occupation of Japan was supposed to be an Allied enterprise, General Douglas MacArthur was designated as the Supreme Commander of the Allied Powers (SCAP) and also Commander-in-Chief of the American Far East Command, running the Japanese occupation for all practical purposes as a U.S. show.

The Soviet Union was so exhausted by the end of the war that its troops occupying Manchuria stripped that area of everything movable and shipped half a million Japanese prisoners (both military and civilian) to Siberia, where they were kept for several years to help rebuild the Soviet economy.[1] Nationalist China, assigned a Big Power status by the Allies, including a permanent seat on the Security Council of the newly established United Nations, soon descended into the throes of a civil war, effectively precluding it from playing more than a marginal role in the affairs of the region. (Chinese Nationalist troops were withdrawn from northern Vietnam in 1947.) Southeast Asia became the scene of a prolonged struggle for independence that further weakened the already exhausted old colonial powers—Great Britain, France, and the Netherlands. And Japan, of course, was a devastated, occupied nation. It would be no exaggeration, therefore, to claim that after World War II there existed a Pax Americana in East Asia and the Pacific.

In 1947-48 the Cold War broke out in Europe and naturally affected Soviet-U.S. relations in Asia and the Pacific. The Soviet challenge to the U.S. position was aggravated by the victory of the Chinese Communists on the mainland in 1949 and the almost immediate signing of a Thirty Year Treaty of Friendship, Alliance, and Mutual Assistance between Mao Zedong and Joseph Stalin. But the United States successfully defended South Korea and Taiwan in the 1950s and made a determined and costly, though fruitless, effort to prevent the takeover of South Vietnam by Communist North Vietnam in the 1960s and early 1970s. This U.S. failure was more than offset, however, by the breakup of the Sino-Soviet alliance and the consequent fragmentation of Communist power in Asia. The causes and the process of the Sino-Soviet conflict are amply documented in the literature (and discussed in the next chapter), so it will suffice here to note that a point of no return between the two countries was reached in the summer of 1960 when Nikita Khrushchev abruptly recalled all Soviet technicians from China (thereby seriously hampering China's industrial development); an open break complete with vitriolic verbal attacks occurred in the summer of 1963; and serious clashes on the Sino-Soviet border took place in the spring of 1969. Yet for a long time the breakup of the Sino-Soviet alliance did not result in a corresponding weakening of Sino-American hostility. Several factors were responsible for this seeming anomaly in the dynamics of international politics.

First, China appeared to be pursuing an aggressive policy abroad and a radical course at home, exemplified by its intervention in the Korean War, the shelling of Quemoy and Matsu islands, and the inauguration of the Great Leap Forward and the communes in 1958. Second, relations were warming between the United States and the Soviet Union—the so-called Spirit of Camp David. Third, the national debate on who lost China in the early 1950s, aggravated by Senator Joseph McCarthy's threatening tactics, made an opening to Communist China (or Chicoms as the mainland Chinese Communists were pejoratively called) very difficult from the standpoint of U.S. domestic politics. More important, perhaps, the Sino-Soviet dispute was first fought out in esoteric terms on the ideological level and, given the perception of a monolithic Communist movement bound by a common Marxist-Leninist ideology, very few scholars, let alone policymakers, correctly assessed the breakdown of the Sino-Soviet alliance.[2] Some conservative commentators even denied the existence of a serious split, arguing that the disagreements were only over means ("*how* to bury us") and not ends.

By the time the dispute erupted in open polemics in 1963, the United States pursued a pro-Soviet policy by successfully negotiating a Partial Nuclear Test Ban Treaty (bitterly opposed by the Communist Chinese who needed atmospheric testing for their as yet untested nuclear weapons). Nevertheless, a signal was sent to Communist China in December 1963 (the so-called Open Door speech of Deputy Undersecretary of State Roger Hilsman to the Commonwealth Club in San Francisco).

On the Chinese side, given the nature of the Chinese anti-imperialist position accusing the Soviet Union of selling out Communist ideals by making deals with the United States, it was difficult for the Chinese leadership to approach the United States or respond to U.S. overtures. This was made even more difficult, if not impossible, by the U.S. escalation of the war in Vietnam, with U.S. bombings of North Vietnam and the eruption of the so-called Great Proletarian Cultural Revolution in China.

All this began to change in the late 1960s with the Soviet invasion of Czechoslovakia and the subsequent promulgation of the so-called Brezhnev

Doctrine, which publicized the self-proclaimed right of the Soviet Union to interfere in the internal affairs of other Communist countries (or come to the defense of socialism as it is phrased). This alone was bound to cause concern to the Chinese leaders, but the steady and dramatic increase in Soviet forces along the Sino-Soviet border was even more ominous. Bloody clashes along the border in March, 1969, initially provoked by the Chinese, added to the tension, as the international atmosphere was filled with rumors, some carefully floated by the Soviets themselves, that a Sino-Soviet war or a Soviet preemptive attack on Chinese nuclear installations was all but inevitable. The United States strongly indicated that it would not acquiesce in violent Soviet actions against China, while the Chinese leadership became convinced that only a rapprochement with, or even an opening toward, the United States would strengthen the weak Chinese position vis-à-vis their northern neighbor.

Ping-pong diplomacy and the secret Kissinger mission to China paved the way to President Nixon's visit to Beijing in February, 1972. The resultant shift in the alignments among the major powers profoundly affected the world strategic balance. The Sino-American Shanghai Communiqué reestablished a certain level in the relations between the two countries, while the Japanese, a few months later, in September 1972, leapfrogged the American accomplishment by establishing full diplomatic relations with China. In the meantime China had become a full member of the United Nations, including having the permanent veto-wielding seat on the Security Council heretofore held by the Taiwan-based Nationalist Chinese government.

The Nixon-Kissinger policy of rapprochement with China was carefully balanced by a détente with the Soviet Union, placing the United States in the enviable position of being courted by both Communist superpowers who were continually at odds with each other. At the same time, the United States attempted to disengage from Indochina without jeopardizing the security of allied regimes in South Vietnam and Cambodia and of neutral Laos. This attempt ended in failure, as Communist North Vietnam overran the South and in due course established its hegemony over the entire Indochina peninsula. The U.S. defeat in Indochina was accompanied by a substantial weakening of U.S. forces in East Asia (President Carter even proposed the withdrawal of U.S. troops from South Korea) and brought about a weak response or no response at all to various Soviet challenges in other parts of the world, most notably in Southwest Asia and Africa. This projection of Soviet power into the Western sphere of influence and the steady increase in Soviet presence and power in East Asia, accompanied as it was by the weakening position of the United States, amounted to a significant change in the correlation of forces in the world and from the Chinese point of view looked ominous indeed.

How did China respond to this dangerous situation? Deng Xiaoping's return to power in the summer of 1977 (following the death of Mao) facilitated the Chinese leadership's resolve to proceed with the ambitious Four Modernizations program to build a solid industrial society by the year 2000 (indeed the initial plans were overly ambitious and had to be drastically scaled down) and to seek closer ties, if not an overt anti-Soviet united front, with the United States, Japan, and Western Europe. This pro-Western policy received further encouragement with Vietnam's entry into Comecon, the Soviet-led economic group, in June, 1978, and a more formal treaty relationship with the Soviet Union in November, 1978 which was followed almost immediately by the Vietnamese invasion of Cambodia and destruction of the pro-Chinese Pol Pot regime. Beijing's response was to send Moscow a message in the form of a Peace and Friendship Treaty with Japan (concluded in August, 1978) and normalization of relations with the United States toward the end of the same year, as well as a limited invasion of North Vietnam in early 1979. Soviet occupation of Afghanistan less than a year later further solidified the relationship between China on the one hand and the United States, Japan, and Western Europe on the other.

In looking over this almost forty-year history of the post-World War II period in Asia and the Pacific, the following four dates have clearly affected the alignment of forces in the area and hence the strategic balance. They stand out as benchmarks:

1. 1947-1948—beginning of the Cold War and reappraisal of U.S. foreign policy (including the assignment of the role of a potential ally to Japan);
2. 1950—signing of the Thirty-Year Treaty of Alliance between the newly emergent Chinese Communist regime and Stalin's Russia, followed shortly thereafter by North Korea's invasion of South Korea;
3. 1960—irrevocable break between Khrushchev and Mao Zedong (which became fully visible in the open break in 1963 and was followed by armed clashes along the Sino-Soviet border in 1969);
4. 1972—beginning of Sino-American and Sino-Japanese rapprochement.

Other events and developments are not so clear-cut, though they have affected the strategic relationships: the gradual evolution of Germany and Japan as economic powers in the Western camp; the several periods of limited détente between the two superpowers, beginning most notably in 1958, 1963, and 1972; the long, costly, and traumatic U.S. involvement and defeat in Vietnam; the formalization and deepening of Sino-American and Sino-Japanese ties in 1978; and the basically short-term Western reactions to Soviet aggressive acts, such as the invasions of Hungary and Czechoslovakia in 1956 and 1968, the attempted stationing of offensive weapons in Cuba in 1962, the invasion of Afghanistan in 1979, and the indirect repression of the Solidarity movement in Poland shortly thereafter.

It will be noted that my last benchmark date, 1972, marks the beginning of China's opening to the United States and Japan, not 1978 which saw the consolidation of Sino-Japanese and Sino-American relations. This is because we need time to watch the duration of a development in order to judge its significance. Time and perspective are the two elements precisely lacking in our attempt to assess the significance of the rapidly evolving and seemingly important events that occurred in the years since 1978, especially as they relate to the strategic balance in East Asia and the Pacific.

Yet many scholars are not as prudent. On the heels of the improved and formalized Sino-American and Sino-Japanese relations in 1978 and the Soviet invasion of Afghanistan in 1979, they have declared the establishment of an anti-Soviet quasi-alliance among the United States, China, Japan, and Western Europe, only to beat a hasty retreat a couple of years later in the light of Sino-American difficulties (the question of Taiwan, U.S. restrictions on the export of high technology to China and the import of textiles from China, and the granting of asylum to a Chinese tennis star, among other problems) and Soviet attempts to break the deadlock in relations with their Chinese neighbors, no doubt attempting thereby to drive a wedge in China's relations with the West. Now we see a spate of articles entitled "China May Return to the Soviet Bloc" (Mineo Nakajima in *Japan Quarterly*),[3] "China Goes It Alone" (Vladimir Petrov in *Asian Survey*),[4] "China Reassesses the Superpowers" (Carol Hamrin in *Pacific Affairs*),[5] and "Sino-Soviet Rapprochement: How Far Will It Go?" (Akio Kimura in *Japan Quarterly*),[6] to mention a few.[7] And Harry Harding (in *Problems of Communism*) speculates on a new phase in Chinese foreign policy beginning in 1983 which he characterized as "Reformist Independent Leanings."[8]

In writing about the present international system and especially the strategic balance in Asia, most scholars largely focus their attention on the "strategic triangle," and generally overlook the role of Japan. An early notable exception is Ralph Clough, who in *East Asia and U.S. Security*,[9] written shortly after the momentous events of 1972, devotes a chapter to "The Four Power System," a "relatively stable . . . subsystem of the world balance of power," embracing the two superpowers, China and Japan.[10] Harold Hinton's 1975 survey of international relations in East Asia, *Three and a Half Powers: The New Balance in Asia*,[11] assigned to Japan the role of at least a half power.[12] And most recently, William Griffith wrote about "the great power Far Eastern triangle" which was becoming "quadrilateral, for Japan is fast becoming a fourth participant. . . ."[13] Otherwise, there must have been literally dozens of books and articles on "the strategic triangle" or "the great-power triangle."[14]

Conceptualization of the Strategic Balance and Asian Alignments

When I got a chance in 1980 to write about the Asian strategic balance (in the lead chapter of the symposium volume, *Asia and U.S. Foreign Policy,* by James Hsiung and Winberg Chai),[15] I stressed the quadrilateral balance in Asia between the two superpowers, China and Japan. But I also argued that rather than conceptualizing the balance as a quadrilateral relationship it made more sense to separate the quadrangle into four triangles: (1) the American-Soviet-Chinese relationship; (2) the American-Soviet-Japanese relationship; (3) the American-Chinese-Japanese relationship; and (4) the Soviet-Japanese-Chinese relationship. I have also noted that in at least two of these four triangular relationships (the Sino-Soviet-American and the Sino-Soviet-Japanese triangles), that of power "A" to power "B" has a direct bearing on their relationship to power "C." For example, Japan's relations with the Soviet Union throughout the 1970s were directly affected by the progress of negotiations on the treaty of peace and friendship between Tokyo and Beijing and particularly by the inclusion or exclusion of the highly charged word "hegemony" (Chinese code word for its northern neighbor) in the text of the treaty. Conversely, the progress of negotiations between Japan and the Soviet Union on the joint development of Siberia was very closely monitored in Beijing, with appropriate warnings dropped from time to time that if Japan proceeded with what could be construed as economic and technological aid to the Soviet in their Far Eastern territory, thereby contributing to the strengthening of the economic and strategic position of the Soviet Union in an area adjacent to China, Japan might lose out in the competition for the exploitation of China's offshore oil resources.

The following year (1981) Lowell Dittmer, in an article in *World Politics,*[16] explored the notion of the strategic triangle in general game-theoretical terms, and then applied his analysis to the Sino-Soviet-American relationship from 1949 to the post-1978 period. He posited three different systemic patterns of relationship: (1) the "ménage à trois," consisting of symmetrical amities among all three players; (2) the "romantic triangle," consisting of amity between one "pivot" player and two "wing" players, but enmity between each of the latter; and (3) the "stable marriage," consisting of amity between two of the players and enmity between each and the third.[17] Dittmer excluded from consideration the fourth pattern of enmity or hostility among all three players, a pattern which in fact in my view has a historical analog in the period from the late 1960s to the turn of the 1970s when China, the Soviet Union, and the United States were essentially in a three-way hostile relationship that resolved itself in China's opening to the United States and in a short-lived Soviet-American détente. In addition to positive and negative relations, Dittmer further distinguished between symmetrical and asymmetrical relationships. After establishing these "Rules of the Game," he looks at the origins of the strategic triangle (1949-71) and "Playing the Game," (since 1971), and offers policy implications, as well as, finally, systemic implications.

Looking at the historical record, Dittmer asserts that during roughly the first decade of the existence of the People's Republic, the pattern of interaction between China and the Soviet Union was that of "stable marriage," while both of them had a negative relationship with the United States. But this period was one of "tight bipolarity" in which there were only two true superpower decision making centers, and China was seen largely as an extension of Soviet power. The following decade (1960-69), according to Dittmer, was an ambiguous, transitional one. The relationship between China and the United States remained negative, whereas that between China and the Soviet Union became increasingly hostile. Dittmer characterizes Soviet-American relations as a détente and "an affair" rather than a stable marriage. Nonetheless, he sees the relationship between the two superpowers as positive, and tight bipolarity in the world structure as disintegrating. Indeed Dittmer credits the demise of polarity between the two camps as directly leading to the establishment of the strategic triangle in his next period, 1970-78. He characterizes the triangular relationship as a "Romantic Triangle," with the United States in the enviable position of the pivot, having positive relations with both China and the Soviet Union, while the two Communist powers continue their conflictual relationship.[18]

Dittmer sees the Sino-American relationship since 1978 as approximating a stable marriage (with the United States as the senior partner), while the Sino-Soviet relationship continues in a conflictual mode and Sino-American relations deteriorate from détente to a confrontation. Of course since Dittmer's article was published in 1981 (and probably written much earlier), he could not have foreseen the deterioration of Sino-American relations since the advent of the Reagan Administration and the halting steps toward some sort of accommodation between China and the Soviet Union.

Dittmer's analysis stimulated my thinking further, and when in 1982 I prepared a paper on recent Soviet-Japanese relations for the annual meeting of the American Association for the Advancement of Slavic Studies in Washington, D.C.,[19] I prefaced it with a schematic examination of Soviet relations in both the Soviet-Chinese-American and the Soviet-Chinese-Japanese triangles. I looked at all eight theoretically possible triangular relationships in each of the two triangles, noting the stable and unstable triangular relationships and trying to identify which of these configurations had historical analogs. It was interesting to note that, in fact, all relationships in both triangles except two had historical analogs. The two exceptions were periods of cooperation among China, the Soviet Union, and the United States (i.e., a ménage à trois) and a situation when China was a pivot, having good relations with both superpowers, while the Soviet Union and the United States were at odds with each other. I have also tried to identify the best and second best as well as the worst and second worst situations for all actors, taking into account also the disparity of power in the two triangles.

In early 1983, Professor Raju Thomas in the introduction to his edited volume, *The Great-Power Triangle and Asian Security*,[20] provided an analysis of the nature of global political relationships. He observed that these relationships within the great-power triangle have undergone radical changes since the end of World War II, and he distinguished four basic phases in the alignment among China, the Soviet Union, and the United States for the past thirty-odd years. Phase One, according to Thomas, covers the period of 1949 to 1963 and is characterized as a time of high tension and a tight bipolar structure, with China aligned with the Soviet Union against the United States. Phase Two covers the decade 1963-72, and while still a period of high tension, it is of an uncertain tripolar structure, with a three-way hostility among the Soviet Union, China, and the United States. Phase Three begins with President Nixon's trip to China in 1972 and continues to 1979, as a period of low tension and a loose bipolar structure, with a Sino-American alignment against the Soviet Union. The present phase since the Soviet invasion of Afghanistan in 1979 is characterized by Thomas as a transitional period of low tension moving from a bipolar to a tripolar structure. He sees alternating hostility and cooperation between the Soviet Union and China, and between China and the United States.[21]

However, the more I thought about these triangular and rectangular relationships, the more I became convinced that the simple cooperation and conflict options were too simple and even misleading for describing real world developments. I have, therefore, added a third, "mixed or transitional" category. This category would describe periods in a relationship when cooperative and conflictual acts alternate or when a relationship undergoes a change in one direction or another.

Strategic Analysis

My own strategic analysis (in addition to the introduction of the third category) differs in certain respects from that of Dittmer and Thomas. (See Chart 1.1) I would start with the 1945-50 period as one of bipolar confrontation between the United States and the Soviet Union. The decade of the 1950s was one of expanded confrontation between the United States on the one hand and the Soviet Union and Communist China on the other, in spite of a brief period of Soviet-American détente that lasted from 1958 to 1960 and coincided with and was not unrelated to, the beginning of the deterioration of

Sino-Soviet relations. The strategic structure during this period was tightly bipolar, with a U.S. alliance group facing a Soviet alliance group, which included China in addition to the countries of Eastern Europe.

The 1960s saw a three-way confrontation among the United States, the Soviet Union, and China, although in 1963 the two superpowers colluded

Chart 1.1 Comparative Strategic Analysis, 1945–1984

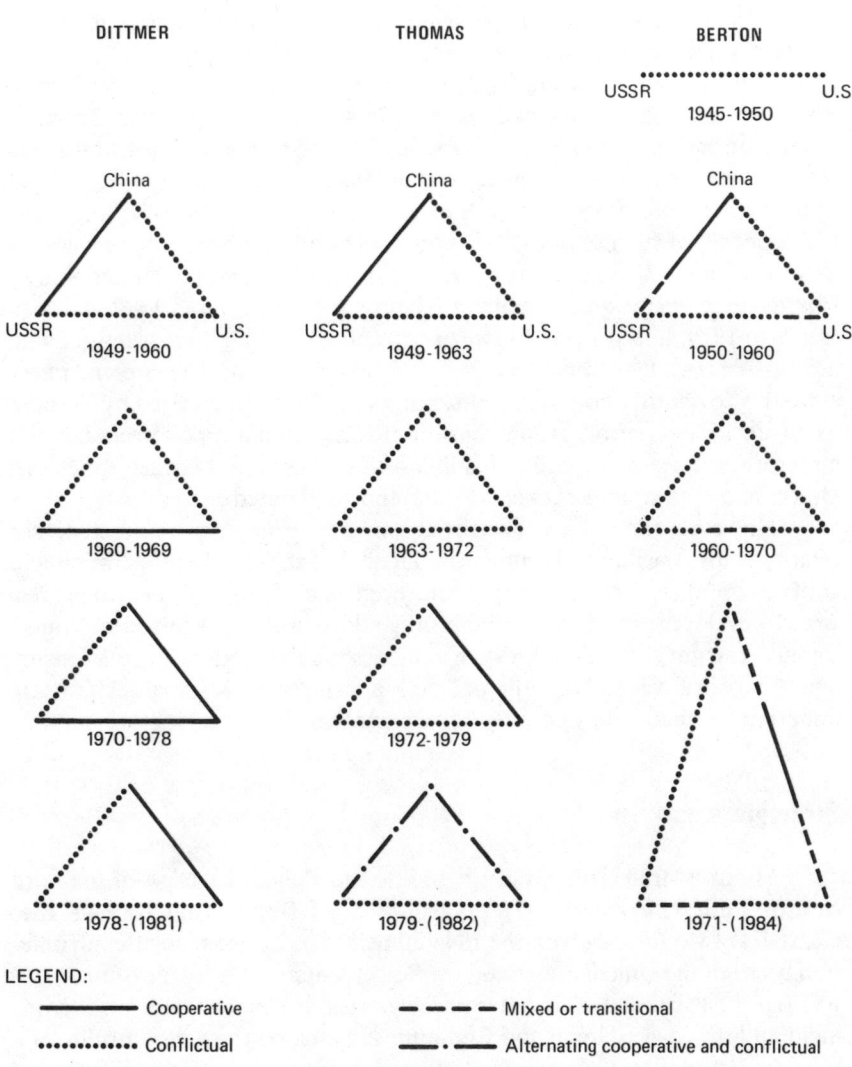

against China in the Partial Nuclear Test Ban Treaty and started a period of détente that collapsed with the Soviet invasion of Czechoslovakia in 1968. The decade of the 1960s continued to be bipolar, though the tight bipolar structure changed into a loosely bipolar one, largely as a result of disintegrating or changing alliance relationships in both camps. Parallel to the fissures in the Sino-Soviet bloc, the Western alliance also became less cohesive, with France going its own way under De Gaulle and all West European allies being dismayed by and unsupportive of the escalating U.S. intervention in Indochina.

I see the period since 1971-72 as one of continued hostility in Sino-Soviet and Soviet-American relations, and a mixed or transitional period in Sino-American relations. To be sure, there have been ups and downs within each relationship. For example, Soviet-American relations started to get better with the Nixon-Kissinger pursuit of agreements on strategic arms limitation within the context of a détente with the other superpower. But Soviet adventurism in the Third World, culminating in the invasion of Afghanistan, soured the relationship and brought it back to controlled conflict or confrontation. Sino-Soviet relations have essentially remained in a conflictual mode in spite of a series of talks in the late 1970s and the early 1980s that gave rise to speculation about the possibility of a thaw in the relations between the two. Sino-American relations warmed up for a short period before and after the Soviet invasion of Afghanistan—almost to the status of a quasi-alliance—only to cool during the first years of the Reagan Administration and to warm up again two to three years later, perhaps partially in response to the challenge of the Sino-Soviet talks.

In terms of systemic structure the present period is latently tripolar, although, because of the great disparity in power between either of the two superpowers and China, we might still find it useful to speak of a strategic bipolarity. We might also look at the tentative Sino-American-Japanese-West European anti-Soviet coalition as a sign of consolidation around the U.S. pole versus the Soviet coalition, which also acquired new members in Vietnam and Afghanistan.

Although Japan is not yet psychologically ready to exercise its immense economic power in the international arena in a diplomatically and politically meaningful way, and to a degree in an independent way, it is becoming the fourth actor in East Asia and the Pacific and is transforming the strategic triangle. Chart 1.2 presents the evolution since 1949 of the Sino-Soviet-American triangle (which can be designated as the global strategic triangle) and the Sino-Soviet-Japanese triangle (the regional strategic triangle), and it provides a schematic representation of the combined relationships among the four powers. Since the shifting fortunes of the strategic triangle have been treated earlier in this chapter, let me briefly describe the changes in the regional triangle.

Chart 1.2 Relations Among China, USSR, U.S., and Japan, 1949–1984

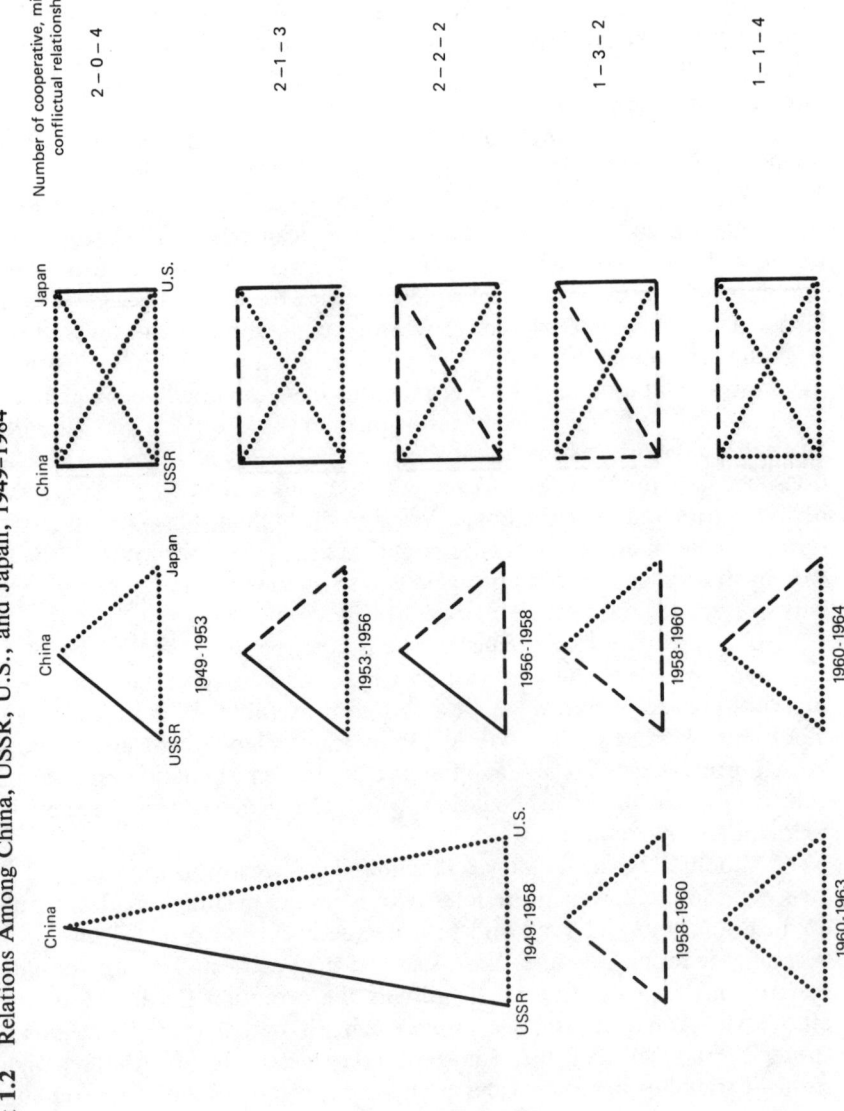

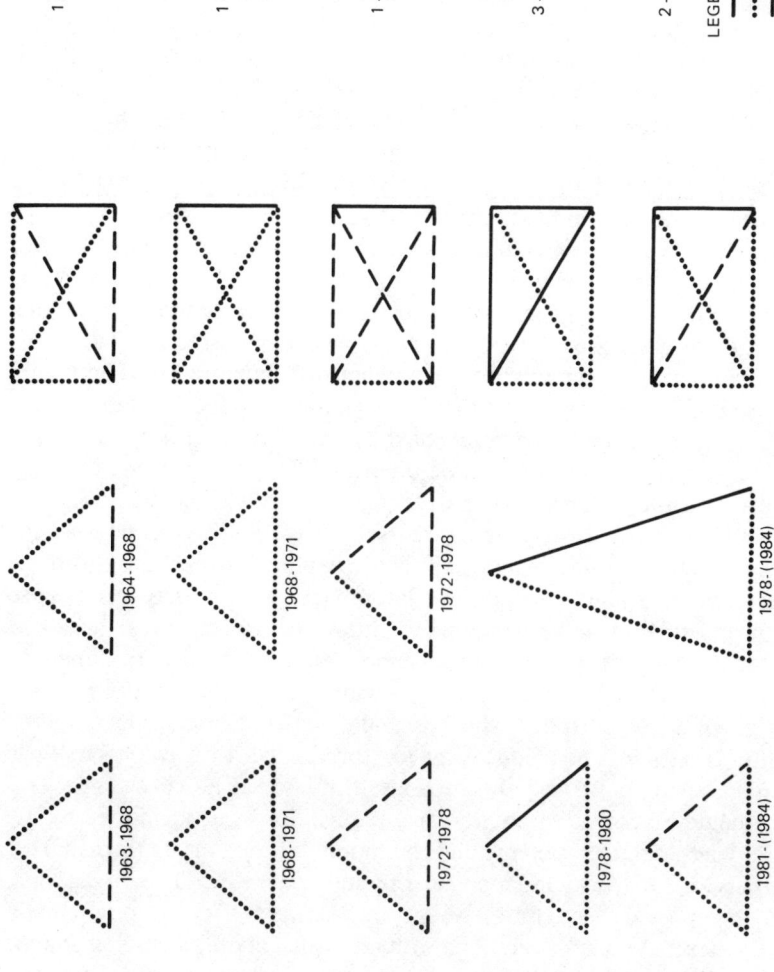

The hostility between *both* Communist powers and Japan lasted only until 1953, when China began to show some interest in establishing informal trade relations with Japan. The Soviet Union, in contrast, continued its hard-line policy toward Japan (characterized by the annual casting of its veto in the United Nations against Japan's admission to the world organization) until 1956. From that date, following the signing of the Soviet-Japanese Joint Declaration which normalized the relations between the two countries, the Soviet Union joined China in moderating its hostility toward Japan and entered into a mixed conflictual-cooperative relationship with its defeated neighbor.

The year 1958 is crucial because important realignments began to occur in both the global and regional triangles. At the regional level, the Chinese Communists broke off their trade relations with Japan (in protest against the pro-Taiwan stance of the Kishi Administration) and contributed to the deterioration of their relations with the Soviet Union; at the same time Soviet-American relations showed signs of improvement.

The year 1960, it seems to me, is also a red-letter year, because several relationships changed in both the global and the regional triangles. Sino-Soviet relations moved to a conflictual phase, Soviet-American relations deteriorated in the wake of the U-2 incident and the aborted Big Two summit, and Soviet-Japanese relations also worsened following the signing of the revised U.S.-Japanese Security Treaty. Sino-Japanese relations improved, however, largely as a result of the disastrous Great Leap Forward campaign and the consequent Chinese need of Japan as a trade partner. These trade relations continued to develop, and in 1962, in addition to the trade with "friendly firms," a more formalized trade channel was inaugurated by the Liao-Takasaki (LT) Memorandum. In response to these expanding Sino-Japanese economic relations, and particularly in response to the near break in its relations with China, the Soviet Union began to court Japan. This was perhaps best symbolized by the visit to Japan of Anastas Mikoyan, long-time Politburo member and First Deputy Premier in charge of foreign trade, which included an audience with Emperor Hirohito. It was indeed a long way for the Soviets to travel from their postwar insistence on trying the Japanese Emperor as a war criminal. Of course, the development of Soviet-Japanese relations was facilitated by the second Soviet-American détente and the signing of the Partial Nuclear Test Ban Treaty in 1963, which Japan, as the only victim of nuclear weapons, strongly supported. The outbreak of the Cultural Revolution in 1966 adversely affected China's relations with all its neighbors, including Japan.

Post-Cultural Revolution developments including the Sino-American and Sino-Japanese rapprochement have been described earlier in this chapter. We turn now to the evolution of the structure of quadrilateral relations. The figures in the right-hand column of Chart 1.2 show the number of positive (cooperative), mixed or transitional, and negative (conflictual) relationships over the years. Of course the structure of the international system is more stable when there are more positive (or at least mixed or transitional) relationships. In this light we can easily see that the most stable period was from 1972 to 1978. The periods that followed, much as they have been praised as beneficial to the United States and the Western Alliance, have unfortunately contributed to instability. In other words, national advantage does not usually contribute to international stability. Settling for second best option (provided it is also your adversary's second best option) is preferable to the best option, which could well be your adversary's worst option. Such a scenario is inherently unstable, and given the relative power of the actors, quite dangerous.

Up to this point I have discussed the strategic balance and Asian alignments at the nation-state level. But Chinese policy toward the other actors in the strategic equation is not just the function of its triangular or quadrilateral relationships with the major powers. At least two other factors have to be taken into account. The first is China's relationships with its neighbors, especially Vietnam, North Korea, and India, and the advanced industrial democracies of Western Europe, Australasia, and Canada. (I am not including Third World relations because these in my view are important only at the rhetorical and symbolic levels and in the United Nations, where the most important problems in world politics are rarely settled.)

The second factor is the dynamics of Chinese domestic politics. Here we must concern ourselves with factional politics, perceptions, and policies. What are the contours of Chinese leadership groups and potential challengers? What are the differing perceptions of the threat to China (both present and long range), of the capabilities and intent of the two superpowers and the changes in their relative power standing and their relationship, and of the role of neighboring states and other important actors on the international scene? What are China's capabilities in dealing with the external environment? And, finally, what is the range of Chinese options, choices, and likely policies? The chapters that follow are addressed to these questions and attempt to provide some answers.

Notes

1. A study of the indoctrination of Japanese prisoners-of-war in Siberia and its effect on Soviet-Japanese relations by the author and his colleagues will be published in the Far Eastern and Russian Research Series of the School of International Relations at the University of Southern California.

2. The rather dismal record of Western scholars with regard to the state and prognosis of Sino-Soviet relations in the 1950s is documented in Loren Paul

Gresham, *Western Analysis of Sino-Soviet Relations During the 1950s,* unpublished M.A. thesis, School of International Relations, University of Southern California, August 1969, prepared under my direction. Of course Franz Borkenau's unpublished analysis of Sino-Soviet relations prepared in February 1952 for the State Department was unavailable at the time. See John E. Tashjean, "The Sino-Soviet Split: Borkenau's Predictive Analysis of 1952," *China Quarterly,* No. 94 (June 1983), pp. 342-361, which includes the complete text of Borkenau's "Analysis of Sino-Soviet Relations." For an analysis of Western writings on the subject, see Donald W. Treadgold "Alternative Western Views of the Sino-Soviet Conflict," in Herbert J Ellison, ed. *The Sino-Soviet Conflict: A Global Perspective*, (Seattle: University of Washington Press, 1982), pp. 325-55.

3. Mineo Nakajima, "China May Return to the Soviet Bloc," *Japan Quarterly,* Vol. 30, No. 2 (April-June 1983), pp. 181-88.

4. Vladimir Petrov, "China Goes It Alone," *Asian Survey,* Vol. 23, No. 5 (May 1983), pp. 580-97.

5. Carol Lee Hamrin, "China Reassesses the Superpowers," *Pacific Affairs,* Vol. 56, No. 2 (Summer 1983), pp. 209-31; rev. version "Emergence of an 'Independent' Chinese Foreign Policy and Shifts in Sino-U.S. Relations," chap. 4 in James C. Hsiung, ed., *U.S.-Asian Relations: The National Security Paradox* (New York: Praeger, 1983), pp. 63-84.

6. Akio Kimura, "Sino-Soviet Rapprochement: How Far Will It Go?" *Japan Quarterly,* Vol. 30, No. 3 (July-September 1983), pp. 248-55; longer version "Sino-Soviet Relations: New Developments and Their Limits," *Journal of Northeast Asian Studies,* Vol. II, No. 1 (March 1983), pp. 17-37.

7. One should also note, however, that scholars such as Donald Zagoria and William Griffith have expressed their doubts about a basic change in the direction of Chinese foreign policy. For example, Zagoria ends his article with the observation that "on the key issues affecting the central balance, China will continue to lean to the West" (Donald S. Zagoria, "The Moscow-Beijing Détente," *Foreign Affairs,* Vol. 61, No. 4 [Spring 1983], pp. 853-73 at p. 873) and Griffith doubts that the "current atmospheric rapprochement . . . will lead to major substantive compromises" (William E. Griffith, "Sino-Soviet Rapprochement?" *Problems of Communism,* Vol. XXXII, No. 2 [March-April 1983], pp. 20-29 at p. 29).

8. Harry Harding, "Change and Continuity in Chinese Foreign Policy," *Problems of Communism,* Vol. XXXII, No. 2 (March-April 1983), pp. 1-19 at p. 8.

9. Ralph N. Clough, *East Asia and U.S. Security* (Washington, D.C.: Brookings Institution, 1975), pp. 44-54.

10. *Ibid.,* pp. 47 and 44.

11. Harold C. Hinton, *Three and a Half Powers: The New Balance in Asia* (Bloomington: Indiana University Press, 1975).

12. William Kintner assigns the same half power role in the strategic triangle to China. See William R. Kintner, "A Strategic Triangle of Two and a Half Powers," *Orbis,* Vol. 23, No. 3 (Fall 1979), pp. 525-34.

13. Griffith, *op. cit.,* p. 28.

14. Gerald Segal, "China and the Great Power Triangle," *China Quarterly,* No. 83 (September 1980), pp. 490-509; "China's Strategic Posture and the Great Power Triangle," *Pacific Affairs,* Vol. 53, No. 4 (Winter 1980-81), pp. 682-97; and

The Great Power Triangle (London: Macmillan, 1982). See also Thomas M. Gottlieb, *Chinese Foreign Policy Factionalism and the Origins of the Strategic Triangle* (Santa Monica: Rand, November 1977) (R-1902-NA); John Gittings, "The Great Power Triangle and Chinese Foreign Policy," *China Quarterly,* No. 39 (July-September 1969), pp. 41–54; Harry Schwartz, "The Moscow-Peking-Washington Triangle," *Annals of the American Academy of Political and Social Sciences,* No. 414 (July 1974), pp. 41–54; Gaston J. Sigur, "The Strategic Triangle: The U.S., the U.S.S.R. and the P.R.C.," in Lloyd R. Vasey, ed., *Pacific Asia and U.S. Polices: A Political-Economic-Strategic Assessment* (Pacific Forum, 1978), pp. 28–35; William E. Griffith, ed., *The World and the Great Power Triangle* (Cambridge, Mass.: M.I.T. Press, 1975); Michel Tatu, *Le grand triangle: Washington-Moscow-Pékin* (Paris: Institut Atlantique, 1970), *Le triangle Washington-Moscow-Pékin et les deux Europe(s)* (n.p.: Casterman, 1972), and "The Great Power Triangle: Washington-Moscow-Peking" in Robert J. Art and Robert Jervis, eds., *International Politics: Anarchy, Force, Imperialism* (Boston: Little, Brown, 1973); Kenneth Lieberthal, *Sino-Soviet Conflict in the 1970s: Its Evolution and Implications for the Strategic Triangle* (Santa Monica: Rand, July 1978) (R-2342-NA); William E. Griffith, "Peking, Moscow and Beyond: The Sino-Soviet-American Triangle," *Washington Papers,* No. 6, 1973; Thomas W. Robinson, "China's Dynamism in the Strategic Triangle," *Current History,* Vol. 82, No. 485 (September 1983), 241–44, 276, 280–81.

15. Peter Berton, "Direction and Analysis of U.S. Foreign Policy," chap. 1 in James C. Hsiung and Winberg Chai, eds., *Asia and U.S. Foreign Policy* (New York: Praeger, 1981), pp. 7–23 at p. 17.

16. Lowell Dittmer, "The Strategic Triangle: An Elementary Game-Theoretical Analysis," *World Politics,* Vol. XXXIII, No. 4 (July 1981), pp. 485–515.

17. *Ibid.,* p. 489.

18. *Ibid.,* pp. 491ff.

19. Peter Berton, "Soviet Policy Toward Japan: Problems, Policies, Push, Propaganda, Prospects," paper presented at the panel on "Soviet Policy Toward East Asia" (Joseph M. Ha, chairman), Fourteenth Annual Convention of the American Association for the Advancement of Slavic Studies, Washington, D.C., October 14–17, 1982.

20. Raju G. C. Thomas, ed., *The Great-Power Triangle and Asian Security* (Lexington, Mass.: Lexington Books, 1983), pp. 1–20 at pp. 4–6.

21. Ronald Keith distinguishes between "trilateralism," or triangular diplomacy (with its attendant "card" playing) and bilateralism which in his view all three actors in the strategic triangle should practice (in conjunction with normalization). Ronald C. Keith, "China and 'Trilateralism'," *International Perspectives,* July/August 1983, pp. 24–26.

A Turn in Sino-Soviet Relations?
——2——
Peter Berton

One of the characteristic features of the international system in the post-World War II era is the volatility of political alignments. To be sure, the United States's close relations with Canada, Western Europe, Israel, Japan, and Australasia have withstood the vicissitudes of international politics for four decades. Yet other relationships have flip-flopped dramatically. Egypt, for example, once a client state of the Soviet Union, is now an important partner of the United States in stopping Soviet expansionism in the Middle East. But by far the most dramatic and far-reaching reversal in political alignments involves the People's Republic of China (PRC). An ally and faithful member of the Soviet bloc and an implacably hostile antagonist of the United States and its alliance system in the early and mid-1950s, Communist China first broke with Communist Russia in the late 1950s and early 1960s, and then came close to becoming an informal ally and potentially important customer and trading partner of the United States, Japan, and Western Europe in the 1970s and 1980s.

How did this come about? Is there a direct connection between China's relationship with each of the two superpowers? Is it in China's best interest in maintain a *very close* entente with one of the superpowers *at the expense* of a correct relationship with the other superpower? Or is a policy of equidistance, or at least evenhandedness, toward the two superpowers preferable? Or does China's interest lie in close relations with the poor and economically backward countries of the Third World, which the late Marshal Lin Biao called the "villages" of the world? Or does China's future lie in close economic and technological relations with the industrialized democracies of Western Europe, Canada, Australasia, and Japan, the late Chairman Mao Zedong's so-called Second Intermediate Zone?

This chapter will briefly touch on the historical roots of Sino-Soviet relations, the ideological dispute provoked by Nikita Khrushchev's reformulations of Marxism-Leninism-Stalinism and his de-Stalinization campaign in the mid-1950s, and the stages in the evolution of the conflict between the two Communist superpowers, along with the divisive and contentious issues between them. More detailed attention will be given the Sino-Soviet relations since 1978, and particularly after the cooling-off of relations between China and the United States with the advent of the Reagan Administration. Finally, I shall try to draw a balance sheet in this triangular relationship, bring in other external and internal factors, and answer the question that is the title of this chapter, "A Turn in Sino-Soviet Relations?"

Territorial, Racial, Historical, and Other Factors

The conflict between China and the Soviet Union was initially called an ideological dispute. This is understandable because the two countries were Marxist-Leninist regimes, ruled by Communist parties, and, more important, engaged in party-to-party (rather than state-to-state) relations that were conducted in highly abstruse and esoteric Marxist jargon. But China and Russia are also neighboring states with a long history of conflicts over territory, dating back even before the 1689 Treaty of Nerchinsk.[1]

There are also racial overtones in their relationship. The Chinese, as proud inhabitants of the Middle Kingdom, treated the Russians, like other foreigners, as barbarians. The Russians cannot forget the centuries-old Mongol yoke and have been apprehensive of the Yellow Peril. Indeed, the word "Asiatic" has a pejorative connotation in Russia, and the Soviet poet Yevgeny Yevtushenko, in a poem composed in March 1969 right after the armed clashes along the Sino-Soviet border, wrote of a new battle of Kulikovo, referring to the first Russian victory over their Asian overlords in the fourteenth century.

In addition, the Chinese Communists have bitter memories of the Soviet-imposed united front with the Guomindang (Kuomintang) Nationalists in the 1920s, which ended in the decimation of the fledgling Chinese Communist Party (CCP). Later, Mao Zedong came to power against the Comintern's wishes, and Joseph Stalin did precious little to help the Chinese Communists during their long stay in the Yanan wilderness. In 1941 Stalin concluded a neutrality pact with Japan,[2] a psychological blow to both the Chinese Communists and Nationalists, and in 1945 he negotiated a wide-ranging treaty with Chiang Kai-shek. (Stalin promised his wartime allies President Roosevelt and Prime Minister Winston Churchill that he would deal only with the Nationalist Government.) The 1945 treaty restored the tsarist spheres of influence in Manchuria and Sinkiang and forced China to acquiesce in the detachment of Outer Mongolia (the so-called Mongolian

People's Republic) from China. (In the late 1930s Mao told Edgar Snow that Mongolia should be returned to China.)

Their occupation of Manchuria in the final days of World War II gave the Soviets the opportunity to strip the area of all industrial equipment, a move that the Soviet Union justified as spoils of war against Japan but which every Chinese irrespective of his political convictions deplored as a setback to postwar industrialization of China. Although the Red Army blocked the movement of Chinese Nationalist forces in Manchuria, and turned over some weapons to the Chinese Communist forces under Lin Biao,[3] the Soviet Union, like everyone else, was surprised at the rapid disintegration of the Nationalist forces and the Communist victory in the Chinese Civil War. Stalin may well have preferred a weak China, mired in civil war, to the establishment of a fraternal Communist regime that placed great emphasis on the unification of the country and the building of a strong industrialized socialist state. In fact, he insisted on the continuation of Soviet special privileges obtained in 1945 from the Nationalist Government and he was not very generous in offering economic aid to the fledgling fraternal neighboring state.

Although the Sino-Soviet treaty negotiated after weeks of wrangling in Moscow was called a Treaty of Friendship, Alliance, and Mutual Assistance, the Soviets provided a loan of only three hundred million dollars over a five-year period, or an annual stipend of a dime per capita. (Contrast this with U.S. generosity in giving over twenty billion dollars in Marshall Plan aid to Western Europe.) In addition to this very small loan, the Soviets imposed onerous joint stock companies, which the Chinese regarded as economic exploitation and which they managed to cancel after Stalin's death.[4]

The unequal contributions of the two Communist neighbors to the prosecution of the Korean War was another cause of Chinese displeasure: the Chinese had to intervene militarily and suffered heavy casualties, while the Soviets provided only material aid, for much of which China had to pay.

The first purge in the PRC in the early 1950s involved the Communist "warlord" of Manchuria Gao Gang, who had extensive contacts with the Soviet authorities across the border, which no doubt was one of the main reasons for his purge.[5] This purge of pro-Soviet elements in the CCP must have contributed to friction between the two parties.

In 1955, the Soviet opening to the Third World, especially the granting of aid to India and Egypt, was probably not welcomed in Beijing. Given the limited amount of available Soviet credits and economic aid, the Chinese Communists would have preferred that these finite resources were first made available within the Soviet bloc to fraternal countries, such as China.

The death of Stalin and the ascension to power of Nikita Khrushchev, who became a member of the Politburo of the Communist Party of the Soviet Union (CPSU) only in 1939, clearly affected Mao's relationship with the Soviet Union. Mao must have grudgingly admired Stalin for his decisive, if ruthless, role in the collectivization of agriculture, forced industrialization, and victory over Germany. But with Stalin gone, Mao probably saw himself as the senior leader in the international Communist movement,[6] a self-assessment that must have complicated his relationship with Khrushchev.

And, finally, even if Mao were prepared for China to play junior partner to the Soviet Union in the Communist bloc's world strategy, surely there should have been some division of labor and some special area, such as Southeast and South Asia, to be assigned to China as its sphere of influence. Yet one of the first in the series of foreign trips that Khrushchev undertook (with his traveling companion Marshal Nikolai Bulganin) was to Afghanistan, India, and Burma—all countries bordering on China.

Ideology and Perception of World Politics

By the time of the Twentieth Party Congress of the CPSU, Khrushchev initiated a number of policies that were counter to previous Soviet practice, and indeed contradicted the ideas of Marx, Lenin, and Stalin.

The most important of these was his declaration that now war was not fatalistically inevitable, contrary to Lenin's dictum that as long as capitalism and imperialism exist war is inevitable. This formulation was made to help Khrushchev in his newly proclaimed policy of peaceful coexistence. The second pronouncement concerned the road to power: contrary to Marx, who postulated that power can only be seized through violence and revolution, Khrushchev proposed that revolution was not the only road to power and that communist parties could conceivably come to power through parliamentary means, that is, through evolution and not necessarily through revolution. This was also part and parcel of the public relations aspect of his peaceful coexistence policy. The third policy change involved the concept of different roads to communism and was contrary to Stalin's insistence on the primacy of the Soviet experience. This was the price that Marshal Tito had extracted from Khrushchev, when the latter made a pilgrimage to Belgrade, to make up for Stalin's obviously unproductive policy of pressuring and ostracizing the Yugoslavs.

Coupled with these policy innovations was Khrushchev's need to dissociate himself from the Stalin regime for domestic political purposes. This he did in a dramatic secret speech at the Congress, denouncing Stalin and setting the stage for the de-Stalinization campaign.

What was the Chinese reaction to these new Soviet policies, which some scholars have termed as Khrushchevism? Taking de-Stalinization (or "the cult of personality" as it was termed in the Soviet Union) first, it seems obvious that although the most extreme features of the Mao cult were still a decade away from full blossoming in the so-called Great Proletarian Cultural Revolution, the whole idea of debunking a supreme leader after his demise was something Mao would not have wanted to support.

Different roads to power could seemingly be endorsed by the Chinese Communists, as it would have legitimized their own unique road to victory in the civil war. Mao understood however that lack of central authority would only weaken the Communist bloc; the Hungarian revolt a few months later underscored this point very graphically. And although only a junior partner of the Soviet Union at the time, Communist China would one day hope to lead the bloc. The peaceful road to power was obviously an option only in open, democratic societies; the Chinese Communist experience was in a totally different social and political setting. But the greatest disagreement was over the question of war and peace. As a revisionist power, facing a rival Nationalist government, the Chinese Communists could not accept Khrushchev's peaceful coexistence formulation and weaken their implied threat of force in the conquest of Taiwan. In fact, in late 1957, Mao misjudged the significance of the successful Soviet missile test and the Sputnik to declare that the "East Wind Prevails over the West Wind," emboldening him to stage the Taiwan Straits crisis the following year.[7]

Beyond all these disagreements over policy, Mao must have been incensed with Khrushchev for not informing him of (much less discussing) these momentous doctrinal changes.

Evolution of the Dispute and the Issues

How did the Sino-Soviet dispute evolve since 1956, the date usually given by the Chinese side as the beginning of their differences with the Soviets? (The Soviet side dates the dispute from 1960 or 1958 when the Chinese allegedly challenged them on a number of issues, foreign and domestic.)[8] I would like to distinguish four periods, with the possibility that the past several years might constitute a fifth:

(1) *1956-1960,* the period from the Twentieth Party Congress of the CPSU to the withdrawal of Soviet technicians from China;

(2) *1961-1963,* from attacks by proxy to open and direct polemics;

(3) *1964-1969,* from personal attacks on leaders to armed clashes on the Sino-Soviet border; and

(4) *since 1970,* a state of stalemate accompanied by polemics, occasional border incidents, and continuous diplomatic and economic contacts.

It is premature to declare that the several rounds of political negotiations since 1979 constitute a different phase in Sino-Soviet relations, unless these negotiations do indeed result in agreements that effect a change in the character of the conflict. So far the contacts have become more frequent and, on the whole, more civil.

1956-1960. The first phase may be characterized as a period of publicly muted disagreements, primarily aired in theoretical journals until the summer of 1960 when Khrushchev pulled out of China all Soviet engineers and technicians working on numerous industrial projects. The dispute involved ideological differences and their implications, discussed earlier, which included China's fears of Soviet-American collusion exemplified by the 1959 "Spirit of Camp David" when Khrushchev visited President Dwight Eisenhower. The Soviets, on their part, were concerned by the ideological challenge implicit in the crash industrialization program known as the Great Leap Forward, and especially the formation of communes, which could be seen as a higher form of social organization than those in existence in the Soviet Union.[9]

We have since learned from Sino-Soviet polemics that in 1958 the Chinese refused the Soviet Union's demands for naval and other bases on Chinese territory and also for establishment of a joint fleet under Soviet command, and that in 1959 the Soviets unilaterally tore up a 1957 agreement on nuclear technology assistance.

1961-1963. The second phase began with what might be called "whipping by proxy," as the Soviets and the Chinese began publicly attacking the Albanians and the Yugoslavs, respectively. The Soviet attacks, which portrayed the Albanians as "dogmatists," were clearly aimed at the Chinese, just as the Chinese attacks on the "revisionist" Yugoslavs were directed at the Soviets. (The 1960 Moscow summit of ruling and nonruling Communist parties papered over Sino-Soviet differences by condemning both revisionism and dogmatism.) For a while the entire international Communist movement played this Albanian-Yugoslav charade depending on whether the Communist party in question supported Moscow or Beijing.[10]

Then, in late 1962, the Chinese chastised the Soviet leadership for both "adventurism" and "capitulationism" in the Cuban missile crisis, and the Soviets subtly questioned Chinese courage in not liberating Hong Kong and Macao from the British and Portuguese colonialists, in contrast to India which drove the Portuguese out of Goa. Western analysts have also noticed that the Soviet Union was scrupulously neutral in the Sino-Indian border dispute and not supportive of its nominal Chinese allies.

Finally, most Chinese grievances against the Soviet Union were made public in the famous 25-point CCP letter of June 14, 1963 to the CPSU (actually a pamphlet entitled "A Proposal Concerning the General Line of the International Communist Movement"). The Soviet response was twofold.

First, the Soviets broke their long silence on July 14 with an "Open Letter from the CPSU Central Committee to Party Organizations and All Communists of the Soviet Union," in which they attempted to respond to the Chinese charges. Second, Moscow quickly came to an agreement with Washington and London on a Partial Nuclear Test Ban Treaty (signed later in July). This treaty prohibited nuclear testing in the atmosphere, which was indispensable for the as yet untested, fledgling Chinese atomic weapons program. Chinese response to the Nuclear Treaty was predictably strident and bitter.[11]

Although unpublicized at the time, tens of thousands of native inhabitants of Sinkiang crossed the Sino-Soviet border in April-May 1962 to join their cousins in the Soviet Central Asian republics. These refugees must have fled in the wake of natural disasters and famine in no small measure caused or aggravated by the ill-conceived Great Leap Forward campaign. Literally thousands of other border violations have been charged by each side to have taken place during these three years.

1964-1969. The CCP began in September, 1963, to make public its response to the July 14, 1963, CPSU letter. The response appeared in the form of long pamphlet-size discussions of the most important issues dividing the two parties, such as the origin of the dispute, Stalin's role in history, Yugoslav revisionism, and war and peace. But in 1964 verbal abuse of one another's policies degenerated into personality attacks, most prominently with the Soviets likening Mao to Adolf Hitler.

The territorial issue was also important in 1964, with Sino-Soviet border negotiations starting and ending. Fuel was added to this issue when Mao, in a talk with a group of Japanese parliamentarians, supported Japanese territorial claims against the Soviet Union.[12] The U.S. escalation of the war in Vietnam was thought to be one development that would help heal the rift between the two Communist protagonists, but Mao resisted the idea of a united Sino-Soviet front against the United States and preferred to oppose both superpowers. (This policy was codified into the so-called Three World Theory a decade later.)

The other arena of Sino-Soviet competition was the international Communist movement. Most Asian Communist parties sided with Beijing, but the majority of the parties sided with Moscow or split into pro-Moscow and pro-Beijing groups. The Soviets further deepened the split with their insistence on holding a world conference of Communist parties in Moscow that would isolate, if not excommunicate, the Chinese party.[13] In the meantime, Mao launched the Cultural Revolution, which not only turned China inward toward self-isolation but further exacerbated relations with its northern neighbor.[14] The dangerous low in Sino-Soviet relations was reached in March 1969 when a series of armed clashes on the border threatened to plunge the two countries into war.[15] Most important, the Soviet Union also began to fortify its frontier and greatly increase the number of divisions along the border and in Mongolia. Brezhnev also began to push the Asian Collective Security plan, which Beijing saw as an "anti-China encirclement scheme."

Since 1970. A meeting between Premiers Alexei Kosygin and Zhou Enlai in late 1969 started a period of stalemate in Sino-Soviet relations.[16] Although the war scare had subsided by 1970, and especially after China's rapprochement with the United States and Japan in 1972, minor incidents along the border occasionally continued to occur. Most of the incidents, however, were probably unprovoked. While the level of polemics has risen and fallen, partly as a result of deliberate policy (such as the Soviet pause after the death of Mao) or in response to domestic events in both countries, bilateral interactions, and international developments, the military buildup has continued. Finally, a certain level of contacts in diplomatic, economic, and river navigation spheres has been maintained over these years.[17]

Let us now examine more closely the different kinds of interactions and the most recent developments in Sino-Soviet relations after 1978. Basically we are talking here of three phases: (1) political talks in the fall of 1979, (2) 1980-1982, cancellation of these talks following the Soviet invasion of Afghanistan, and (3) resumption of Sino-Soviet "consultations" since the fall of 1982.

China's relations with the Soviet Union are conducted at different levels. This is true, of course, of any bilateral relationship. But in the case of Sino-Soviet relations, particularly in view of the closed nature of their societies, their ideological heritage and mode of communication, and the intensity and duration of hostility between them, it is very important to categorize the different types of relationships and assess their relative importance.

Some scholars have argued that Communist states have three kinds of relationships:

(1) *People-to-people* relations—official and semiofficial contacts and exchanges, usually of groups and delegations. This form of contact was especially important to the PRC during the first two decades of its existence, when its network of diplomatic ties was largely limited to the Soviet bloc, a few Western countries, and selected Third World states.

(2) *Party-to-party* relations—the common mode of communication and relationship among the ruling Communist party-states, where the respective Communist party hierarchies deal with the most important problems of interstate relations. For example, resolution of Soviet-Czechoslovak difficulties during the Prague Spring was attempted through a joint meeting of the two Politburos. But when Communist party-states experience difficulties between each other, they usually break off party relations and *downgrade* their relationship to official state-to-state relations.

This was the case between the PRC on the one hand and the Soviet Union and its East European satellites on the other. In fact, Beijing returned unopened all condolence messages on the death of Mao from the CPSU and other fraternal parties, stating that there were no relations between the CCP and the other parties.

(3) *State-to-state* relations—normal diplomatic relations between Communist and non-Communist countries as well as among Communist states that have broken party-to-party relations, such as Sino-Soviet or Soviet-Yugoslav relations.

In the case of present Sino-Soviet relations, we have only people-to-people and state-to-state relations. Party-to-party relations are nonexistent. But I would like to distinguish further between the following types of interactions:

(1) *signals* contained in speeches, statements, interviews, and articles in newspapers and journals—official, semiofficial, or unofficial;

(2) *visits and exchanges* (official, semiofficial, or private) of government officials, scholars, specialists, journalists, athletes, friendship societies activists, and so on;

(3) *routine contacts*—mostly regular sessions between official delegations regulating trade and transportation, navigation on boundary rivers, and border control;

(4) *political talks*—preliminary and plenary, whether called consultations or negotiations;

(5) *border incidents*—minor or major, provoked or unprovoked; and

(6) *military movements*—changing the size, disposition, and weapons of troops, including strategic forces.

Political Negotiations in 1979

The political negotiations between China and the Soviet Union since the late 1970s began as a consequence of the conclusion of the 1978 Sino-Japanese Peace Treaty. The 1950 Sino-Soviet Treaty of Alliance was explicity directed against Japan, and, consequently, the Japanese negotiators obtained an understanding from their Chinese counterparts that China would not extend that treaty beyond its 1980 expiration date. (Of course for all practical purposes the 1950 treaty ceased to have any meaning after the escalation of the Sino-Soviet dispute in the early 1960s and especially after the 1969 border clashes.) In accordance with the treaty's provisions, China notified the Soviet Union one year in advance that it would not be extended. To soften the impact, the announcement was first confidentially communicated to the Soviet ambassador in Beijing, Ilya Shcherbakov,[18] on March 31, 1979, and then officially announced on April 3 as an action taken by the Standing Committee of the National People's Congress. While making the point that "the treaty has long ceased to exist except in name, owing to violations for which the Chinese side is not responsible," the Chinese government also called for the normalization of Sino-Soviet relations on the basis of the five principles of peaceful coexistence and proposed that negotiations be held to resolve outstanding issues between the two countries.[19]

Since it was China that proposed to resume negotiations with the Soviet Union,[20] the Chinese action should be placed in the context of the international political alignments of the time. It was a defensive action on the part of the Chinese, since Leonid Brezhnev warned China in January, 1979 that if the Chinese leaders did take action to abrogate the treaty, they should acknowledge responsibility for the consequences.[21] This warning came after the Vietnamese invasion of Cambodia, and before the Chinese punitive action against Vietnam. We should also remember that the Soviets countered the Sino-Japanese rapprochement with closer relations with Vietnam, first to admit Vietnam into Comecon and later to conclude a Treaty of Friendship and Cooperation, in essence a quasi-military alliance against China. The Soviet Union also protested the conclusion of the China treaty to Japan and characterized the relations among China, Japan, and the United States as "signs of the first step leading to a new military alliance."[22] The subsequent normalization of relations between China and the United States announced in December 1978 must have only reinforced this perception.

Thus, while it was China which proposed to the Soviet Union to start negotiations, Moscow probably saw merit in the proposal because it would allow it to counter the emerging Sino-Japanese-American entente. (The Soviets were also continuing to pressure Japan to sign a treaty of good neighborliness and cooperation.)[23] Although official and unofficial Soviet comments indirectly chided China for ingratitude by reminding the Chinese of Soviet economic assistance in the 1950s and the Sino-Soviet treaty's strategic role during the Korean War and the Taiwan Straits crisis in 1958, accused the Chinese leadership of pursuing a diametrically changed policy, and declared that they were solely responsible for the termination of the treaty, Foreign Minister Andrei Gromyko, in a note handed to Chinese Ambassador Wang Youping on April 17, accepted the Chinese proposal for negotiations. (Ironically, on the same day the *People's Daily* blasted Soviet published reactions with a long Commentator's article entitled "What Reason Is There for Moscow to Fly into a Rage?") On May 5, Chinese Foreign Vice Minister Yu Zhan, in a memorandum to the Soviet ambassador in Beijing, responded that China was ready to discuss ways to expand trade, scientific and technological cooperation, and cultural contacts with a view to improving relations.[24] In June, in a television speech in Hungary, Brezhnev declared that if China was really sincere in its desire for negotiations, the Soviet Union on its part was prepared to make a serious and earnest effort.[25]

These moves and countermoves with regard to the impending negotiations, where to hold them, what to discuss, and at what level dragged on for months. (In the meantime, minor skirmishes along the Sino-Soviet border were reported and duly protested, the Strategic Arms Limitation Talks [SALT] II agreement was signed in Vienna by Brezhnev and Jimmy Carter in June, and Vice-President Walter Mondale visited Beijing in August and announced that President Carter would visit China the following year.)

Sino-Soviet talks were finally held in Moscow between September 27 and November 30 (five preparatory talks and six formal sessions) at the vice ministerial level, the Soviet Foreign Vice Minister Leonid Ilyichev and his Chinese counterpart, and the former Chinese ambassador in Moscow, Wang Youping. During these negotiations, Sino-Soviet polemics continued in the press as well as in the debates in the United Nations General Assembly, albeit in a somewhat toned-down fashion. On the positive side, both sides have made reference to some historical documents from the early, friendly period in their relations, as if to underscore that a return to a more proper relationship were possible. Reflecting lack of agreement on the major issues and even on the agenda for future talks, no announcements were made regarding the progress achieved at these meetings. Nevertheless, both sides agreed to resume negotiations in Beijing in early 1980.

Later revelations suggest that both sides have agreed on an expansion of trade relations and of scientific, technological, cultural, and sports exchanges, but have completely disagreed on the approach to resolving outstanding issues. On the one hand, the Chinese wanted the Soviets to substantially reduce their forces on the Sino-Soviet border, withdraw their troops and missiles from the Mongolian People's Republic, stop Soviet support of Vietnam's invasion of Cambodia, and seriously negotiate the border issue.[26] The Soviets, on the other hand, tabled their 1978 proposal of a document on the principles to regulate relations between the two countries, which could serve as a replacement for the 1950 treaty. These principles have included "complete equality, mutual respect for state independence and sovereignty, territorial integrity, noninterference in each other's internal affairs, the nonuse of force or threat of force, and mutual benefit."[27]

The basic reason for the discrepancy in the Chinese and Soviet approaches to their negotiations is that in regard to China the Soviet Union is a status quo power that wants to freeze the existing conditions by treaties and agreements guaranteeing the nonuse of force, while China vis-à-vis the Soviet Union is a revisionist power that feels itself threatened and almost encircled from the north, west, and southeast, and wants changes to effect a break in the encirclement and a reduction of the military threat to northeast and north China, including its capital, Beijing.

We should not forget that since the outbreak of the Sino-Soviet dispute, the Soviets moved a number of divisions (including tank divisions) and missiles into Mongolia, increased the number of divisions on the Sino-Soviet border from ten or twelve to over fifty, and have targeted China with at least a thousand nuclear missiles. All this is far beyond legitimate Soviet defense needs. China cannot keep up with the quantitative and qualitative increase in Soviet forces and has to run to keep in place. Some U.S. analysts do not preclude the possibility of limited Soviet military action aimed at lopping off some areas of China inhabited by national minorities whose cousins live across the border in the Soviet Central Asian republics. One is reminded of General Aleksei Kuropatkin's plan in 1912 to annex all Chinese territory north of the line joining Tashkent and Vladivostok.[28]

Sino-Soviet negotiations did not resume in 1980. The Soviet invasion of Afghanistan at the end of December 1979 put an end to this exercise, and China canceled the talks in mid-January, as it welcomed U.S. Defense Secretary Harold Brown. Later in the year Premier Hua Guofeng traveled to Japan, while Vice Premier Geng Biao went to the United States. China also joined the United States, some West European countries, and Japan in boycotting the Moscow Olympic games. On April 10, 1980, the Sino-Soviet Treaty of Friendship, Alliance, and Mutual Assistance quietly expired.

Resumption of Talks in 1982

It was three years before Sino-Soviet political negotiations restarted (in October, 1982) in Beijing at the vice ministerial level. The Chinese Foreign Ministry emphasized, however, that the meeting between Soviet Foreign Vice Minister Ilyichev and his Chinese counterpart Qian Qichen were "consultations," rather than negotiations aimed at normalization of relations.

The intervening period was, on the whole, full of polemics on both sides, but the Soviet Union made some attempts to improve relations which proved unsuccessful. Annual river navigation talks continued, and so did bilateral trade, although at a lower volume. In March, 1981 Moscow proposed that the two countries discuss the implementation of confidence building measures in the Far East that might lead to a relaxation of tension.[29] And six months later the Soviet Union suggested the resumption of border talks. The Chinese response was unenthusiastic. They were also quite incensed by the stationing of Soviet troops in the Afghan panhandle bordering on China[30] and especially by the conclusion in June, 1981 of a Soviet-Afghan border treaty that Beijing declared "illegal" and "invalid" because it affected a disputed area of the Sino-Soviet border.[31] The Chinese view of the boundary question was authoritatively presented by the director of the Institute of International Studies in Beijing,[32] eliciting an angry Soviet reply.[33] The Soviets have estimated that in 1981 the Chinese published over twenty articles on the Sino-Soviet territorial and boundary question,[34] Chinese leaders made over one hundred anti-Soviet statements, and *People's Daily* printed over 2,500 anti-Soviet items.[35]

Why did China agree to resume talks with its northern neighbor in the fall of 1982 while Soviet troops were still in Afghanistan? Did the Soviet Union make some concrete concessions to China? Did it make any promises? Was China disappointed with the state of Sino-American relations following the Reagan Administration's pro-Taiwan rhetoric and arms sales plans? Or was it a combination of these and other factors?

Let us look first at the first factor—the Soviet Union. Although the Soviets ignored the Chinese call for concrete deeds, especially in terms of their military posture on the Sino-Soviet border and in Mongolia, Brezhnev did extend a warm invitation to the Chinese to return to the negotiating table.[36] The Brezhnev offer was made during a speech on a visit to Tashkent, the capital of a Soviet republic bordering on China. The reference to Sino-Soviet relations was made in the context of a tour d'horizon of Soviet policy in Asia and following an appeal to "our Japanese neighbors":

> Now for our relations with *China*. This is a complicated question.
>
> The fundamental position of our Party and the Soviet state on the question of Soviet-Chinese relations was set forth clearly in the decisions of the 25th and 26th CPSU Congresses. Here I would like to mention the following additional considerations.
>
> *First.* Despite the fact that we have openly criticized and continue to criticize many aspects of the Chinese leadership's policy (especially its foreign policy) as not corresponding to socialist principles and norms, we have never tried to interfere in the internal life of the Chinese People's Republic. We have not denied and do not now deny the existence of a socialist social system in China—although Peking's fusion with the imperialists' policy in the world arena is, of course, at variance with the interests of socialism.
>
> *Second.* We have never supported and do not now support, in any form, the so-called "two Chinas concept," and we have completely recognized and continue to recognize the CPR's sovereignty over the island of Taiwan.
>
> *Third.* There has been no threat to the Chinese People's Republic from the Soviet Union, and there is none now. We have not had, and do not now have, any territorial claims against the CPR, and we are prepared at any time to continue talks on outstanding border questions with a view to reaching mutually acceptable decisions. We are also prepared to discuss the question of possible measures to strengthen mutual confidence in the area of the Soviet-Chinese border.

Fourth. We well remember the time when the Soviet Union and people's China were united by bonds of friendship and comradely cooperation. We have never considered the state of hostility and alienation between our countries to be a normal phenomenon. We are prepared to reach an agreement—without any preliminary conditions—on measures, acceptable to both sides, to improve Soviet-Chinese relations on the basis of mutual respect for each other's affairs and mutual benefit—and, needless to say not to the detriment of any third countries. This offer extends to economic, scientific and cultural relations as well as the political relations—as soon as both sides are ready for concrete steps in any of these spheres.[37]

Only a year before, on February 23, 1981, at the Twenty-Sixth CPSU Party Congress, although alleging that Soviet "feelings of respect and friendship for the Chinese people remain unchanged" and that "our proposals aimed at normalization of relations with China remain on the table," Brezhnev also had this to say about China:

China's own leaders themselves call the system . . . during the . . . cultural revolution "a most cruel feudal-fascist distatorship." We have nothing to add to this evaluation. . . . China's foreign policy . . . is aimed at exacerbating the international situation and at making common cause with imperialist policy.[38]

China did not reject the Soviet offer out of hand. In a response to the Tashkent speech, the Chinese Foreign Ministry spokesman took note of Brezhnev's statement about improving Sino-Soviet relations, firmly rejected his accusations that China was colluding with the imperialists, and declared that China attached importance to the Soviet Union's actual deeds rather than its words.[39] On May 14, Premier Zhao Ziyang, in an interview with a Japanese press delegation, reiterated the Foreign Ministry stand on the Tashkent speech, but also stressed that China opposed Soviet hegemonism and its policy of external expansion.[40]

Vice-president George Bush visited China in May, but the question of arms sales to Taiwan continued to plague Sino-American relations. On the heels of the Bush visit, Mikhail Kapitsa, the head of the First Department of Far Eastern Affairs of the Soviet Foreign Ministry, visited Beijing as a guest of the Soviet ambassador and presumably had some informal meetings with appropriate Chinese officials. Coincidentally, three months later, in mid-August, Kapitsa's counterpart, Yu Hongliang, director of the Soviet Union and East European Affairs Department of the Chinese Foreign Ministry, paid a similar unofficial visit to the Soviet capital at the invitation of the Chinese ambassador which was made during the Sino-American negotiations that led to the August 17 joint memorandum on the Taiwan problem.

It seems that the Yu visit led to the Chinese decision to resume vice ministerial talks in October without waiting for concrete Soviet "deeds," which most analysts would agree did not take place: Soviet forces were not thinned out along the Sino-Soviet border, Soviet missiles were not withdrawn from Mongolia, and there was no visible change in the Soviet support for Vietnam and its policy in Cambodia. And, of course, Soviet troops were still in Afghanistan, which was the original reason for breaking off the first round of negotiations in early 1980.

In and of itself the Brezhnev Tashkent offer was not crucial in changing Chinese policy toward negotiations with the Soviet Union, but it did come at a time of Sino-American friction and it cleverly reminded the Chinese that the Soviet Union had never questioned Chinese sovereignty over Taiwan and had never engaged in a Two-China policy. Brezhnev also held out the carrot of the economic, technological, and scientific benefits China might get from closer collaboration with the Soviet Union, making the Chinese leadership aware that the Soviet Union might contribute in an important way to the success of the Four Modernizations, especially since so many of the Chinese industrial plants built in the 1950s with Soviet assistance could be relatively easily and cheaply modernized at a fraction of the cost of importing Japanese and Western techology.[41] Soviet economic and technical assistance would make limited Chinese financial resources go a longer way.

Last, but not least, preparations were being made for the Twelfth Party Congress of the CCP, the first such congress since 1977. It is on occasions such as these that rhetoric is important, that symbolism is important, and that practical compromises—whether in domestic economic policy or in foreign policy—must be camouflaged. Officially, China never tired of reminding everybody that it was a poor, developing Third World country and that it did not aspire to superpower status, although in reality it did not give up its veto-wielding seat as a permanent member of the Security Council of the United Nations. And, since China's relations with Third World countries were somewhat neglected and one encountered less reference to the Three Worlds Theory during the heyday of its overly optimistic reliance on economic, technological, and, to a smaller extent, security assistance from the United States, Japan, and Western Europe, a party congress would be an occasion when all the right symbolism and rhetoric could be provided. Thus, Hu Yaobang's section on foreign policy in his long report to the Congress was entitled "Adhering to an Independent Foreign Policy."[42] Most of the speech was devoted to China's "lofty international duty," the propostion that "China never attaches itself to any big power," the Five Principles of Peaceful Coexistence, and to the Third World. Yet three countries received special treatment in the form of separate paragraphs discussing China's relations with, in this order, Japan (30 lines), the United States (33 lines), and the Soviet Union (27 lines). Japan was warned that "some forces in Japan are whitewashing the past Japanese aggressions against China and other East Asian countries and are carrying out activities for the revival of Japanese militarism," but that

> together with the Japanese people and with far-sighted Japanese public figures in and out of government, we will work to eliminate all hindrances to the relations between our two countries and make the friendship between our two peoples flourish from generation to generation.[43]

The United States came in for some severe criticism for its Taiwan policy, or as Hu Yaobang put it, "a cloud [that] has all along hung over the relations between the two countries," and he concluded by saying that

> Sino-US relations can continue to develop soundly only if the principles of mutual respect for sovereignty and territorial integrity and non-interference in each other's internal affairs are truly ahdered to.[44]

Hu Yaobang's reference to the Soviet Union likewise contained serious complaints but also the hope that its northern neighbor would somehow mend it ways with deeds:

> The relations between China and the Soviet Union were friendly over a fairly long period. They have become what they are today because the Soviet Union has pursued a hegemonist policy. For the past 20 years, the Soviet Union has stationed massive armed forces along the Sino-Soviet and Sino-Mongolian borders. It has supported Viet Nam in the latter's invasion and occupation of Kampuchea, acts of expansion in Indochina and Southeast Asia and constant provocations along China's border. Moreover, it has invaded and occupied Afghanistan, a neighbor of China, by force of arms. All these acts constitute grave threats to the peace of Asia and to China's security. We note that Soviet leaders have expressed more than once the desire to improve relations with China. But deeds, rather than words, are important. If the Soviet authorities really have a sincere desire to improve relations with China and take practical steps to lift their threat to the security of our country, it will be possible for Sino-Soviet relations to move towards normalization. The friendship between the Chinese and Soviet peoples is of long standing, and will strive to safeguard and develop this friendship, no matter what Sino-Soviet state relations are like.[45]

China was ready to play with all three other actors in the stategic quadrangle.

Japanese Prime Minister Zenko Suzuki visited Beijing at the end of September, reciprocating the visit of Premier Zhao Ziyang and commemorating the tenth anniversary of the establishment of diplomatic relations between the two countries. High-level U.S. visitors did not arrive until early in 1983, but the Sino-Soviet vice ministerial talks between Ilyichev and Qian Qichen began in Beijing on October 5.

The Soviet diplomat stayed in Beijing for three weeks, but no official disclosure about the talks was made in either capital, except to note that the next round would be held in a few months in Moscow. Brezhnev made comments about the need to improve relations with China before and after the Ilyichev talks.[46] Although he died two weeks later, the occasion of his funeral provided an opportunity for the new Soviet leader Yuri Andropov to show special attention to the Chinese Foreign Minister Huang Hua who represented China at the Brezhnev rites. (Actually, most countries were represented by heads of state, prime ministers, vice-presidents, and the like, and China's representative, a foreign minister, was one of the lowest rank.) Huang Hua also met with Gromyko, the first Sino-Soviet ministerial meeting in a very long time.[47] The exchange of greetings on October 1, China's National Day and the anniversary of the October Revolution (actually November 7), were somewhat warmer than in previous years, and the Chinese ambassador attended the Red Square celebrations for the first time in about two decades.[48] The sixtieth anniversary of the establishment of the U.S.S.R. in December was likewise commemorated by China with a special cable from the National People's Congress and the State Council and with high-level Chinese attendance of the celebrations at the Soviet Embassy in Beijing. Soviet coverage of China was deliberately correct and several Soviet officials dropped hints about the progress being made at the Sino-Soviet talks. Chinese references were much more guarded and Chinese criticism of the Soviet Union was toned down but not absent. And the third anniversary of the Soviet occupation of Afghanistan was not left unnoticed by the Chinese press.[49]

Talks in 1983-84

The second and third rounds of talks were held in March and October 1983 in Moscow and Beijing, respectively. No progress was reported at either session insofar as the substantive issues—or what the Chinese side calls "the obstacles" to normalization—were concerned. But during the second round a trade accord was reached which was supposed to increase bilateral Sino-Soviet trade for 1983 from three hundred million to eight hundred million dollars. Equally important, and of symbolic significance, after almost twenty years direct trade was to resume in the border regions such as Inner Mongolia and Chita Oblast, across the Amur and Ussuri rivers, and in the Sinkiang—Central Asian borderlands. The negotiations also led to another accord on the exchange of students and of experts in the fields of agriculture, science, and technology. The Chinese would send agricultural experts, while the Soviets would help China remodel or update the industrial plants built with Soviet assistance in the 1950s.

The talks were described as "beneficial," even though the sessions must have been frustrating. The Chinese pressed their demands on the removal of the Soviet threat in the north, southeast, and southwest, and the Soviets hid behind the principle of not discussing problems affecting third countries (Mongolia, Vietnam, Cambodia, and Afghanistan)[50] and pushed a treaty—or an agreement, or even a joint declaration—pledging nonaggression and security on the borders which the Chinese in turn would reject on the grounds that "such a document is meaningless while the three major obstacles remain."[51]

In what kind of atmosphere did the talks take place? On the bilateral level, the Soviets released in January, 1983 an article in the *New Times* responding to "dozens of articles denigrating the political course of the U.S.S.R.," which had appeared in *People's Daily* in November and December 1982, and complaining bitterly about Chinese "unfounded territorial claims."[52] The Chinese duly responded, and in general the Soviet and Chinese media continued their usual polemics. On the international level, the second round was preceded by the visits to China in February of Secretary of State George Schultz and Susumu Nikaido, the secretary-general of the ruling Liberal Democratic Party and special envoy of Prime Minister Nakasone, and was followed by a high level Chinese economic mission to Japan.

The third round of Sino-Soviet talks, in October, also took place amid important Sino-Japanese and Sino-American diplomatic activity. The Third Sino-Japanese Ministerial Conference was held in Beijing in early September and Secretary of Defense Caspar Weinberger visited China at the end of the month, while General Secretary Hu Yaobang and Foreign Minister Wu Xueqian made a very successful week-long trip to Japan, which led to a mutual pledge "to work together for an enduring harmony which will last through the next century and beyond."[53]

Although news reports alleged that the Soviets offered to freeze its military buildup along the Chinese frontier, remove nuclear weapons from border areas, and establish a Moscow-Beijing communications hot line,[54] it seems that the only tangible result of the third round of talks was an agreement to resume after almost twenty years what is called "tourist exchanges." In reality these began with an exchange of activists from the Soviet-Chinese Friendship Society and the Union of Soviet Societies for Friendship with Foreign Countries on the one hand and the Chinese

People's Society for Friendship with Foreign Countries and the Chinese-Soviet Friendship Society on the other.[55]

Perhaps more important than the regular Ilyichev-Qian round was China's attempt to play triangular diplomacy in officially inviting the Foreign Vice Minister Mikhail Kapitsa to Beijing, billed by Xinhua News Agency as "the first high-ranking Soviet government official to come to China on an official visit in over twenty years," just before the scheduled Weinberger visit. No breakthrough was reported, or probably anticipated, and at the end of the visit a meeting between the Soviet and Chinese foreign ministers was scheduled to take place during the autumn session of the United Nations. In the aftermath of the shooting down of the Korean airliner, however, Gromyko canceled his trip to New York and the Sino-Soviet ministerial meeting did not take place.

Soviet media coverage of the Weinberger and the Hu Yaobang visits was on the whole restrained insofar as China was concerned, concentrating mostly on U.S. and Japanese motives. Foreign Minister Wu Xueqian, however, came in for some shrill criticism for his statement in Hokkaido in which he supported Japan's territorial claims against the Soviet Union,[56] and for what *Izvestiia* called "Tendentious Statements" regarding his analysis of the breakdown of the arms control talks in Geneva.[57]

The fourth round of Sino-Soviet "consultations" took place in Moscow, March 12-26, 1984, between two delegations headed by the same veteran negotiators, Ilyichev and Qian Qichen. The talks were described as having proceeded in a "frank and calm atmosphere," and both sides were said to believe they had been "useful." Although both sides pointed out that since the consultations began in the latter part of 1982, economic, trade, scientific, cultural, and sports ties and exchanges had increased, no mention was made of any progress on substantive issues, even though it was announced that an exchange of views had taken place on the "normalization of Sino-Soviet relations, bilateral contacts and world issues."[58] The fifth round of talks took place in Beijing in October 1984, during which the Chinese were reported to have omitted mention of their previous three preconditions.

Since the March 1984 talks were held in Moscow shortly after the death of General Secretary Yuri Andropov, it should be noted that compared to the 1982 Brezhnev funeral, the Chinese delegation to the Andropov rites was upgraded and headed by Vice Premier Wan Li, who in accordance with protocol was thanked for coming by his counterpart, the Soviet first vice chairman of the Council of Ministers, Geidar Ali Aliev. No special attention was shown to the Chinese guests by the new Soviet leader Konstantin Chernenko, in contrast to Andropov's gesture to Huang Hua fifteen months earlier, and in spite of more effusive condolences expressed by the Chinese government.[59] However, Andropov's death coincided with the visit to Beijing of a Soviet trade delegation headed by Vice Minister of Foreign Trade Ivan Grishin, who came to negotiate the 1984 agreement on the exchange of goods and payments. The new agreement calls for Sino-Soviet trade of 1.2 billion dollars, an increase of 60 percent.[60]

What is far more important, however, is that these Sino-Soviet vice ministerial talks were held during the visit to Beijing of the Japanese Prime Minister Yasuhiro Nakasone, and bracketed by Premier Zhao Ziyang's visit to the United States in January and President Reagan's visit to China in April. *Pravda* observed that "crude distortions" were made of Soviet foreign policy and in all instances nervously commented on U.S. and Japanese attempts to draw China into a strategic alliance against the Soviet Union.[61] Although in all these commentaries the blame was largely placed on the Americans and the Japanese, and China was treated with restraint, the cumulative effect of all these visits, and especially President Reagan's signing of the Sino-American accord on nuclear technology (along with the scheduled visit to Washington of the Chinese Defense Minister), must have sufficiently alarmed the Soviet leadership that they decided to send a warning signal to China. This took the form of the postponement, on twenty-four hours notice, of the visit to Beijing by Ivan Arkhipov, first vice chairman of the Soviet Council of Ministers. He would have been the highest ranking Soviet official to come to China in fifteen years, since Premier Kosygin's visit in the fall of 1969.[62] More significant than his current position, Arkhipov in the 1950s was the general advisor for the Soviet experts in China, and his visit could have resulted in an important upgrading of industrial plants built with Soviet assistance, one tangible card that the Soviets hold vis-à-vis the Four Modernizations. Of course, the Arkhipov visit can be rescheduled and further progress can be made in the next round of talks on subsidiary issues. But true to its clumsy practice, the Soviet Union has again chosen to act tough and defiant. Refusing to concede on the three substantive issues, the Soviet Union's best hope to lure China away from the Western alliance is to use the economic carrot of increased trade, and especially the modernization of the Chinese industrial plants built with Soviet assistance. It seems that we can always count on the aged, suspicious, and embattled Soviet leadership to act in the only way it knows how in the dog-eat-dog, kto-kovo survival politics of the Soviet domestic scene. But international politics are not Soviet domestic politics, and time and again Soviet pressure policies have backfired, most spectacularly and continuously in the case of Japan, and more recently during the general elections in West Germany. It is no coincidence that *all* advanced industrial powers are solidly aligned against the Soviet Union. The inflexible Soviet leaders seem to be helping the West also in its dealings with China.

It was a smart Soviet move in 1981 and 1982 to attempt to bring China back to the negotiating table at a time of a cooling in Sino-American relations and even for a while in Sino-Japanese relations (over the issue of revised Japanese textbooks minimizing Japanese aggression against China). Whether it was wise for the Soviets to stonewall on the three "obstacles" and refuse to reduce the Soviet military presence at least on China's borders in the north and in Mongolia is another question. There was probably much domestic opposition, especially from the military establishment, to give up tangible assets in exchange for intangible Chinese goodwill for what the Soviet Union fears is a strong irredentist China on its borders.[63] Soviet policy vis-à-vis China is basically threefold: (1) prevent, or at least delay, China's becoming a first-class industrial, military, and nuclear power; (2) prevent other powers from aligning themselves with China and helping it achieve a true great power status through its Four Modernizations; and (3) create a military posture to pressure China in the short run, and prepare for growing Chinese power in the long run. Thus one can see the Soviet dilemma and the risks involved as they perceived them. And it is in this light that we can understand Soviet uneasiness, or even rage, when the United States is willing to provide China with weapons and especially weapons technology. The Chinese, in contrast, are going ahead with increased contacts in spite of the postponement of the Arkhipov visit. Foreign Vice Minister Qian visited Moscow at the end of June 1984.

Future Scenarios

In dealing with future scenarios of Sino-Soviet relations, it is extremely important to think in terms of the leadership characteristics on both sides. The Soviet leadership group seems much more durable and cohesive as compared with China, where, in the last dozen years, we have seen the passing from the political scene of such personalities as Mao Zedong, Zhou Enlai, Liu Shaoqi, Lin Biao, and more ephemeral types such as the Gang of Four and Hua Guofeng. In fact, the degree of opposition to the present ruling Deng-Hu-Zhao triumvirate is a matter of debate among scholars. What kind of leaders will emerge in the post-Deng period? Who will lead the Soviet Union after the Brezhnev generation passes from the political scene? The political, ideological, and philosophical makeup of the ruling groups is an extremely important factor in the formulation of foreign policy.

In a book on Sino-Soviet relations, Yung-hwan Jo and Ying-hsien Pi suggested a rather useful typology (adapted from Thomas Robinson)[64] of leadership groups in both China and the Soviet Union. And while I think that it is convenient to think in terms of hard-line, middle-, and soft-line Soviet leadership and radical, "muddle through," and pragmatic Chinese counterparts, I would further make the distinction in each case between foreign and domestic policy. A group can combine a hard-line foreign policy approach with the relatively liberal stance on economic reform. In the mid-1930s Stalin combined a moderate "popular front" foreign policy with a very repressive regime at home. So I would argue that both the foreign and the domestic policies of the ruling group must be considered in our attempt to analyze future interactions between China and the Soviet Union. For example, if the Soviet leadership attempts to introduce serious economic reforms, China will have a breathing spell and will experience less pressure from its northern neighbor. Conversely, the reordering of the Four Modernizations in terms of a higher priority for military modernization, with a corresponding increase in the allocation of resources to the military, will stiffen the Soviet position on the need to maintain large forces on the Sino-Soviet border.

Mineo Nakajima, a prominent China specialist on the faculty of the Tokyo University of Foreign Studies, argues that the convergence of Soviet and Chinese *domestic* policies should steer China toward a rapprochement with the Soviet Union.[65] He contends that the logic of the reforms of the Four Modernizations, accompanied as they are by de-Maoization, will bring China simultaneously to the Soviet New Economic Policies of the 1920s and the age of de-Stalinization of the 1950s.[66] He claims that "the Soviet Union offers the only practical model for China"[67] and that "China will pattern itself on the Soviet model."[68] Nakajima notes that Soviet experts (such as Vice Foreign Minister Qian Qichen) are gaining increasing prominence, and he makes a great deal of the full posthumous rehabilitation of Marshal Peng Dehuai, whose sympathies with Khrushchev, he claims, "were unmistakable,"[69] and the fact that several of Peng's associates (most notably the present Defense Minister Zhang Aiping) have not only been rehabilitated but are back in positions of power. He also cites as significant the rehabilitation and reappointment to important positions in two strategically important Manchurian provinces, Liaoning and Heilongjiang, of the disgraced associates of Gao Gang, the Communist "warlord" of Manchuria purged by the central government in the early 1950s.

This analysis assumes that pro-Soviet elements in the Chinese leadership in the 1950s have remained pro-Soviet and that experts on the Soviet Union are somehow by definition sympathetic to Moscow's policies. Yet, veteran anti-Communist Richard Nixon led the United States into a rapprochement with Communist China and Soviet expert Richard Allen can hardly be accused of harboring pro-Communist sympathies and using his position in the National Security Council to promote policies of détente and rapprochement with Communist powers.

On the systemic level, the reader is referred back to chapter 1, where I have discussed the dynamics of the strategic triangle and quadrangle. These relationships were treated in terms of cooperative, conflictual, and mixed or transitional modes. But the reality of bilateral relations is much more complex. In assessing the future of Sino-Soviet relations, I would like to go beyond these three modes and suggest the following seven types of relationships:

(1) formal alliance;
(2) informal or quasi-alliance;
(3) entente, rapprochement, or reconciliation;
(4) neutral, correct equidistant relationship;
(5) détente or tolerable relationship;
(6) confrontation or Cold War (border clashes); and
(7) war (limited or general).

If one looks at the 1978 to early 1980 period, the relationship between China and the United States can be characterized as Type 2, informal or quasi-alliance directed against the Soviet Union. Sino-Soviet relations since 1969 are Type 6, a Cold War-like confrontation with occasional border clashes.

Are these two types of relationships the best for China under the circumstances? First, I would argue that the short-lived anti-Soviet quasi-alliance among China, the United States, Japan, and Western Europe was the result of undue aggressiveness on the part of the Soviet Union[70] coupled with the Chinese perception of an indecisive and weakening United States. For China to become a participant, albeit an informal one, in a hostile coalition against its much stronger and quite threatening neighbor is not optimum policy. (For related reasons, some U.S. scholars have argued that the United States should adopt an equidistant posture toward the two Communist superpowers, instead of joining China in an anti-Soviet united front.)[71] The advent of a strongly anti-Soviet new U.S. administration with its trillion and a half dollar rearmament program improved China's chances of getting some concessions from the Soviet Union, while Reagan's pro-Taiwan gestures have come just in time to strengthen Chinese resolve to keep a little distance from the United States. Thus I would suggest it is in China's best interest to improve its relationship with the Soviet Union from Type 6 to Type 5—a détente-type tolerable relationship—while at the same time lower the relationship with the United States from Type 2 to Type 3, still retaining close relations but not in the context of an anti-Soviet front.[72]

In the present deep-freeze in Soviet-American relations, China has more room to maneuver. But playing one superpower against the other is not without pitfalls. What are Chinese calculations if and when the two superpowers reach some sort of accord on both the European theater and global balance of nuclear forces? Unlikely as it seems now, what if the United States and the Soviet Union restore their relations even to a fraction of the Nixon-Kissinger détente stage? China would most likely seek redress outside the strategic triangle, probably in closer ties with Japan and secondarily with Western Europe, Canada, and Australasia (Chairman Mao's Second Intermediate Zone). In fact, inasmuch as I see a quadrilateral relationship, China can continue to maintain a Type 2 relationship with Japan (and possibly with the other members of the Western alliance),[73] as this would be seen by the Soviets to be less threatening than a Sino-American coalition.

As I have already stated, vis-à-vis the Soviet Union, China is a revisionist irredentist power that wants to effect some changes in the territorial status between the two countries and lessen the Soviet threat to its security, especially in the north. The Soviet Union at the minimum wishes to freeze the status quo vis-à-vis China, preserving its territory and military advantage. In fact, time has not been on China's side: in early 1978 China spoke of one major obstacle to the normalization of relations with its northern neighbor, namely the Soviet military pressure on the northern border and in Mongolia. By late 1978, with the Soviet-Vietnamese alliance, there were two obstacles, and by early 1980, with the Soviet occupation of Afghanistan, there were three obstacles.

I would look at the future of Sino-Soviet relations in the following three-part time frame:

(1) *Tactically* (short range)—China will talk about an independent stance in foreign policy,[74] emphasizing from time to time the importance of relations with the Third World, and will try to extract some substantive concessions from the Soviet Union by holding out a promise not to go all the way with the United States and its allies.

(2) *Strategically* (middle range)—China needs a peaceful environment for the success of its Four Modernizations, and it needs technology and capital that only the United States, Japan, and the West can provide.[75]

(3) *Long Range*—as China develops its industrial base, its economic infrastructure, and its military forces, it can safely seek equidistance or even-handedness toward the Soviet Union and the West.

As for now (to answer the question in the title of this chapter), there is no fundamental turn in Sino-Soviet relations, as yet. There is likely to be some rhetorical posturing, some loosening of Sino-American ties away from the anti-Soviet united front, and some openings to the northern neighbor. But the Soviet Union is likely to give up its tangible military-strategic advantages and it is unable to fully satisfy China's economic, technological, and financial needs. China's future in the short and middle range still lies with the West.

Notes

1. Mark Mancall, *Russia and China: Their Diplomatic Relations to 1728* (Cambridge, Mass.: Harvard University Press, 1971) and O. Edmund Clubb, *China and Russia: The "Great Game"* (New York: Columbia University Press, 1971).

2. See "The Japanese-Soviet Neutrality Pact" by Chihiro Hosoya (translated and with an introduction by Peter A. Berton) in James William Morley, ed., *The Fateful Choice: Japan's Advance into Southeast Asia, 1939-1941* (New York: Columbia University Press, 1980), pp. 1-114.

3. See "Soviet Assistance in the Strenghtening of the Revolutionary Base in Manchuria" in O. B. Borisov and B. T. Koloskov (pseud.), *Sovetsko-kitaiskie otnosheniia, 1945-1970* (Moscow: Mysl', 1972), pp. 28-44, or the English translation *Soviet-Chinese Relations, 1945-1970,* edited with an introductory essay by Vladimir Petrov (Bloomington: Indiana University Press, 1975), pp. 52-62.

4. For difficulties (especially on economic issues) encountered by the Chinese delegation during negotiations with the Soviet Union in 1950, see Wu Xiuquan, "Memoirs of a Veteran Diplomat: Sino-Soviet Relations in the Early 1950s," *Beijing Review,* Vol. 26, No. 47 (November 21, 1983), pp. 16-21 and 30.

5. It should be noted that on the occasion of the sixtieth anniversary of the founding of the CCP, *Pravda* listed Gao Gang among the "outstanding revolutionaries who represented proletarian Marxism-Leninism and internationalism" in the Chinese party as opposed to the "petty-bourgeois, great-power and chauvinistic [line] epitomized in the activities of Mao Zedong and his followers." I. Aleksandrov, "On the Sixtieth Anniversary of the Communist Party of China," *Pravda,* July 1, 1981. *K.D.K. Information (Tokyo),* No. 81/8 (August 1981), p. 3. Gao Gang was also commemorated in December 1980 as "a true Marxist and faithful friend of the Soviet Union" who advocated close cooperation with the Soviet Union, for which he was persecuted to death. Quarterly Chronicle and Documentation, *China Quarterly,* No. 86 (June 1981), p. 396.

6. Mikhail Kapitsa, a senior China specialist in the Soviet Foreign Ministry, wrote that "after Stalin's death, Mao Zedong began claiming to be the leader of the world communist movement. In China, posters depicting the profiles of Marx, Engels, Lenin, Stalin, and Mao Zedong were put out in vast numbers." M. Ukraintsev (pseud.), "Soviet Chinese Relations: Problems and Prospects," *Far Eastern Affairs* (Moscow), No. 3, 1982, pp. 15-24 at p. 15.

7. Mao also made a rather unfortunate remark about his conviction that mankind will survive a nuclear war. Speech in Moscow, November 18, 1957, *Peking Review,* Vol. 6, No. 36 (September 6, 1963), p. 10. In the Taiwan Straits crisis, it is significant that Soviet support for China came *after* the crisis had been defused.

8. The Chinese began their version of the history of the dispute by observing that "it takes more than one cold day for the river to freeze three feet deep," that it all started in 1956, and that the Soviet version was "a big lie." *The Origin and Development of the Differences Between the Leadership of the CPSU and Ourselves* (Peking: Foreign Languages Press, 1963).

For a very readable account of Sino-Soviet differences, see Klaus Mehnert, *Peking and Moscow* (New York: Mentor Books, 1964). See also Donald W. Treadgold, ed., *Soviet and Chinese Communism: Similarities and Differences* (Seattle: University of Washington Press, 1967).

9. For a classic study, see Donald S. Zagoria, *The Sino-Soviet Conflict, 1956-1961* (Princeton: Princeton University Press, 1962). Relevant documentation can be found in G. F. Hudson, Richard Lowenthal, and Roderick MacFarquhar, eds., *The Sino-Soviet Dispute* (New York: Praeger, 1962).

10. William E. Griffith, ed., *Albania and the Sino-Soviet Rift* (Cambridge, Mass.: M.I.T. Press, 1963) and Alexander Dallin, ed., *Diversity in International Communism: A Documentary Record* (New York: Columbia University Press, 1963).

11. Peter Berton, comp., *The Chinese-Russian Dialogue* (Los Angeles: University of Southern California, 1963), 2 vols. (see especially a 16-page chronology of Sino-Soviet relations, June, 1949-October, 1963), and William E. Griffith, ed., *The Sino-Soviet Rift* (Cambridge, Mass.: M.I.T. Press, 1964).

12. Peter Berton, "Background to the Territorial Issue [between China and the Soviet Union]," *Studies in Comparative Communism*, Vol. 2, Nos. 3 & 4 (July/October 1969), pp. 130-48; Dennis J. Doolin, *Territorial Claims in the Sino-Soviet Conflict* (Stanford: Hoover Institution Press, 1965); and George Ginsburgs and Carl F. Pinkele, *The Sino-Soviet Territorial Dispute, 1949-1964* (New York: Praeger, 1978).

13. William E. Griffith, ed., *Sino-Soviet Relations, 1964-1965* (Cambridge, Mass.: M.I.T. Press, 1967) and John Gittings, *Survey of the Sino-Soviet Dispute* (London: Oxford University Press, 1968). For the impact of the Sino-Soviet dispute on the Communist world, see Adam Bromke, *The Communist States at the Crossroads Between Moscow and Peking* (New York: Praeger, 1965); and Adam Bromke and Teresa Rakowska-Harmstone, eds., *The Communist States in Disarray, 1965-1971* (Minneapolis: University of Minnesota Press, 1972).

14. Thomas M. Gottlieb, *Chinese Foreign Policy Factionalism and the Origins of the Strategic Triangle* (Santa Monica: Rand, November 1977, R-1902-NA).

15. Thomas W. Robinson, "The Sino-Soviet Border Dispute: Background, Development, and the March 1969 Clashes," *American Political Science Review*, Vol. 66. No. 4 (December 1972). pp. 1175-1202; Richard Wich, *Sino-Soviet Crisis Politics: A Study of Political Change and Communication* (Cambridge, Mass.: Harvard University Press, 1980); and Alfred D. Low, *The Sino-Soviet Dispute: An Analysis of the Polemics* (Rutherford, N.J.: Fairleigh Dickinson University Press, 1976).

16. Other scholars further subdivide this period. Kenneth Lieberthal writing in 1978 disinguished the periods of (1) 1969-73 (Soviet attempts to contain China, while encouraging potentially pro-Soviet leaders); (2) August 1973 to September 1976 (no new Soviet offers); and (3) the post-Mao phase (waiting for China to take up seriously pending Soviet offers). (Kenneth G. Lieberthal, *Sino-Soviet Conflict in the 1970s: Its Evolution and Implications for the Strategic Triangle* [Santa Monica: Rand, July 1978, R-2342-NA]). Writing in 1983, Chi Su sees five stages: (1) late 1960s to July 1971 (Henry Kissinger's secret trip to China); (2) July 1971 to late 1973; (3) late 1973 to May 1978 (National Security Advisor Zbigniew Brzezinski's trip); (4) May 1978 to January 1980 (Defense Secretary Harold Brown's trip); and (5) since January 1980. (Chi Su, "U.S.-China Relations: Soviet Views and Policies," *Asian Survey*, Vol. XXIII, No. 5 (May 1983), pp. 555-79). James Hsiung in the present volume comes up empirically with the following subphases: (1) 1969-71, (2) 1972-74, (3) 1975-77, and (4) 1978-80 (end of data). (See chap. 7, below.)

17. Border talks were conducted annually from 1969 to 1978, with sessions lasting from two to five months. The Soviet delegation tabled a number of drafts of treaties and agreements, which were rejected by the Chinese side. Border river navigation talks are supposed to be held annually, but only five sessions (the 16th to

the 20th) were held between 1970 and 1977, when a limited agreement was reached on the Ussuri River navigation. Annual trade talks are held to set the level of bilateral trade and these meetings have been rotated between Beijing and Moscow.

18. The choice of Shcherbakov was very significant in highlighting the importance the Soviet Union paid to the Vietnam factor in Sino-Soviet relations. After serving as minister-counselor in the Soviet Embassy in Beijing in 1963–64, Shcherbakov spent a decade as the Soviet ambassador in Hanoi.

19. Foreign Broadcast Information Service (FBIS), *Daily Report*, PRC, April 3, 1979, p. C1.

20. Vice Premier Geng Biao confirmed that the proposal for the Sino-Soviet talks was initiated by China "in order to keep interstate relations between China and the Soviet Union after the expiration of their alliance treaty." Interview with the visiting director general of the Japanese NHK broadcasting agency on August 11, 1979. *K.D.K. Information*, No. 9/79 (September 1979), p. 4.

21. *Asian Security 1979* (Tokyo: Research Institute for Peace and Security, 1979), p. 68. In November 1980 Deng Xiaoping was reported to have said: "Khrushchev only played with words, whereas Brezhnev threatens us with strength." *Christian Science Monitor*, November 15, 1980, cited in Quarterly Chronicle and Documentation, *China Quarterly*, No. 85 (March 1981), p. 198.

22. *Krasnaia zvezda*, September 17, 1978, cited in *Asian Security 1979*, p. 37.

23. The draft of the Treaty on Goodneighbourhood and Cooperation between the Soviet Union and Japan can be found in Rodger Swearingen, *The Soviet Union and Postwar Japan: Escalating Challenge and Response* (Stanford: Hoover Institution Press, 1978), pp. 289–91.

24. *Asian Security 1980*, pp. 12–13.

25. *Ibid.*, p. 13.

26. M. Ukraintsev (pseud.), "Soviet-Chinese Relations: Problems and Prospects," *Far Eastern Affairs*, No. 3, 1982, pp. 15–24 at p. 17.

27. Prof. M. Ukraintsev (pseud.), "Entering the Fourth Decade (Notes on the PRC's Foreign Policy)," *Far Eastern Affairs*, No. 4, 1981, p. 50.

28. For the Soviet military buildup, see the annual *Asian Security* published since 1979 by the Research Institute for Peace and Security in Tokyo; Harry Gelman, *The Soviet Far East Buildup and Soviet Risk-Taking Against China* (Santa Monica: Rand, August 1982, R-2943-AF) and *Soviet Expansionism in Asia and the Sino-Soviet-US Triangle* (Marina del Rey, Calif.: Security Conference on Asia and the Pacific, March 1983); Jonathan D. Pollack, *The Sino-Soviet Rivalry and Chinese Security Debate* (Santa Monica: Rand, October 1982, R-2907-AF); C.G. Jacobsen, *Sino-Soviet Relations Since Mao: The Chairman's Legacy* (New York: Praeger, 1981); especially chap. 1, "The Strategic Context," pp. 18–40; and Part Two, "The Military Dimension: Comparisons and Scenarios," in Douglas T. Stuart and William T. Tow, eds., *China, the Soviet Union, and the West: Strategic and Political Dimensions in the 1980s* (Boulder, Colo.: Westview Press, 1982).

29. Ukraintsev, "Soviet-Chinese Relations," pp. 21–22. On similar Soviet moves toward Japan, see Hiroshi Kimura, "The Soviet Proposal on Confidence-Building Measures and the Japanese Response," *Journal of International Affairs*, Vol. 37, No. 1 (Summer 1983), pp. 81–104.

30. Li Yun, "Afghanistan: Soviet Occupation of the Wakhan Area," *Beijing Review*, Vol. 24, No. 7 (February 16, 1981), p. 10.

31. See the statement of the Soviet Foreign Ministry in *Pravda*, August 12, 1981, in *Current Digest of the Soviet Press* (*CDSP*), Vol. XXXIII, No. 32 (September 9, 1981), p. 16; "China-USSR: The Disputed Area of the Pamirs," *Beijing Review*, Vol. 24, No. 37 (September 14, 1981), pp. 21-23; John W. Garver, "The Sino-Soviet Territorial Dispute in the Pamir Mountains Region," *China Quarterly*, No. 85 (March 1981), pp. 107-118; and James G. Monroe, Jr., "Garver's Pro-Soviet Tilt: Do the Data Tell the Truth?" and John W. Garver's reply in *China Quarterly*, No. 88 (December 1981), pp. 686-90.

32. Li Huichuan, "The Crux of the Sino-Soviet Boundary Question," *Beijing Review*, Vol. 24, No. 30 (July 27, 1981), pp. 12-17 and p. 31, and No. 31 (August 3, 1981), pp. 13-16.

33. P. Dalnev, "Peking's Words and Deeds: The Essence of the Difficulties at the Soviet-Chinese Border Negotiations," *International Affairs* (Moscow), No. 11, 1981, pp. 68-85.

34. *Ibid.*, p. 68.

35. O. Borisov (pseud.), "The Situation in the PRC and some of the Tasks of Soviet Sinology," *Far Eastern Affairs*, No. 3, 1982, pp. 3-14 at p. 13.

36. The Soviet proposal to resume negotiations made six months earlier, in September 1981, did not elicit outright Chinese rejection.

37. *Pravda* and *Izvestiia*, March 24, 1982, in *CDSP*, Vol. XXXIV, No. 12 (April 21, 1982), p. 6.

38. *Pravda* and *Izvestiia*, February 24, 1981, in *CDSP*, Vol. XXXIII, No. 8 (March 25, 1981), pp. 6-7.

39. Radio Beijing, March 27, 1982, and a comment by Xinhua Correspondent in *Beijing Review*, Vol. 25, No. 14 (April 5, 1982), p. 11. "Deeds rather than words" is a familiar Chinese formula in responding to Soviet offers. See, for example, "Renmin Ribao" Commentator, "Real Deeds, Yes; Hollow Statements, No!" *Peking Review*, Vol. 21, No. 13 (March 31, 1978), pp. 14-16; and "As a Chinese saying goes, 'Judge a man by his deeds, and not his words.' We want action from the Soviet Union." Mu Youlin, "Sino-Soviet Relations," *Beijing Review*, Vol. 25, No. 29 (July 19, 1982), p. 3.

40. "Premier Zhao on Sino-Japanese Relations and Other Questions," *Beijing Review*, Vol. 25, No. 21 (May 24, 1982), p. 5. For a Soviet reaction to the Zhao visit to Japan, see Yuly Yakhontov in *Pravda*, June 6, 1982, in *CDSP*, Vol. XXXIV, No. 23 (July 7, 1982), p. 22.

41. According to Soviet claims, under Soviet technical assistance, 256 industrial projects were completed in China, which in the early 1960s accounted for 30 percent of China's total output of commodities, 40 percent of steel, 50 percent of rolled steel, 80 percent of motor vehicles, more than 90 percent of tractors, 25 percent of electric power, 55 percent of hydroelectric powergenerating equipment, and so forth. Eighty-five other projects were completed with the assistance of other socialist countries. Alekseyev commentary, "Important Factors in the Development of People's China Along the Socialist Road," Radio Moscow in Mandarin, September 27, 1982, in FBIS, *Daily Report*, USSR International Affairs, China, September 30, 1982, p. B 3. The extent of Soviet aid to China during the 1950s is discussed in S. Manezhev and L. Novosyolova, "The Role of External Factors in China's Economic Development," *Far Eastern Affairs*, No. 2, 1983, pp. 38-50.

42. Hu Yaobang, "Create a New Situation in All Fields of Socialist Modernization," *Beijing Review*, Vol. 25, No. 37 (September 13, 1982), pp 11–40. Two months later, an article by Huan Xiang, Vice President of the Academy of Social Sciences, was entitled "Adhere to Independent Foreign Policy," *Beijing Review*, Vol. 25, No. 46 (November 15, 1982), pp. 21-23.

43. Hu Yaobang, *op. cit.*, p. 30.

44. *Ibid.*

45. *Ibid.*, p. 31.

46. Speech in Baku on September 26 and address to military leaders in Moscow on October 27, 1982.

47. See FBIS, *Daily Report*, PRC International Affairs, Soviet Union and USSR National Affairs, Death of Brezhnev, November 11-19, 1982.

48. The Soviet greeting ended with "We *sincerely* wish the Chinese people. . . ." The Chinese reciprocated: "The Chinese side is *sincerely* striving to eliminate all obstacles. . . ." (Emphases added.) FBIS, *Daily Report*, USSR International Affairs, China, September 30, 1982, p. B 5, and PRC International Affairs, Soviet Union, November 8, 1982, p. C 1.

49. "The Afghan People Will Certainly Triumph," *Renmin Ribao* editorial, December 27, 1982 cited in FBIS, *Daily Report*, PRC International Affairs, South Asia, December 27, 1982, pp. 71-2 and Shi Jingfan, "The Afghan Situation in the Three Years Since the Soviet Invasion," *ibid.*, pp.72-3.

50. An article in the *Beijing Review* pointed out that from 1959 to 1977 the leaders of the Soviet Union and the United States held many summit talks and in at least seven of them they discussed the problems of Germany, Indochina, the Middle East, Europe, and other "third countries." (Vol. 26, No. 12 [March 21, 1983], p. 12).

51. *K.D.K. Information*, No. 4/83 (April 1, 1983), p. 1.

52. Observer, "What Is the Purpose?" *New Times* (Moscow), No. 3, January 1983, pp. 12-14.

53. "Hu's Visit to Japan a Success," *Beijing Review*, Vol. 26, No. 49 (December 5, 1983), p. 16.

54. Michael Parks in the *Los Angeles Times*, October 28, 1983, Part I, p. 5. See also Nayan Chanda's report ("A Glacially Slow Thaw," *Far Eastern Economic Review*, Vol. 122, No. 44 [November 3, 1983], pp. 31-33) of a Sino-Soviet agreement to modernize a factory in Harbin constructed with Soviet aid in the 1950s, and Richard Nations' ("Feeling for a Ceiling," *ibid.*, pp. 32-33) on the Soviet SS20 missiles, which have been raised as an issue in the Sino-Soviet talks.

55. The Soviet delegation was headed by Dr. Sergei Tikhvinsky, who is also serving as the first vice chairman of the Central Board of the Soviet-Chinese Friendship Society. "On a Mission of Friendship," *Izvestiia*, November 15, 1983, p. 5, in *CDSP*, Vol. XXXV, No. 46 (December 14, 1983), p. 9.

56. P. Dalnev, "Generosity at Someone Else's Expense," *Pravda*, November 30, 1983, p. 5, in *CDSP*, Vol. XXXV, No. 48 (December 28, 1983), p. 20.

57. A. Petrov, *Izvestiia*, December 6, 1983, p. 5, in *CDSP*, Vol. XXXV, No. 49 (January 4, 1984), pp. 20-21.

58. "Sino-Soviet Talks Seen as Useful," *Beijing Review*, Vol. 27, No. 15 (April 9, 1984), p. 11.

59. The Brezhnev condolence message was two lines long. It stated that he "unfortunately passed away," and expressed deep condolences. The Andropov message was five times as long. It began with "We were shocked to learn of the untimely death," conveyed profound condolences, quoted Andropov's desire for an improvement in Sino-Soviet relations, and expressed the Chinese government's sincere desire and hope to further develop these relations. FBIS, *Daily Report*, PRC International Affairs, Soviet Union, November 12, 1982, p. C 1, and USSR National Affairs, Death of Andropov, February 13, 1984, p. P 20.

It should also be mentioned that on the occasion of the sixty-sixth anniversary of the October Revolution celebrations in 1983, China for the first time in many years sent its holiday greetings and warm wishes to "the Government of the Soviet Union and the Soviet people" instead of only to the Soviet people. *Ibid.*, PRC International Affairs, Soviet Union, November 8, 1983, p. C 1.

60. "Sino-Soviet Trade to Climb by 60%," *Beijing Review*, Vol. 27, No. 9 (February 27, 1984), p. 11; *Izvestiia*, February 11, 1984.

61. *Pravda*, January 20, March 29, and April 28, 1984. For a Soviet view of the Sino-American rapprochement in the second half of the 1970s, see S. K. Merkulov, *Amerikano-kitaiskoe sblizhenie* (*vtoraia polovina 70-kh godov*) (Moscow: Nauka Publishers, 1980), 120 pp.

62. Radio Moscow, May 9, 1984.

63. Harry Gelman, in his prepared statement presented before the Subcommittee on Asian and Pacific Affairs of the House of Representatives on August 2, 1983, argued that the Soviet Union is unlikely to sacrifice "concrete geopolitical advantages around China's periphery." Harry Gelman, "Soviet Policy Toward China," *Survey*, Vol. 27, No. 118/119 (Autumn/Winter 1983), p. 165.

64. Yung-Hwan Jo and Ying-hsien Pi, *Russia Versus China and What Next?* (Lanham, Md.: University Press of America, 1980), p. 129, partially based on Thomas W. Robinson, "Future Domestic and Foreign Policy Choices for Mainland China," *Journal of International Affairs*, No. 2 (1972), pp. 192-215.

65. A PRC scholar on a visit to the United States made a similar point that "some in the Kremlin seem to recognize that China's new generation of leaders is determined to rebuild a Soviet-type system and view this decision as the basis of a Sino-Soviet reconciliation." Edmund Lee (pseud.), "Beijing's Balancing Act," *Foreign Policy*, No. 51 (Summer 1983), pp. 27-46 at p. 31.

66. Mineo Nakajima, "China May Return to the Soviet Bloc." *Japan Quarterly*, Vol. XXX, No. 2 (April-June 1983), pp. 181-87.

67. *Ibid.*, p. 186.

68. *Ibid.*, p. 185. Professor Nakajima cites an article entitled "China Should Learn from the Soviet Union," in *Chishi Niendai* (The 1970s), a Hong Kong magazine allegedly often articulating the views of Deng Xiaoping.

69. Nakajima, *op. cit.*, p. 182.

70. This represents Michel Tatu's fourth principle of triangular relationships: "Excessive aggressiveness on the part of one actor will provoke the collusion of the two other actors." Michel Tatu, *Washington-Moscou-Pékin et les deux Europe(s)* (n.p.: Casterman, 1972), p. 26.

71. Perhaps the most prominent advocate of equidistance is Robert Scalapino of the University of California at Berkeley. See, for example, Robert A. Scalapino's

"Approaches to Peace and Security in Asia: The Uncertainty Surrounding American Strategic Principles," chap. 1 in Sudershan Chawla and D. R. Sardesai, eds., *Changing Patterns of Security and Stability in Asia* (New York: Praeger, 1980), pp. 1–21.

72. It could be also argued, of course, that maintaining an implacable position vis-à-vis the Soviet Union is not only a sign of weakness but also a form of deterrence, which China would lose if it were to improve its relations with its northern neighbor without obtaining Soviet concessions on the crucial disposition of forces.

73. Premier Zhao Ziyang visited six West European countries May 29-June 16, 1984. See *Beijing Review* (June 25, 1984), pp. 6–12.

74. Chou Enlai, I believe, used to tell foreign visitors (including Henry Kissinger) to watch what the Chinese do and not what they say. Western analysts generally date China's more independent stance in world affairs from 1982 and the Twelfth CCP Congress. But on December 6, 1983, in his report on international affairs to the National People's Congress Standing Committee, Foreign Minister Wu Xuqian contended that China has been pursuing an independent foreign policy since the Third Plenum of the Eleventh Central Committee in December 1978, the time of China's most important agreements with Japan and the United States. At the same time, in December 1983, Huan Xiang, the director of the Beijing Institute of Foreign Affairs told a reporter from *Der Spiegel* that "our policy does not run equidistant from the two superpowers, because it is the Soviet Union that poses the direct threat to our country's security." In general, Western analysts overinterpret casual remarks made by Chinese leaders to foreign visitors, without evaluating the context of such meetings. It is obvious that different emphasis will be placed by the Chinese leaders depending on whether they are talking to an African head of state, an Italian Communist Party delegation, a U.S. secretary of state, a Yugoslav journalist, or a Japanese minister of finance.

75. Here a quotation from Sun Tzu might be appropriate: *Yuan jiao jin gung*—"Ally yourself with a distant state in order to attack (successfully) a close neighbor."

The Reagan Administration Turnaround on China
— 3 —

Stephen Uhalley, Jr.

There was a significant breakdown in relations between the United States and the People's Republic of China in 1983-84 as compared to the year 1979 when, seven years after President Richard Nixon's historic reopening of relations with China in 1972, the two countries had finally formally exchanged diplomatic recognition. That first year (1979) of the formal relationship proved, in fact, to be for some time the high point of relations as trade and other exchanges suddenly increased dramatically. Then came the U.S. presidential campaign in which candidate Ronald Reagan's sympathies regarding the PRC and Taiwan respectively became evident to all. When Reagan won election it was widely expected that the warmth of the relationship as developed during the Carter Administration would not be continued. Unsurprisingly, in fact, relations declined. By early 1983 relations had reached a low ebb and were continuing to deteriorate.

This is how matters stood despite the notable effort that had culminated in the August 17, 1982 communiqué designed to resolve for the time being the problem of U.S. arms sales to Taiwan. However, that ambiguous accord soon produced disagreement over what it meant and continued Chinese complaints that the United States was not adhering to the agreement.

In addition to this key issue regarding arms sales to Taiwan were other problems that exacerbated the deteriorating relationship. These included disagreement over textile quotas, the perplexing Qing Dynasty Huguang Railway bonds court case, the handling of tennis star Hu Na's defection, and the PRC's application for Asian Development Bank membership.

Other issues and developments were complicating and souring the relationship even more. On the Chinese side, there was increasing dissatisfaction that the United States was not fulfilling its commitment to help China's modernization program more meaningfully, primarily by facilitating the transfer of high technology. This disappointment may have influenced newer Chinese assessments of the global situation as a whole, contributing to the adoption in 1982 of a self-consciously independent foreign policy and the renewal of Sino-Soviet talks. For its part, the United States by late 1982 was placing less emphasis on the China relationship, particularly as a reliable counter to the Soviet Union. This change in the U.S. posture was accompanied by greatly increased critical evaluations of China by Americans. Both sides, it appeared, were beginning to regard each other more soberly and more realistically than may have been the case for much of the period since 1972. This contributed to the strain in the relationship, but it probably also augered well for the evolution of sounder or more realistic relations in the future.

Thus, by 1983 the U.S.-P.R.C. relationship was maturing into a more complex one. The reasons for the apparent deterioration were correspondingly complex. Similarly, the explanation for the sudden improvement of relations in the course of 1983 is more complicated than may appear to be the case in early readings of the available evidence. It is tempting to surmise, for example, that the United States obligingly reacted to the limited Chinese responsiveness to Soviet talk initiatives by finally deciding to facilitate technology transfer to China. Or, one might infer that the Reagan Administration was concerned about the paucity of notable foreign policy successes generally and was aware of an increasing vulnerability to impending presidential electoral campaign changes that the Chinese relationship, painstakingly improved by Presidents Nixon, Ford, and Carter, was being jeopardized by Reagan. Hence it decided to turn an otherwise expected campaign deficit into an asset by doing what was necessary to improve relations with Beijing. Conversely, the Chinese, satisfied with the prospect of the improved access to eagerly desired high technology, soon resolved or otherwise suspended or muted comments, for the time being, on other issues including the Taiwan problem. Of course, there is, in fact, something to each of these allegations, and in one way or another each has a part, with perhaps appropriate rephrasing in a suitably fuller complex explanation of what led to the apparently sudden improvement of relations.

It is well known that U.S.-P.R.C. relations faltered in the early Reagan Administration, partly because of public comments made by the President himself, both earlier while he had been campaigning for the presidency as well as after taking office. These comments conveyed the impression, probably very accurately, that Reagan would continue to be sympathetic to and supportive of Taiwan. In fact, some of Reagan's earlier campaign remarks were probably injudicious and unrealistic. For example, the suggested reinstitution of official ties with Taiwan was no longer an achievable prospect. But, in fact, since taking office Reagan began, inexorably, to modify his views, although he is not likely to jeopardize seriously an old ally, which he believes Taiwan to be. At the same time, as part of modifying his personal position he has accepted that U.S. relations with the PRC should continue to follow the lines already established by previous administrations. But in pursuing this fundamental policy orientation he has tried to convey the impression of being more deliberate than former President Carter and more careful not to concede what is unnecessary. Not even Reagan's primary anxiety regarding the Soviet Union has led him to be particularly susceptible to any desire to align with China in a close strategic relationship. Former Secretary of State Alexander Haig, who had strongly advocated moves in that direction, was early eased out of the Administration. This did not preclude some informal cooperation with Beijing, but there was no strong compulsion on the part of Reagan to move determinedly in this direction or to pay an unreasonable price for it. In short, Reagan came, over time, to see the desirability of a regular relationship with the PRC, but he saw this relationship in a framework that more clearly gave ample consideration to other U.S. interests and obligations.

As for Chinese leaders in Beijing there undoubtedly was anxiety among them when Reagan was elected. Perhaps expecting the worst anyhow, Deng Xiaoping decided to adopt a harder line himself, in effect testing Reagan to determine just what would be the new parameters in the relationship and to see what might be gained by such an approach. Thus when Reagan provided the pretext, with his provocative remarks, the trumpeting over Taiwan began. The tense atmosphere in the U.S.-P.R.C. relationship over the ensuing months prompted the Soviet Union to enter the new game; in the year before his death, President Leonid Brezhnev had repeatedly appealed to Beijing to renew the Sino-Soviet dialogue. Deng took up this option, and in the fall of 1982, the talks, which had actually begun in 1979 only to be suspended by the Soviet invasion of Afghanistan that December, again resumed.

Ironically, the apparent deterioration of U.S.-P.R.C. relations actually began under the Carter Administration. The Taiwan Relations Act, although this was not the responsibility of the Administration, quickly took the bloom off the rose of the normalization of the U.S.-P.R.C. diplomatic relations at the outset of 1979. However, it was the Carter Administration that initially authorized U.S. companies to discuss with Taiwan the sale of the advanced FX jet fighter, and it granted diplomatic immunity to members of the Coordination Council for North American Affairs, which agency unofficially represents the Republic of China in the United States.[1]

In fact, except for the occasional discordant, candid remarks by Reagan, his new administration actually tried to keep U.S.-P.R.C. relations on an even keel. As early as March 1981 the Administration made clear that relations with Taiwan would not be upgraded, and that it shared the commitment to the Shanghai communiqué of 1972 and the normalization agreement of 1978.² During his visit to China in June 1981, Secretary Haig gave assurances to Chinese leaders regarding arms sales to Taiwan. Haig also informed the Chinese that Reagan was going to relax controls on high technology equipment for export to China and would even consider arms sales to China. But the Chinese were not responsive to these signals. This was partly attributable to domestic political maneuvering within China during 1981, but also to the desire to test Reagan further, particularly with the hope of altogether terminating U.S. arms sales to Taiwan. Thus the October 1981 Cancun meeting between Reagan and Premier Zhao Ziyang was unproductive, as was Foreign Minister Huang Hua's visit to Washington that same month.

Nevertheless, Reagan persisted. Assistant Secretary of State John Holdridge visited Beijing in January 1982, bearing the concessionary news that the FX fighter would not be sold to Taiwan and initiating the discussions that eventually led to the important August 17, 1982 communiqué.

In this tense interim period Reagan dispatched three personal letters to Zhao, Deng, and Party Chairman (at the time) Hu Yaobang respectively, and visits to Beijing were made by Vice-president George Bush and Senator Howard Baker. The resulting August 17 communiqué was a somewhat rushed compromise that did not really settle the arms sales issue. But time had run out. Reagan needed to inform Congress on his decision to continue coproduction of the F-5E in Taiwan (information he had already shared with Beijing), and Deng needed something positive in hand for the Twelfth Party Congress. But as Michel Oksenberg has pointed out, the document did make explicit what had been implicit in the 1972 Shanghai Communiqué and the normalization agreement.³ The Chinese reaffirmed their policy of seeking peaceful reunification of Taiwan. The United States disavowed any intention to infringe on Chinese sovereignty or to pursue a "two Chinas" or a "one China, one Taiwan" policy. The United States also said it did not seek to carry out a long-term policy of arms sales to Taiwan, that such sales would not exceed in quality or quantity the levels supplied since 1978, and that it intended gradually to reduce its sales.⁴

The August 17 communiqué was followed by disagreement over interpretation, and Chinese commentators continued to accuse the United States of various violations. By the end of the year 1982 the atmosphere was not healthy, and this was exacerbated by other developments. Not all of these were directly controllable by the Reagan Administration, but each received great media attention and sharp criticism by the Chinese.

In September 1982 a federal judge in Alabama ordered China to pay $41.3 million plus interest for defaulted 1911 Qing Dynasty Huguang Railway bonds. The five percent bonds were issued for construction of the railway that still runs between Beijing in the north of China and Guangdong in the south. The suit was taken to court in 1979 by nine plaintiffs but was later certified a class action extending benefits to 280 bondholders. China refused to appear in the case on the grounds of sovereign immunity. The significance of the case became even greater with the threat to attach two Chinese jetliners in the United States.[5] This fear of attachment obviously could have a serious effect on U.S.-P.R.C. trade. The case also provoked an emotional response among some Chinese. For example, a writer in the Hong Kong *Wen Wei Po* sometime later asked about alleged "blood debts" owed by the U.S. government in China, alluding to various historic actions in which the United States participated, including the suppression of the Boxer Rebellion.[6]

Another important issue that came to a head at the beginning of 1983 was disagreement over the level of textile imports into the United States. This was a sensitive issue because of the high level of unemployment in the U.S. textile industry and the U.S. need to consider the ramifications for other major suppliers of textile products. As a consequence, Chinese leaders had been cautioned over the preceding several months not to expect to be able to increase their share of the market faster than 1.5 to 2 percent per year. However, the Chinese, pointing to the annual deficit in their trade with the United States, and conscious of their late entry into the American market with these foreign exchange-earning products, demanded an increase of six percent.[7] As a result, the agreement lapsed on January 1, 1983. The United States then applied quotas on thirty-two Chinese products and further limited the PRC's share of the textile market. The Chinese retaliated by placing an embargo on U.S. cotton, synthetic fibers, and soybeans, and reducing purchases of wheat and other agricultural products. This affected fifteen percent of U.S. exports to China. However, it clearly was not a serious retaliation. Even though U.S.-P.R.C. trade declined in early 1983, the temporary decline was attributable to other factors and there remained throughout this period evidence of strong Chinese interest in economic relations with the United States.

The visit of Secretary of State George Shultz to Beijing February 2-6, 1983, was an important one, although neither at the time nor for sometime afterward did there appear to be much concrete evidence of success. However, in retrospect it can be seen that it was another signal effort of the Reagan Administration to place U.S.-P.R.C. relations on better footing. Unfortunately, soon after the Shultz visit was concluded President Reagan made yet another public comment that temporarily clouded the goodwill generated during the Shultz visit. In an interview with the magazine *Human Events,* Reagan summed up the August 17 communiqué saying: "If the day ever comes that those two (China and Taiwan) find that they can get together and become one China, in a peaceful manner, then there wouldn't be any need for arms sales to Taiwan. And that's all that was meant in the communiqué. Nothing was meant beyond that." The immediate Chinese response was that the remark indicated "a grave step backward."[8] This verbal flare-up along with the various unsettled and unsettling issues in early 1983, distracted attention from the significance of the Shultz visit.

Secretary Shultz made a strong favorable personal impression on Chinese leaders. He listened carefully to their representations and patiently and politely explained U.S. positions, stressing the difficulties U.S. policymakers face in dealing with certain bilateral issues. He also suggested that some of the difficulties may stem from an insufficient understanding of the differences in the respective legal systems and societies, and urged the Chinese to learn more about how the U.S. system operates. Shultz stressed repeatedly that he sought to build "mutual trust and confidence." He strongly reaffirmed the administration's commitment to limit and gradually reduce arms sales to Taiwan, although he refused to provide a timetable or details of the limits. One of the objectives of the visit was restoration of the dialogue on international issues which had been regarded as a useful aspect of the relationship but which had lapsed. It was restored. But an agreement to Shultz's suggestion that Defense Secretary Casper Weinberger visit Beijing was deferred by his hosts. Nor was a date set for a visit by Premier Zhao Ziyang to Washington. Shultz did not claim any specific or tangible accomplishments from his visit, but he did correctly see it as a setting "the stage for new advances."[9]

Later that month Assistant Secretary for East Asian and Pacific Affairs Paul Wolfowitz told the Subcommittee on Asian and Pacific Affairs of the House Committee on Foreign Affairs that "developing a strong, stable and enduring U.S.-China relationship is an important element of President Reagan's foreign policy." Wolfowitz reiterated that both Shultz and Reagan have made it clear that the United States would "adhere to the communiqués that we and previous administrations have negotiated." But he also stressed that we have made clear to the Chinese that we have a deep interest in the well-being of the people of Taiwan, as reflected in the Taiwan Relations Act, and will continue the productive, unofficial relationship we have with them.[10]

On March 5, 1983 Secretary Shultz made a particularly significant speech to the World Affairs Council in San Francisco. It was notable because it suggested a new U.S. orientation that now regarded Asia as a whole, with less emphasis placed on a strategic relationship with China. Greater attention was given to Japan's role and relationship with the United States. References to China were considerate, but that country was now placed in a regional, rather than global context, as being first and foremost a part of Asia and only secondarily as a counterweight to the Soviet Union. Shultz did seem to make even clearer in this presentation the desirability of aligning the United States with China's modernization program, and he saw China as an integral economic force in Asia. On the other hand, Shultz acknowledged that "frustration and problems in our relationship are inevitable." This is not just attributable to the Taiwan problem but goes to the "differences between our social systems."[11]

Other issues conspired to make U.S.-P.R.C. relations appear worse than they actually were in the spring and summer of 1983. The disclosure in mid-March that arms sales to Taiwan would increase to as much as $800 million in fiscal 1983 and $780 million in 1984 brought expectable protests from the Chinese. This is because the August 17, 1982 communiqué had committed the United States to limit the quality and quantity of arms to Taiwan to the sales level reached in 1979, which was $600 million. The U.S. argument was that the newly released estimates were inflation-adjusted, and that the 1979 figure so adjusted would be $830 million. Although there were protests, including a charge of "double-dealing" by the Beijing *China Daily* during the visit of a delegation of U.S. congressmen led by House Speaker Thomas O'Neil, these did not become strident. The U.S. contention was, after all, not unreasonable, and was accompanied by reaffirmations of the intention to live by its commitments "over time."[12]

Much more serious was the matter of the defecting tennis star, Hu Na, whose case dragged on for eight months before she was finally granted asylum on April 4, 1983. This had become widely publicized, and a "face" issue for Beijing. There also was some division among U.S. officials regarding the case. Hu sought refuge claiming that she would be persecuted in China because she had repeatedly refused to join the Communist Party. Chinese Foreign Ministry spokesman Qi Huaiyuan charged that the incident was "long premeditated and deliberately created" by the United States.[13] Furthermore, in retaliation, China cancelled 19 government-sponsored sports and cultural exchange programs. Ironically, on the same day as this measure was announced China's new ambassador to the United States, Zhang Wenjin, presented his credentials to President Reagan. The Chinese retaliation was measured and limited; it did not affect tourism or the student exchange program which at this time included eight to ten thousand Chinese students in the United States and three hundred U.S. students and two hundred and fifty U.S. experts in China.[14]

The distinct change of direction came in May, 1983. At a meeting of the Politburo that month it was said that General Secretary Hu Yaobang gave a talk criticizing Deng's "open door" policy, and asking for closer ties with the Soviet bloc.[15] However, only that March the second round of talks with the Soviets had concluded in Moscow without notable success. It was at this juncture then that the United States came through. Secretary of Commerce Malcolm Baldridge visited Beijing that same month bringing the message that restrictions on exports of sophisticated technology to China was to be liberalized in a meaningful way. The Pentagon's veto over export licenses to China would be curtailed by placing China in the same class under the U.S. Export Administration Act as other countries considered to be friendly or allied with the United States, including India, Egypt, or Yugoslavia. Up to this time China had been in a category of its own under the Act, but was actually regarded as a "controlled destination" similar to Soviet bloc countries. Hence, this new decision eliminated a contradiction between U.S. supportive assertions regarding China's modernization, stability and security and the tough export controls on high technology that were applied only to "enemies" and to China. It underscored U.S. intentions to support more clearly China's economic development objectives. Furthermore, whereas some of the issues troubling the relationship were not directly controllable by the Administration, this was a highly important one that the executive branch of the U.S. government did have the authority to deal with as it wished.[16]

This gesture impressed Deng, perhaps just at a time when he needed such a concession that could be used to persuade domestic critics that his open door policy and lean to the United States was justified after all. In any case, this was regarded as an important gain for Deng because the several months of testing Reagan's position had led him to believe that the President was sincere about promoting a sound relationship but was not likely to give things away just to quiet Chinese criticisms and demands. In fact, Deng was concluding that the U.S. position was reasonable enough under the circumstances, albeit with blemishes here and there. The Soviet relationship might continue to be explored for what it was worth. But the U.S. tie was too valuable to jeopardize by continued undue criticism. Furthermore, it was becoming increasingly apparent that Reagan may not be merely a one-term president whose term could be waited-out. As the U.S. economy showed signs of improvement, the Chinese reasoned that their accommodation might just as soon begin earlier than later, and this might confer benefits. Hence, even though there were other problems that would surface and rankle, a decision was made to be more indulgent with the Reagan Administration, and more solicitous of the U.S. relationship.

Thus, when Pan American World Airways decided to resume flying to Taiwan in June 1983, while the Chinese were upset and did indicate their displeasure, their retaliatory measures were again strictly limited. Emergency landing rights and flights over South China were cut off. But Beijing's demands that the Reagan Administration replace Pan Am by another carrier for flights to China was refused, and the matter has remained suspended.[17] Of course, Beijing was aware that its profitable CAAC flights could be in turn retaliated against should it unilaterally terminate Pan Am's China service.

Beijing had hoped too to gain membership in the Asian Development Bank (ADB) and formally made its request in February, 1983. In its application, however, it demanded that the Republic of China's membership be cancelled. The United States disagreed. In fact, Secretary Shultz hinted that the United States might withdraw or reduce its contribution to the ADB if Taiwan was expelled. The U.S. position is based on the charter of the ADB which is different from many other international organizations in stating that the ADB is not to be influenced by the political character of members. In August, 1983, the U.S. House of Representatives actually passed a bill favoring termination of U.S. contributions to the ADB if Taiwan is expelled. Beijing did not pursue the matter vigorously.[18]

In June 1983, Beijing decided to crack down on another aspect of the Taiwan problem. It warned various nations not to allow "Taiwan's unofficial offices" in their countries to issue visas or continue to issue visas from their offices in Taiwan. Beijing held that these practices represent an effort by Taiwan to establish *de facto* official relations with nations that have normal relations with China. The United States responded by claiming that the Coordinating Council for North American Affairs' offices in the United States were functioning "consistent with their status."[19] Again, Beijing did not press the matter.

Not only were newer issues handled with less stridency than previously, but as the atmosphere improved some of the tougher problems were being reexamined with the intention of resolving them if at all possible. Hence the textile quota negotiations were now quickly resolved with China accepting a growth in sales to the United States of between 2 and 3 percent per year. This rate was slightly higher than that accorded to other Asian suppliers, but it was much lower than the 6 percent originally demanded by Beijing.[20] Both sides moved off dead center in the Huguang Railway bonds case. During the summer China retained a U.S. law firm to represent it in the case, without, however, accepting the court's jurisdiction in the matter. Nevertheless, the move did suggest that the Chinese had decided to pursue the case on legal grounds. In response to this Chinese gesture to play by U.S. rules, Secretary Shultz then made a friend-of-the-court brief in the case, asking that the default judgment be set aside for foreign policy reasons and that China be allowed to appear in court.[21] Obviously, both governments began to cooperate actively on this sensitive issue in order to prevent it from becoming unmanageable.

The warming relationship became even more apparent during Senator Henry Jackson's visit to China in late August 1983. Jackson bore yet another letter from President Reagan to Deng Ziaoping expressing again the U.S. desire to strengthen relations with China. Deng was clearly pleased and told Jackson: "We welcome this." Deng also noted that relations had improved significantly after three years of increasing strain. Jackson acknowledged that "a very difficult period had been weathered" and said that the "opportunity is now present to expand our relations." He even ventured that U.S.-P.R.C. relations were "at an important juncture with the possibility of resuming strategic cooperation as well as improving bilateral ties." Jackson also reaffirmed that "Reagan made several major decisions to improve relations with China, and he is now committed to a one-China policy." With regard to arms sales to Taiwan, Jackson indicated that the process of reducing sales and eventually ending them was under way, and this was being facilitated because Congress "is moving realistically toward a one-China policy."[22]

The U.S.-P.R.C. relationship blossomed even further with the visit of Secretary of Defense Casper Weinberger in late September, 1983. The visit was of symbolic significance because the Pentagon had been a particular bête noir with regard to techology transfers to the PRC. Yet here was the Pentagon's chief, a noted anticommunist, in the company of Deng Xiaoping, with both men relaxed and amiable with each other. More than symbolism was involved in this exceptionally successful visit. Weinberger was able to assure the Chinese leaders that about 75% of China's shopping list of 65 weapons and military related technology had been approved. Furthermore hope was held out for some of the remaining items which were to be discussed in detail in the months ahead by military specialists on both sides.[23]

Because of the costs of such hardware the Chinese were interested primarily in opportunities for coproduction and reverse engineering. There may be a possibility for limited coproduction of some U.S.-designed items if a sufficient quantity of equipment is purchased. Copying of U.S. equipment is generally discouraged but this becomes less important an issue as technology becomes dated. In any case, the United States remained opposed to any reexportation of U.S. arms. Weinberger tried to make it clear during his visit that whatever arms sales arrangement that might be made with China would not constitute a military alliance. Obviously, neither side was interested in going so far, nor in having the impression given that such a direction is being consciously pursued. But set in motion was a projected $1 billion annual flow of U.S. civilian and military technology to China, as well as plans for visits and military exchanges between the two countries beginning in 1984.[24]

Weinberger also was able to announce that Premier Zhao Ziyang would visit the United States in January, 1984 and that President Reagan would then visit China in April, 1984. This announcement was the most solid evidence of all that relations were maturing remarkably well, a crowning adornment for the successful Weinberger visit.

The euphoria of the Weinberger trip was sustained by the visit of Foreign Minister Wu Xueqian to Washington the following month. This visit included an unscheduled dinner at the home of Secretary Shultz on the evening before official meetings began, a very cordial talk with President Reagan, and an exceptional official banquet at the White House.[25] It was apparent that both sides wished to prevent anything that might detract from the renewed momentum in the relationship or threaten the success of the forthcoming Zhao and Reagan visits. Maintaining the necessary even keel was not easy.

In Congress, for example, two opposed trends were working their way out. On the one hand, wording was changed in the U.S. Export Administration Act to shift China into the so-called V category of friendly countries as had been agreed to by the Administration. The House also voted to change the wording of the Foreign Aid Bill in order to remove characterizations of China as an enemy or a member of the international communist conspiracy—vocabulary that had been popular in the 1950s. But on the other hand, the Senate Foreign Relations Committee passed a resolution on "Taiwan's future," which led on November 18 to the summoning of Ambassador Arthur Hummel to the Ministry of Foreign Affairs to receive a strong protest. One week later, Hummel was again summoned to receive yet another protest against an alleged "two Chinas plot," this one as evinced in an appropriations bill passed by the Senate and House on November 17 and 18 respectively. The Chinese took exception to a subsection of the bill which held that "Taiwan, Republic of China, should remain a full member of the Asian Development Bank, and that its status within that body should remain unaltered no matter how the issue of the People's Republic of China's application is disposed of."[26] General Secretary Hu Yaobang was then moved to say that without an acceptable U.S. response to the PRC's protests both the Zhao and Reagan trips would be cancelled.[27]

However, these flare-ups were readily contained. On November 21, the Reagan Administration's guidelines on high technology, including dual-use technology, were finally published in the Federal Register—which in turn had been facilitated by Beijing's agreement to obtain U.S. permission before undertaking to transfer technology of United States' origin to other countries.[28] Also, on November 30, Reagan personally repudiated the congressional pro-Taiwan formulation and acknowledged again that the PRC was "the sole legal government of China."[29] In the meanwhile, on the Chinese side, General Secretary Hu's originally quoted remarks suggesting cancellation of the Zhao and Reagan trips were publicly toned down.[30]

There were still difficulties with textiles, which might have upset preparations for the impending Zhao visit. However, U.S. textile manufacturers were persuaded to drop charges of unfair trade practices by China in return for a tightening of textile import controls by the Reagan Administration.[31] Also serving to illustrate the complications of the evolving relationship even as both sides sought to put the best face on things, negotiations for a new shipping agreement between the two countries broke down in December.[32]

Overall, however, by the beginning of 1984 a new positive momentum had again been established in U.S.-P.R.C. relations. Thus Premier

Zhao Ziyang did visit the United States in January and this proved to be a well-handled event on both sides. Zhao was cordially received by Reagan, yet the visit was not given so much publicity, nor was an impression given that the United States was conceding anything unnecessarily, so as to provoke too many of the President's more conservative supporters. The continued support of the latter remained desirable especially in 1984, an election year. The two leaders acknowledged differences but did not dwell on these. Regarding Taiwan, both agreed to abide by the terms of the August 17, 1982 communiqué. Otherwise, greater attention was given to this issue in the Chinese media than in the United States. Zhao was encouraged in talks with congressional leaders not to be unduly apprehensive regarding the pro-Taiwan sentiment in Congress. Neither side pushed the idea of a strategic relationship, and, in fact, Reagan acknowledged China's independent foreign policy line. Of course, this did not deny that there is a strategic dimension to the relationship, but each leader emphasized economic rather than military cooperation.[33]

Accordingly, the two leaders signed a science and technology agreement that extended for five years the original 1979 agreement. They also signed an industrial and technological agreement, the first such agreement China had undertaken with any trading partner.[34] While such a document is largely rhetorical it did underscore the desire of the principal leaders on each side to secure their economic relationship and to make it clearer to the respective implementing bureaucracies and other interested parties that this is the case. In the meanwhile, more specific agreements continued to be negotiated. There were expectations that a tax treaty would be ready for signatures when Secretary of the Treasury Donald Regan visited China in March, 1984. Another desirable agreement, on investments, was expected to take much longer to negotiate.

There were, however, optimistic expectations that President Reagan would be able to sign an important treaty on nuclear cooperation during his visit to China in April. This would provide nuclear technology the Chinese particularly desire and it would mean big dollar sales for U.S. companies. At the very least, Reagan was to sign a new cultural exchange agreement.

Military relations were not ignored.[35] However, since Secretary Haig left office this topic came to be handled much less demonstratively. The Weinberger visit of September, 1983 reestablished a format whereby the Chinese could explore possible purchases from an enlarged list of dual-use technology and both sides could continue to engage in limited forms of military cooperation. However, this was done with greater consideration both of China's own priorities and financial and absorptive capabilities as well as of the sensitivities of other countries in Asia. Furthermore, there has been less of a tendency by either Washington or Beijing to provoke the Soviet Union unnecessarily. Fortunately, for its part, the Soviet leadership has been appropriately responsive to the quieting down of this issue, giving little emphasis to it.

In the meanwhile, the Sino-Soviet talks continued. Sessions were held in Moscow in March and in Beijing in October, 1983. The latter meeting was preceded by a visit to Beijing by Soviet Vice Foreign Minister Mikhail Kapitsa, who arrived just before Secretary Weinberger's visit. Kapita was the highest ranking Soviet official to visit China in over 20 years. The Soviet Union appeared to be interested in an improvement of relations and it made what it likes to call "confidence-building" proposals to China. This did produce positive results. Both sides agreed to double their trade from the current annual level of $815 million (which in itself was up from only $312 million the year before). The Soviets undertook to renovate a factory they had built in Harbin, in the 1950s, and there was to be an expansion of scientific, technical, and academic exchanges, and the resumption of cultural exchanges. But most heralded at the time were Soviet proposals to freeze the Soviet military build-up along the frontier, remove nuclear weapons from border areas, and establish a Moscow-Beijing communications hotline.[36] The Chinese took these latter proposals under advisement, but there remained the problems of Afghanistan and Kampuchea which the Soviets continued to sidestep. Nevertheless, sufficient progress was experienced to encourage both sides to continue the talks into 1984.

In all, the Sino-Soviet relationship did improve. To some degree this only made good sense to many observers, including Americans.[37] But the improvements were not substantive enough to warrant undue U.S. concern. Hence the warming of the Sino-Soviet relationship did not seem to have been a particularly significant factor in Washington's own efforts to improve U.S.-P.R.C. relations. There certainty does not appear to be anything approaching an overreaction in the Reagan Administration to the Sino-Soviet maneuvering, although concern continued to focus on Soviet designs generally, and it was recognized that while U.S.-Soviet relations are at a low ebb the Chinese can take some advantage of the fact.

Very clearly then, a significant change has taken place in the Reagan Administration's China policy, the turn coming rather noticeably in mid-1983. It was heralded by Secretary Shultz's China visit in February, but can be pinpointed to Secretary of Commerce Baldridge's assurances to the Chinese in May that there would be a serious liberalization in the transfer of technology to China. The Chinese response to this has been genuinely positive because the move obviously facilitates their modernization program. But also reflected in the improvement is Deng's decision that Reagan had been tested far enough, and that even though some troublesome issues remain, Deng believed it would be prudent to appear more graciously responsive to an Administration that might well be continued for another term.

The Reagan Administration's handling of this turnaround was actually rather remarkable, or, at least looked more remarkable because Deng cooperated. However this may be, Reagan did manage to improve the complex China relationship despite the concerted efforts of a vocal pro-Taiwan lobby, and without giving the impression that too much was being given in the bargain. The August 17, 1982 communiqué did draw accusations of "appeasement" but subsequent events have underscored the ambiguity of that agreement however often it may be reaffirmed. And the liberalizing of technology sales only gave U.S. companies a chance to share a market that was otherwise being monopolized by others. Thus Reagan managed to preclude possible charges by election year opponents that he was threatening to lose China, and instead achieved a modest plus in a foreign policy otherwise devoid of notable successes. He turned a likely election campaign deficit into an asset—including an invaluable trip to China with all its symbolic underscoring of a foreign policy success and generous publicity during the reelection campaign. Yet even as U.S.-P.R.C. ties thickened the Reagan Administration has attempted to make clear that it is deeply aware of the great differences that exist betwen the two countries and their respective political and social systems. By so doing, Reagan still retained the loyalty of many of his conservative supporters, their undiminished pro-Taiwan sentiment notwithstanding. Moreover, the quickening ties with China were engineered in such a way—by both Washington and Beijing—as not to provoke the Soviet Union unduly.

This improvement in U.S.-P.R.C. relations suggests greater sophistication by the players of the premier global three-person game. Thus, both sides were somewhat solicitous of the third player, the Soviet Union, even though each remained apprehensive of the latter's ambitions. Moreover, the United States demonstrated greater concern for the reactions of other affected Asian nations. And it simultaneously emphasized the greater value it placed on its relationship with yet another major world-class player—Japan—whose relations with both China and the Soviet Union are also of great significance.

Much of the success of these crucial changes in Reagan's policy in Asia is probably attributable to its stress upon economic relationships. This emphasis accords with China's most urgent priorities and is always welcomed by Japan. And although the Soviet Union is not for the time being exactly invited to the feast, it does not perceive its relative exclusion as threatening to it as a more explicit emphasis on U.S.-P.R.C. military relations would be.

Notes

1. Michel Oksenberg, "A Decade of Sino-American Relations," *Foreign Affairs* (Fall 1982), 191.
2. *Ibid.*, 192.
3. *Ibid.*, 194.
4. Text in *Beijing Review (BR)*, August 23, 1982, 14–15.
5. See Karl P. Herbst, "Railway-Bond Case Threatens U.S.-China Trade," *Asian Wall Street Journal (AWSJ)*, June 22, 1983, p. 6.
6. *Wen Wei Po*, March 31, 1983, in *Foreign Broadcast Information Service*, March 31, 1982, W-1.
7. John Copper, "The Lessons of Playing Tough with China," *Asian Studies Center Backgrounder*, Washington, D.C.: The Heritage Foundation, August 23, 1983, 2.
8. *BR*, March 7, 1983, 14.
9. Don Oberdorfer, Peking, February 5, 1983, *Washington Post (WP)*, February 6, 1983, A-1.
10. "Developing an Enduring Relationship with China," Current Policy No. 460, Bureau of Public Affairs, U.S. Department of State, February 28, 1983.
11. See Richard Nations, "A Tilt Toward Tokyo," *Far Eastern Economic Review (FEER)*, April 21, 1983, 36–37.
12. See Robert Manning, Washington, "Still Up in Arms," *FEER*, April 14, 1983, 44.
13. Michael Weisskopf, "China Hits Decision on Asylum," Peking, April 5, 1983, *WP*, April 6, 1983, A-21.
14. *The New York Times*, April 8, 1983, p. 1.
15. See, for example, Michael Parks, "Chinese Leaders Reported Split Over U.S. Ties," Peking, *Los Angeles Times*, May 23, 1983, p. 1.
16. Richard Nations, "Raising the Barriers," *FEER*, June 16, 1983, 16–18.
17. AP, Washington, in *The Honolulu Star Bulletin*, June 16, 1983, A-17.
18. John Copper, *op. cit.*, 6.
19. *Ibid.*, 5–6.
20. Art Pine and Amanda Bennett, "Textiles Pact Might Smooth Sino-U.S. Ties," *AWSJ*, August 1, 1983, 1.
21. *AWSJ*, August 5–6, 1983, 3.
22. Michael Parks, "Strides Seen in U.S.-China Relations," Peking, Los Angeles Times Service, *Honolulu Star Bulletin*, August 28, 1983, A-30.
23. David Bonavia, Peking, "Weinberger's Bouquet," *FEER*, October 13, 1983, 18–19.
24. Knight-Ridder Service, Shanghai, *Honolulu Advertiser*, September 30, 1983, A-17.
25. Richard Nations, Washington, "The Wooing of Wu," *FEER*, October 27, 1983, 20.
26. *BR*, November 28, 1983, 9, and December 5, 1983, 10.
27. AP, Washington, *Honolulu Star-Bulletin*, November 29, 1983, A-4.
28. Richard Nations, *FEER*, December 1, 1983, 17.
29. *Ibid.*, December 22, 1983, p. 23.

30. Amanda Bennett, Peking, *AWSJ*, December 20, 1983, p. 1.
31. Richard Nations, *FEER*, December 22, 1983, p. 23.
32. *The Honolulu Advertiser*, December 19, 1983, C-1.
33. Richard Nations, *FEER*, January 26, 1984, 24.
34. *Ibid.*, 49.
35. One of the most thoughtful discussions of the pros and cons of this issue took place at a workshop sponsored by the U.S. Senate's Committee on Foreign Relations and the Congressional Research Service of the Library of Congress on October 28-29, 1981, a period when much concern was being expressed about such cooperation. See the publication resulting from this workshop: *The Implications of U.S.-China Military Cooperation*, January 1982, Washington, D.C.: U.S. Government Printing Office, 1981. A subsequent, shorter treatise of value is Robert G. Sutter, *Chinese Nuclear Weapons and American Interests—Conflicting Policy Choices*, Report No. 83-187F, Washington, D.C.: Congressional Research Service, The Library of Congress, September 27, 1983.
36. Nayan Chanda, Hong Kong, *FEER*, November 3, 1983, 31-33.
37. See, e.g., Donald S. Zagoria, "The Moscow-Beijing Detente," *Foreign Affairs* (Spring 1983), 871-873; *China Policy for the Next Decade: Report of the Atlantic Council's Committee on China Policy*. Washington, D.C.: The Atlantic Council of the United States, October 1983, pp. 42-43; and *The PRC's New Policy Directions: An Assessment,* Honolulu, Hawaii: Pacific Forum, 1983, p. 3.

Implications of Changing Sino-Japanese Relations for the Future of the U.S.-Japan Nexus

—— 4 ——

George O. Totten

The great reversal in Sino-Japanese relations since the establishment of the People's Republic of China came with Japan's formal recognition of the government in Peking as the sole legitimate government of China. This occurred on September 29, 1972. The new Japanese Premier, Kakuei Tanaka, fresh from a summit meeting with the U.S. President, Richard Nixon, carrying his blessing, but at the same time going further than the United States was to do for the next six years by recognizing the PRC, apologized to the Chinese for what Japan had done in China. The apology was a bit lame, but, given the stakes involved, was accepted by the Chinese. At the same time, Japan derecognized the Republic of China and promised to sign a peace treaty with the PRC government.

These acts received almost unanimous approbation in Japan and, especially since it had the blessing of the Americans, was greeted by a sigh of relief. Japan had really been thrown into a state of turmoil by the "shock" of Nixon's new approach to China, announced in July of 1971, about which he had not consulted the Japanese government, and which was followed up by his visit in February and enunciation of the famous Shanghai Communiqué. In that document, with China's Premier Chou En-lai, President Nixon, this former active supporter of the Committee of One Million to Keep Communist China out of the United Nations, agreed to work for full recognition of Peking by the United States of America. In their characteristic panic, a number of Japanese journalists had raised the question of whether the United States was going to reverse its policy and favor supporting China over Japan as the bulwark of peace in East Asia, which had been the United States' original policy at the end of World War II. After all, the United States in 1972 was engaged in war in Vietnam and Japan was doing little to help, whereas China had the longest border in the world with the Soviet Union and could more obviously help contain it.

Looking back from 1984, however, such Japanese fears seem almost laughable. The U.S.-Japan "nexus," based, as it is, both on formal security arrangements and a vast economic and cultural exchange, has held fast. Moreover, the relations of both Japan and the United States with China appear to have benefited U.S.-Japan relations.

The Effect of the Sino-American Rapprochement on Japan

Ever since the establishment of the PRC in 1949, the Japanese government and people had never been fully happy with the United States' belligerent policy toward this new "Red" China. During the U.S. occupation, the Japanese wanted to regain their sovereignty more than anything. The obvious method was to please the U.S. policymakers. After the Peace Treaty with the United States was signed in September 1951, the Yoshida government under U.S. pressure, signed a separate peace treaty with the ROC on Taiwan, even though it knew this was considered a hostile act by Peking.

Through the 1950s and 1960s the Japanese increasingly resisted the U.S.-imposed economic boycott of China. They developed the principle of "separating economics from politics." This enabled the Japanese government to take a strong policy of political nonrecognition of the PRC, while at the same time countenancing some trade with China. Despite U.S. opposition to the trade, the United States did not press the issue too hard. In 1962 the so-called Liao-Takasaki* agreement was reached, under which annual negotiations were held. The Chinese attempted to use these to push for eventual Japanese recognition, and their attempts elicited widespread support within Japan. Of course, there were ups and downs in the response. During the early part of the Great Proletarian Cultural Revolution, even the Japanese intellectuals reacted adversely and the Japanese Communist Party turned against Mao Tse-tung (Mao Zedong). However, the Japanese government's policies toward China, especially its maneuvers to keep Beijing from taking China's seat in the Security Council were unpopular among the Japanese people. They became a factor in Premier Eisaku Sato's fall in 1972. He had cosponsored the unsuccessful U.S. resolution to keep Taiwan in the U.N. in October, 1971. The Chinese refused to deal with him. It was amazing how well things went for his successor, Tanaka. When the latter returned home from Peking after recognition of the PRC, he was greeted

---

*This refers to the memorandum signed by Liao Chengzhi and Tatsunosuke Takasaki on December 9, 1962 for a five-year period providing for semiofficial trade, known as "L-T trade."

fervently not only by his party colleagues, but also by leaders of all the opposition parties, except ironically for the Japanese Communist Party.

Interestingly enough opposition party leaders (outside of the Communists) had worked together with Foreign Minister Masayoshi Ohira and Premier Tanaka to effectuate the normalization of relations with China. They considered it a suprapartisan issue, knowing it was so popular. But still there was an important group of pro-Taiwan "hawks" of high Liberal Democratic Party (LDP) leaders who put up a last-ditch fight against normalization. They were largely undermined by the willingness of the mainland Chinese to agree to Japan's continuing its lucrative trade and other nonpolitical contacts with Taiwan.[1]

The significance of cooperation between ruling Liberal Democratic Party leaders and opposition figures lay in the fact that the recognition of China removed one of the elements in the fundamental foreign policy cleavage between the dominant LDP and its opponents. And this had important implications for the opposition's attitudes toward the United States and the U.S.-Japan Security Treaty which had been at the heart of the foreign policy controversy in Japan at least from almost a year before it was signed in September, 1951 in San Francisco. That treaty was considered a precondition by the United States for granting the Peace Treaty. Even the Peace Treaty was criticized by the opposition for not being "comprehensive" in that the Soviet bloc and some the other allies against Japan did not sign it. The opposition accused the conservative parties of selling out to one side in the Cold War, an act that could involve Japan again in a world conflict. They argued that Japan should instead play the role of a bridge between East and West, between socialism and capitalism, and work hard to reduce world tensions and bring about world disarmament. This emotional issue climaxed in riots in 1960 that brought down the government of Premier Nobusuke Kishi after he had gotten it ratified.

From 1951 to the 1970s leftist opinion in Japan considered that in general U.S. interventionism was more dangerous to world peace than the Soviet brand. With the Vietnam War still raging in 1972 this was rekindled as an emotional issue. But with the recognition of China, whose fear of Soviet expansionism had become so great, the left in Japan was much affected, especially when the Chinese stopped criticizing Japanese "militarism" and quietly let it be known that they now favored the U.S.-Japan Security Treaty. China's interest in its own reunification with Taiwan and concern with its borders with the Soviet Union prompted it to encourage the Japanese to stuggle for the return of Japan of certain "northern islands" which the Soviet Union had occupied after the end of World War II. In Japan leftists had long played down that issue and it was mostly rightwingers who called for their return. But in recent years the left-wing parties, including the Japanese Communists, have joined with the government in demanding the islands' return. In all this, general Japanese attitudes toward the Self-Defense forces have become more positive. Larger and larger sectors of the population see them not as semi-American mercenaries, but as necessary forces for providing some sort of trip-wire against possible Soviet aggression. This is not to say that even now Japanese concerns about a Soviet threat are as great as those of Western Europeans, but they are growing.

The Sino-Japanese Peace Treaty

Nevertheless, although a peace treaty was promised by Tanaka during the normalization negotiations in 1972, it was delayed time and again until August 12, 1978. This was during the rising tension in Afghanistan but before the full-scale Soviet invasion in the wake of the bloody palace coup in Kabul of September, 1979. At that time the Japanese government did not want to antagonize the Soviet Union unnecessarily. One of the bones of contention that had held up the treaty (although it had not been an issue in the first few years) was the so-called "anti-hegemony" clause. The Chinese were using the phrase as a code word for the Soviet Union at the time, although it could apply to any big country, especially the United States. Pro-Taiwan groups in Japan, normally very anti-Soviet, ironically argued that signing the treaty with such a clause would antagonize the Soviet Union. But they lost out and the treaty was signed.[2]

They lost out because of a compromise suggested by Deng Xiaoping, the main figure on the Chinese side pushing for the treaty. He said that the treaty did not imply joint action by China and Japan against a hegemony-seeking power, and China and Japan had their own foreign policies. In the very short treaty Article II pledges that neither China nor Japan would "seek hegemony" and both are "opposed to efforts by any other country . . . to establish such hegemony." But Article IV blandly states, "The present treaty shall not affect the position of either contracting party regarding its relations with third countries."[3] The Japanese thus claimed that the treaty was not "anti-Soviet," but interestingly enough both Moscow and Washington regarded it as such. This pleased Washington and angered Moscow. Soviet threats against Japan for signing the treaty had the effect of bringing China, Japan, and the United States together. Nevertheless, Soviet fears of a military alliance between China and Japan against the Soviet Union did not materialize.

This Treaty of Peace and Friendship between Japan and the People's Republic of China was seen mainly as a peace treaty by the Chinese and as a friendship treaty by the Japanese. That is why it has the double name. The Japanese considered that Japan had already signed a peace treaty with

China (the one with the ROC in 1952) and had acknowledged the cessation of a state of war between China and Japan in the normalization treaty. The Chinese overcame some Japanese objections by waiving any demands for reparations and by separately negotiating trade agreements (specifically those of February, 1978 and March, 1979).

Four years later referring to the Treaty, Zhao Ziyang, the new Chinese Premier, when he visited Japan in June 1982, proposed three principles for the development of Sino-Japanese relations: (1) peace and friendship, (2) equality and mutual benefit, and (3) long-term stability.[4] While he did not mention it, there were two factors that gave an edge to Sino-Japanese relations over Sino-American. One was that there was no Taiwan irritant in Sino-Japanese relations. The other was that Japan still enjoys a great cultural heritage from China.

So far we have seen that the United States' volte-face in relations with China helped remove one sore spot in U.S.-Japan relations, which was U.S. containment of China. Oddly enough the Japanese who were located so near China compared to Americans never felt the "threat" from "Red" China to the extent the Americans did. We have also seen that normalization of relations with China helped reduce the criticism of the opposition parties in Japan toward the U.S.-Japan Security Treaty and toward the Japanese military forces. Thus, the U.S.-China rapprochement did have a beneficial effect on U.S.-Japan relations.

Has Japan Helped Improve U.S.-Chinese Relations?

It can be argued that Japan's recognition of the PRC in 1972 created the formula for the normalization of U.S.-China relations in 1979. In the years subsequent to Japan's derecognition of Taiwan, despite Taiwan's initial adverse reaction and certain later incidents, Taiwan-Japan trade and cultural relations have continued and flourished. Thus, it was clear that the same thing could occur with a shift in the United States' diplomatic relations to Peking.

By signing the Treaty of Peace and Friendship with China in August 1978, the Japanese reminded Washington that this item still remained on the agenda for the Carter administration. Pressures were building up among U.S. businessmen who felt at a disadvantage in competing with the Japanese and with other nationals in China who had established formal diplomatic ties with Peking. Similar pressures were coming from cultural groups and the academic world in the United States who were interested in large-scale exchange. Without much preparation, but encouraged by the Japanese, who had in a sense "run interference" for the Americans, President Carter on December 15, 1978, together with Chinese Premier Hua

Guofeng, announced to a surprised world that the United States and China would normalize relations as of January 1, 1979.[5]

The lack of preparation by the Carter Administration for this move was evident in that it had no draft legislation prepared for continuing its unofficial relations with Taiwan. When a belated draft reached the Congress no real explanatory work had been done by the administration. As a result the Taiwan Relations Act (TRA) on which not just a pro-Taiwan lobby and conservative Congressman worked, but also liberals, such as Jacob Javits, Republican of New York, went to the very edge of undoing the normalization of relations with the PRC.[6] Normalization was based on the agreement that the United States, like Japan, would have no official diplomatic relations with Taiwan. In addition, unlike the case with Japan, the United States had military ties with Taiwan, notably the Mutual Defense Treaty (MDT) of 1954. This was to terminate with a one year statement of intent in accordance with the terms of the Treaty. The MDT thus officially ended December 31, 1979. But the TRA almost revived pledges of that treaty and even went further in extending coverage to protect Taiwan from boycotts and embargoes, not mentioned in the MDT. Of course, China objected to this and called for its abrogation.

Normalization seemed to unleash a pent-up desire for people from both China and the United States to visit each other. In 1979, 308 official Chinese delegations visited the United States, while 40,000 Americans went to China. In 1980 about 10,000 Chinese came to the U.S., while over 70,000 Americans visited China. After that, the growth of the number going in both directions has skyrocketed. The same is true with business.

Ameicans found, however, that in almost every field Japanese had often gotten into China and made the most desirable contacts first. Yet the Chinese welcomed the Americans in an even more friendly manner than the Japanese. In the late 1970s the Chinese had become "dizzy" with visions of accomplishing the "four modernizations" that far outstripped reality. They had to retrench. Nevertheless, economic growth has taken place; not only has trade increased enormously, but a number of joint ventures with U.S. and other foreign capital and technology have been started. In these circumstances, at least so far, U.S. and Japanese businessmen have not found themselves in any more competitive position with each other than with business people from other countries doing business with China. While Japanese have often gotten the best business suites in the hotels, new, modern, hotels are being built. Americans have learned from Japanese experience, but often Americans have come in with new and more innovative proposals that startle the Japanese and Europeans who had resigned themselves to the slowness of Chinese bureaucratic ways. What startled the Japanese and Europeans even more was seeing the Chinese responding to Americans in new ways.

One area Japanese have not entered is arms sales. Americans have been hesitant about arms sales to China, and China about purchasing arms from the U.S. Defense Minister Zhang Aiping has indicated China does not want to become dependent on foreign arms and would rather produce its own arms even at great cost. What China needs most, he indicated, was technology. After two years' delay the United States at the moment is negotiating with the Chinese on this matter and has agreed to selling some technology that could have military use.

Japan's corollary to not selling arms to China is that it does not sell arms to Taiwan, whereas the United States govenment does. It is in this area that the greatest damage to U.S.-Chinese relations has occurred in both 1982 and 1983. The solution to this lies in the promise by the U.S. to phase out such sales.[7] How the United States actually interprets this and carries it out will greatly affect Sino-American relations and indirectly Sino-Japanese ties in ways difficult to predict.

The Prospects for the U.S.-Japan Nexus

How will Sino-American and Sino-Japanese relations affect the very special ties between the United States and Japan?

(1) Both the United States and Japan consider that a strong China is crucial to peace and stability in Asia.

(2) Both see that China might play some role in reducing tensions on the Korean peninsula. Both understand that China does not have much leverage for movement in the matter, because North Korea could shift away from its slight tilt toward China to tilt or turn to the Soviet Union. But China is cautiously responding to some feelers from South Korea. Japan has intermittent direct contacts with North Korea but is very constrained by its formal ties with South Korea. Since the United States has no relations with North Korea, China might serve as a go-between. China made a step in this direction when Premier Zhao Ziyang visited the United States in January, 1984. He brought with him a proposal from North Korea proposing tripartite talks among Washington, Seoul, and Pyongyang. The U.S. response was to suggest China be involved as well, but North Korea would not have China participate without some participation from the Soviet Union.

(3) The United States and Japan are the two greatest sources of technology transfer to and trade with China.

(4) While English is the most widely studied foreign language in China, Japanese is number two. Since English is used by many countries and Japanese only by one, it can be argued that China is investing proportionally more in studying Japanese to learn just from Japan than in studying English which is the most important international language in the

world today. However, one must realize that Japanese is a key to learning about the West almost as much as English is.

Thus, the interests of the United States and Japan tend to run parallel with regard to China.

What are the problems for the U.S.-Japan nexus that Sino-Japanese relations hold?

The appearance of issues that would sever Japan from the United States or cause friction between them that China could profit by should be considered dangers to the U.S.-Japan nexus. However, at present my view is that China desires to see harmony between Japan and the United States, since both are allied against the Soviet Union, even though Japan officially tries to hide that from both the Soviet Union and her own people.

At the same time China does not wish to see increased tensions between the Soviet Union and other countries. China wants to see Japan and the United States as well as Western Europe militarily prepared. In this area there is no cause for friction.

A likely source of friction is China's siding with Third World countries against the superpowers, which could include the United States. A recent example of this is China's condemnation of the United States' invasion of Grenada, although in that case China was in the company of many of the so-called Second World nations as well. There are innumerable economic and security questions of "class struggle" in the Third World on which China would side with the peasants and workers against dictators supported by landlords, industrialists, and the military, whereas the United States would support the status quo. Japan is likely to stay out of such situations as much as possible, but her business interests might tend to support the status quo. Nevertheless, Japan would be slightly closer to China on such issues, thus, this would be an area of possible but relatively unimportant frictions between the United States and Japan.

Another area of possible friciton is in the area of disarmament. China is planning to become involved in the moves for the reduction of nuclear armaments. This leads China to give moral support to antinuclear struggles in Europe and the U.S. China will push for reductions by both superpowers to reduce their arsenals by one half. When that is achieved China wants the rest of the nuclear powers to meet to consider how to reduce nuclear arms all around. Such moves, however, will not be confined to nuclear weapons but extend to conventional and other new weapons from chemical and biological to lasers and satellites.[8]

Since the most important initial stimulus to the rapprochement between China and the United States was the recognition of the Soviet Union as a common threat, it is perhaps most fitting to conclude with a short comment on the question: How will the U.S.-Japan nexus be affected by closer Sino-Soviet relations?

A definite movement in ameliorating Sino-Soviet relations has become apparent. But since relations are so bad, change will take place slowly. Many of the ideological differences between the Soviet Union and China have subsided, and so has the ideological fervor on both sides. What remains are traditional and historical rivalries and distrusts. The Chinese will have to see real concessions by the Soviets in terms of reductions of troops and weapons along the borders before there is movement in the negotiations. For this the Soviets will ask a price. If the price is not too great, the Chinese can comply. This would lead to a reduction of tensions. If this should lead to mutual East-West arms reductions, this would allow China to concentrate more on its economic development. Such a situation would be beneficial to both Japan and the United States and open up new opportunities to avert a worldwide catastrophe.

Notes

1. For a detailed account of Japan's recognition of the PRC, see Haruhiro Fukui, "Tanaka Goes to Peking: A Case Study in Foreign Policymaking," in T.J. Pempel (ed.), *Policymaking in Contemporary Japan* (Ithaca and London: Cornell University Press, 1977), pp. 60–102.
2. Haruhiro Fukui, "Japan and China: Peace at Last," *Current History* (November 1978), 149–54.
3. This was part of the so-called Four Principles proposed by Foreign Minister Miyazawa in 1975 and rejected then by China. The inclusion of this clause indicated a change in the domestic climate in China. This position was argued by Tatsumi Okabe, "Japan's Relations with China in the 1980s," in Gaston J. Sigur and Young C. Kim (eds.), *Japanese and U.S. Policy in Asia* (New York: Praeger Publishers, 1982), p. 101. For Miyazawa's Four Principles, see *Ibid.*, Note 4, p. 116.
4. "Zhao Ziyang Congli Fangwen Riben," *Xinhua Yuebao,* 6 (1982), 164.
5. It may be of interest that a serendipitous incident occurred to me on that date. I was teaching in Sweden and had prepared a short broadcast in Swedish for Sveriges Radio on prospects for normalization, indicating this could occur sooner than people realized. It was broadcast on December 14. This next morning early I received telephone calls from both the U.S. and Chinese Embassies in Stockholm informing me of the news of the Carter-Hua statement. My short talk was then rebroadcast on the 15th with a few words added by the announcer that the normalization had just occurred. The talk could not have been more timely.
6. See Jacob K. Javits, "Congress and Foreign Relations: The Taiwan Relations Act (of 1979)," *Foreign Affairs,* 60 (Fall 1981), 54–62.
7. "United States Arms Sales to Taiwan: Joint Communiqué of the United States and the People's Republic of China, August 17, 1982," *Weekly Compilation of Presidential Documents* (Washington, D.C.: U.S. Government Printing Office).
8. See "China on Disarmament" and "China's Disarmament Proposal" in *China & the World* (2) (1982) (translated and reprinted from the Chinese quarterly *Journal of International Studies,* published by *Beijing Review),* 5–18 and 19–21 respectively.

Southeast Asia in the Sino-Soviet Tangle
—— 5 ——
Sheldon W. Simon

At various times since the founding of the People's Republic of China, Beijing has been surrounded by threats to its security from all sides: the United States and Taiwan to the east, the Soviet Union to the north, Vietnam to the south, and India to the west. At least since the fall of Lin Biao in 1971, the Chinese leadership has been concerned about managing these threats in a manner that would reduce their potency and insure against their coalescence. To accomplish this end, as Harry Harding recently noted, Chinese leaders ask a consistent set of questions: which powers are rising and becoming hegemonic? What are their strategies for global domination? What are their strengths and weaknesses? What united front can be mobilized against them?[1]

China perceived that the United States had passed the zenith of its power in Asia by the early 1970s at the same time the Soviet Union seemed to unrelentingly expand its politicomilitary influence in the region. Judging that the United States would no longer be a threat to China under these conditions, Sino-U.S. cooperation against Moscow became a strategic necessity; and Beijing "leaned to the West." China urged the United States to maintain a military presence in the region and also moved to improve relations with The Association of Southeast Asian Nations (ASEAN) and Japan—policies that were accelerated when the Soviets invaded Afghanistan and facilitated the Vietnamese occupation of Kampuchea.

China has borne political costs, however, in its "anti-hegemonic" united front with capitalist states against the Soviet Union and its regional ally, Vietnam. Most important has been a loss of prestige in the Third World and among radical movements. The latter increasingly see China as a status quo power, abjuring assistance to third world revolutionaries in order not to antagonize the Western states on which Beijing depends for developmental aid and investment. The former are wary of China's "punishment" meted out to Vietnam which they sometimes interpret as an imperialist act by a large state against a smaller neighbor—one that only recently successfully emerged from decades of battle against foreign domination.[2]

Since 1981 PRC analysts have come to see the Soviet Union as overextended with commitments in Poland, Afghanistan, Indochina, Cuba, and parts of Africa on top of Moscow's internal economic difficulties. This complex of problems reduces the degree and imminence of the Soviet threat to China and for the first time permits Beijing to effect a more balanced foreign policy between the two superpowers.[3]

Since 1981, then, the PRC has been "fine tuning" its relations with the Third World, the Soviet Union, and the United States, hoping to maximize benefits from each while erasing the image that it had joined the U.S. camp. This does not mean, however, that China has forsaken its basic desire for close ties with the West for both security and development. Rather, Chinese leaders see the opportunity to reduce tensions with the Soviet Union and stabilize its northern borders at the same time. Thus, the PRC has dropped its strident calls for an anti-hegemony united front against the Soviet Union and has appealed instead for cooperation with all "friendly" countries in achieving China's goals of political and economic independence.[4]

The Chinese have also been heartened by the Reagan Administration's strong anti-Soviet stance, in all probability concluding the U.S. posture is so deeply ingrained that the PRC need no longer keep reinforcing it. With the Americans bent on long-term opposition to Soviet expansion, the PRC can move into the pivot position between Moscow and Washington, opening up new options in relations with both. China has publicly listed its conditions for normalization of relations with the Soviet Union. They are couched in terms designed particularly to appeal to the Third World and ASEAN. Two of the three conditions would require the Soviets to withdraw from Afghanistan and stop assisting Vietnam in its occupation of Kampuchea. Interestingly, the Chinese insist that the cessation of aid to Vietnam is the most important of the three—perhaps in hopes of driving a wedge between Moscow and Hanoi by holding out the possibility of normalizing relations with the Soviet Union if only the latter loosens its ties to Vietnam.[5] By moving toward more stable regional relations, Deng Xiaoping is also able to press ahead with his domestic political agenda of restructing central and local institutions. This major turnover of party/government personnel would be much more difficult in an atmosphere of regional tensions.

From Moscow's perspective, détente with China might also be welcome. It could help ease the Soviet Union's two-front problem by undercutting any strategic cooperation between Beijing and Washington. Nevertheless, Moscow's inexorable military buildup over the last two decades and its growing Asian deployments of air, ground, naval, and rocket forces can only mean that relations with China will remain tense and that Beijing will continue to court the United States and Japan to help redress the balance between a militarily weak PLA and ever-growing Asian Soviet might. As long as the Soviets believe military forces to be their primary diplomatic instrument, they will remain unwilling to negotiate third world accommodations.[6] Moreover, Soviet deployments in third world regions are likely to increase because of Moscow's sense that these are relatively safe possibilities given the Soviet Union's strategic parity with the United States.

At bottom, the Soviets are unwilling to accept the Chinese view that it should be the suzerain power vis-à-vis the Southeast Asian mainland. By aligning with Vietnam, the Soviets are now associated with the most powerful military establishment in Southeast Asia. They have also acquired naval and air base facilities that provide substantial ability to threaten the still limited PLA navy along the entire Chinese coast. Given the strategic advantages to the Soviet Union of this situation, it seems unlikely that Moscow will voluntarily reduce its presence and influence in Vietnam.

In some ways, then, China's apprehensions about Soviet encirclement appear justified. The Soviet occupation of Afghanistan, its close ties to India, and the Moscow-Hanoi alliance plus close relations with Laos and Cambodia do constitute a kind of "encirclement" or at least the potential of influencing these states to resist Chinese pressures. The Soviet-Vietnam relationship is central to Moscow's aims of encircling China and increasing Soviet naval capability in the South China Sea-Indian Ocean region to challenge U.S. maritime supremacy in Asia. Thus, Soviet ships in the Indian Ocean rely extensively on supplies and reinforcements from the Pacific Fleet which, in turn, benefits from the use of storage facilities in Vietnam. From airfields in Vietnam, Soviet bombers could attack southern China and U.S. bases in the Philippines—viewed by China, ASEAN, and Japan as essential to the defense of the region against the Soviet Union.[7]

Additionally, the Soviet Pacific Fleet is now the largest of its naval contingents, containing one-third of all Soviet submarines (120), one-fourth of all principal surface combatants (80), and one-third of all naval aircraft, including the longrange Backfire bombers equipped with antiship cruise missiles.

Although Soviet assets deployed from Vietnam are of considerable use in peacetime, they would be vulnerable in the event of war to U.S. forces based in the Philippines or Guam. As Paul Dibb has noted, a U.S. carrier battle group could readily destroy Soviet air and naval forces operating from Vietnamese bases. For similar reasons, it is most unlikely that Soviet forces would be able to interdict the Malacca Strait. In any event, Japanese tankers could be rerouted through Indonesian or even Australian waters.[8] Of more concern is the Soviet Union's use of bases in Vietnam as intermediate staging points for rapid response to a political crisis in Southeast Asia. Noteworthy in this regard are reports in December 1983 of the deployment of about ten TU16 Badger medium-range bombers at Cam Ranh Bay equipped with Kingfish and Kelt air-to-surface missiles. This is the first time that Soviet strike aircraft appear to be regularly stationed in Indochina, although they are not accompanied by fighters.[9] Offsetting ASEAN and ANZUS (Australia-New Zealand-U.S.) naval and air forces in the region are essential if this Soviet capability is to be neutralized.

Politically, there have been costs as well as benefits to the Soviets in their Vietnam alliance. On balance the latter outweigh the former, however. With the assurance of Soviet guarantees against China, Vietnam invaded Kampuchea and consolidated its position in Laos, effectively destroying any significant Chinese influence in Southeast Asia. Even China's limited incursion into Vietnam could be interpreted as underlining the credibility of the Soviet guarantee since Beijing withdrew soon after the Soviets threatened unspecified retaliation.[10] To maintain its credibility as a regional power, then, China has continued to "bleed" Vietnam, a policy that serves well the Soviet plan to maintain Vietnam's dependence.

The ASEAN states, too, though ambivalent about China's strategy toward the Kampuchean conflict, have resisted granting legitimacy to the regional Soviet military buildup in the aftermath of the Vietnamese occupation. Thus, the ASEAN five have rejected requests for port calls by the Pacific Fleet and have backed Thailand in its protest to the Soviet Union when the *Minsk* carrier task group sailed into the Gulf of Thailand in November 1980. Subsequently, Malaysia agreed to the staging of Australian P3 Orion reconnaisance aircraft and drew up plans to build another air base on the east coast of the Peninsula at Gong Kedak, although the latter has been postponed for financial reasons. (Malaysia already has one air base on the east coast at Kuantan from which aircraft monitor the country's 200-mile exclusive economic zone in the South China Sea.) Malaysia will be deploying a substantial proportion of its forty recently purchased A-4 Skyhawks at Kuantan to counter a potential Soviet-Vietnamese threat from the South China Sea.

The Sino-Vietnam Confrontation

The falling out between Beijing and Hanoi began almost immediately after the end of the Second Indochina War. Le Duan led a delegation to the

PRC in September 1975 to seek economic aid. Deng Xiaoping told him, however, that unless Vietnam supported China's antihegemony policy, PRC assistance would not be forthcoming.[11] In effect, Deng insisted on extending the Sino-Soviet conflict into PRC-Vietnam relations. Vietnam, of course, refused and moved closer to the Soviet Union, essentially for lack of any alternatives.

China's limited invasion of Vietnam in February-March, 1979 is less important for its mixed military results than its political demonstration that China was willing to take risks and absorb costs to oppose Soviet and Vietnamese plans for the region. Beijing was reassuring ASEAN and the United States of its continued opposition to the expansion of Soviet influence by flagellating the "small hegemonism."

PRC backing for the Pol Pot regime has been a more difficult political issue, however. The only way that China could justify support for the notorious Khmer Rouge and muster international sympathy at the same time was to adhere to legalistic principles and insist on a U.N. role in solving the Kampuchean conflict. In this way China hoped to generate external pressure on Vietnam that it could not exert by itself. Only by capitalizing on the regional implications of the Kampuchean conflict and the Soviet Union's role within it could Beijing hope to enlist the support of the international community.[12] While Beijing did not inflict a military defeat on Hanoi, it has imposed all the military and economic burdens of a two-front security threat. China has also contributed to the survival of the Khmer Resistance on the Thai border. By maintaining pressure on Vietnam, Beijing believes that Hanoi will be permanently weakened as a military power in the area; and as long as VPA forces remain in Kampuchea, Hanoi will also be politically isolated, prevented from effecting a rapprochement with ASEAN.

Interestingly, since 1982, China expresses less concern about the military implications of the Soviet use of Vietnam's bases. Chinese media assert that the number of Soviet vessels using Cam Ranh is small and that their primary role is to monitor regional maritime activity. Noting that no Soviet fighter aircraft have been stationed in Vietnam, *Renmin Ribao* concludes: "Judging from a comparison of the strength of both sides, it would still be difficult for the Soviet Navy to wage a fight against the United States in these areas."[13] Soviet bloc sources have gone even further by stating that China had told the Soviet Union that if Vietnam withdraws from Kampuchea, China might be willing to accept some Soviet military presence in Vietnam. Of course, this suggestion could well be nothing more than a ploy designed to raise Vietnamese fears about a Soviet sellout, particularly since the Chinese believe that if the Soviet Union stops its aid to VPA forces in Kampuchea, then Hanoi will ask the Soviets to remove their naval and air contingents from Vietnam.[14]

Nevertheless, the Chinese continue to follow a dual-track strategy: urging negotiations to maintain international support for the Democratic Kampuchean seat in the United Nations and increasing military pressure on Vietnam by supporting insurgents. Western analysts state that in addition to supplying the Khmer Rouge, the Chinese have also set up a network to support the Lao resistance, a battalion of which has been trained in Yunnan province.[15]

The Chinese finesse the question of what happens to Kampuchea if the Vietnamese pull out and the only militarily significant force is the Khmer Rouge? Virtually all observers predict a return to civil war and chaos and go on to argue that the Khmer Rouge must not be permitted to play any role in a post-Vietnam Cambodia. While sensitive to Pol Pot's past record, the PRC insists that the Khmer Rouge have reformed and, in any event, are now part of a broader noncommunist coalition:

> Under the circumstances in which Vietnam refuses to withdraw its troops, to think too early about the problems following a Vietnamese troop withdrawal [is to] meddle in others affairs by making arrangements for Kampuchea's future. . . . [This] cannot but disperse people's energy and will not help bring about a solution of the Kampuchea problem.[16]

China insists it is prepared to restore normal relations with Vietnam when the latter's forces are removed from Kampuchea.[17] Whether this means that Beijing would be willing to do so several years from now in the event that the Heng Samrin pro-Vietnam government has acquired sufficient military and administrative capacities to no longer require VPA forces remains to be seen. Interestingly, Vietnam offers a mirror image policy to China, promising to withdraw all its forces from Kampuchea when stability and security reigns along the Thai border and China ends its threat on Vietnam's northern boundary.[18]

The Soviet-Vietnam Connection

Vietnam moved reluctantly into the Soviet camp through a series of post-1975 hardships: the total withdrawal of Western assistance to the South at the end of the war; a costly armed conflict with Kampuchea leading to the termination of Chinese assistance; the devastation wrought in the northern provinces by the early 1979 Chinese invasion; a succession of bad harvests through 1981; and a continued U.S. embargo of trade and aid.

Soviet bloc economic assistance for 1982 was estimated at over $1.5 billion, two-thirds of which came from the Soviet Union.[19] But, most of this consists of loans that must be repaid. Soviet bloc aid has been directed primarily to industrial and infrastructure projects. Most of the products of the former are earmarked to repay the loans. Nevertheless, the debt continues to mount with Vietnam owing the COMECON countries $1.3 billion by 1981. Over 60 percent of Vietnam's export receipts go into debt servicing.

Vietnamese authorities acknowledge that the Soviet Union supplies their country with virtually all of its import needs in steel, petroleum, grain, nitrogenous fertilizer, cotton, and trucks. Other COMECON states provide consumer goods and machinery. Vietnam's ability to import was seriously curtailed in 1981, however, when the Soviet Union increased the selling price of its oil by 300 percent.

In addition to mortgaging much of its mineral, marine, and tropical agricultural production to repay the Soviet bloc, Hanoi has also resorted to the widespread use of labor contracts under which Vietnamese workers are sent to COMECON countries as indentured laborers, an estimated 40 percent of their wages going to repay Vietnam's outstanding debt. Up to 100,000 Vietnamese may be in the Soviet Union and Eastern Europe under this arrangement over the next several years.

The total Soviet overseas economic burden is mounting. According to a study by Paul Dibb at the Australian National University, it was estimated at $3 to 5 million per day for Vietnam plus another $300,000 per day for Cambodia. This is comparable to the amount for Ethiopia but considerably less than the $12 million per day for Cuba, $55 million to subsidize Eastern Europe, and an unknown but very substantial expenditure in support of Soviet forces in Afghanistan. This heavy drain on the Soviet economy has led to a more niggardly attitude toward aid to Vietnam since 1982 as well as pressure on Hanoi to undertake administrative reform so that Soviet assistance will be more efficiently utilized.[20] Nevertheless, Moscow's subventions to Hanoi are still less than ten percent of its total foreign aid burden and appear to remain a good investment for the strategic returns.

Most important of all for the Soviets are undoubtedly the Vietnamese base facilities acquired for the Pacific Fleet. Soviet Task forces led by a guided missile cruiser and including nuclear-powered submarines form at Da Nang and Cam Ranh Bay. The Chinese claim the Soviets have begun construction on another naval base on Can Son Island in the South China Sea about 80 miles southeast of Vinh Loi in Vietnam. In 1983 up to 20 ships a day (half combatants) may be found in Cam Ranh Bay. Soviet TU-95 reconnaissance aircraft are equipped to watch for U.S. submarines as well as surface shipping. According to U.S. photographic intelligence the Soviets have constructed a pier for nuclear submarines, underground fuel storage tanks, and an onshore electronic monitoring station.[21]

Vietnamese officials insist, of course, that Soviet use of the bases in no way compromises the SRV's independence. Somewhat disingenuously, Foreign Minister Nguyen Co Thach asserts:

> We could not have safeguarded our independence without aid from the Soviet Union; and the Soviet Union does respect our independence. We offered the Soviets the facilities that Singapore gives to others. . . . We give them facilities, yes, but the base is Vietnamese. And, you know, our worry is justified because the Philippines bases were used against us during the past decade; but the bases in Vietnam have never been used against anyone in Southeast Asia.[22]

Nevertheless, both the Vietnamese and the Soviets may be apprehensive over the possibility of the other drawing it into hostilities not of its own making. Thus, Hanoi may fear the prospect of Soviet actions in other parts of Asia leading to retaliation against the bases in Vietnam. Moscow, in turn, would be concerned that a Vietnamese attack on Thailand would have grave repercussions on Soviet relations with ASEAN, Japan, and the United States as well as raising the prospect of a Chinese retaliatory attack on Vietnam. This scenario would be particularly unwelcome to the Soviets at a time when they are hoping to effect a détente with China and improve relations with the ASEAN countries. Hence, Soviet Foreign Minister Gromyko's strong backing of the Vietnamese proposal for a Southeast Asian regional conference which would lead to a ratification of the status quo in exchange for discussion of ASEAN's peace zone proposal.[23]

ASEAN and Sino-Soviet Concerns

The ASEAN states find themselves in a very uneasy situation vis-à-vis Chinese and Soviet diplomacy in Southeast Asia. Initially hopeful in the early to mid-1970s that both major communist states could be persuaded to accept the region as a Zone of Peace, Freedom and Neutrality (ZOPFAN) upon the end of the Vietnam War, the five witnessed instead the extension of Sino-Soviet conflict directly into Indochina and indirectly into ASEAN itself. As the frontline ASEAN state, Thailand has welcomed China's threats to Vietnam and aid for the Khmer Resistance even though ASEAN as a group believes Chinese involvement in the Indochina imbroglio serves only to provide additional opportunities for Soviet meddling in the region.

Beijing's aggressive intrusion into Vietnam, its support for the Cambodian insurgents, and even its appeal to ethnic kinsmen throughout Southeast Asia to invest in China's "Four Modernizations" rekindle worries over the long-term nature of the "Chinese threat." With about 18 million Chinese in Southeast Asia and the belief that regional communist parties have disproportionately been led by Chinese, most ASEAN states manifest a highly suspicious attitude toward the PRC. Beijing's unwillingness to withdraw moral support publicly from these movements (for both domestic political reasons having to do with Deng Xiaoping's credibility as a revolutionary and for foreign policy fears that the Soviet Union and Vietnam could fill the breach if China left the scene) has meant that many ASEAN leaders still believe China is a potential source of subversion to the polities.[24]

The above assessment particularly characterizes the views of Indonesia and Malaysia. Thailand and Singapore respond that regardless of China's long-term ambitions, it currently has little capability of power projection. Rather, the imminent danger to Southeast Asia is the Soviet Union and its growing navy bent on control of the Strait of Malacca and the Straits of Sunda and Lombok in Indonesia.[25] Accordingly, Indonesia and Malaysia insist that China is the problem and that the United States must avoid arms sales to the Chinese, while Thailand and Singapore seek to persuade ASEAN's friends that the Vietnam-Soviet relationship is the main threat to peace.

The PRC has attempted to dispel doubts about its intentions in Indochina. Beginning in late 1980, Beijing reaffirmed its support for U.N.-supervised free elections and an independent nonaligned Kampuchea after a Vietnamese withdrawal. In February, 1981, Chinese Premier Zhao Ziyang journeyed to Thailand to express China's willingness to participate in an international guarantee of Kampuchea's neutralization, including a pledge that Kampuchean territory would not be used to threaten other countries.[26]

Vietnam, on its part, wishes to avoid a direct confrontation with ASEAN (and China) by refraining from attacking Khmer Resistance sanctuaries across the Thai border. In all probability the Soviets would refuse to back such attacks in any event.[27] Moreover, China continues to exert military pressure on Vietnam whenever the latter has temporarily encroached on the Thai border during dry season operations against the Khmer Resistance. Most recently in April, 1983, China launched an artillery offensive on the Vietnam frontier in response to Vietnamese raids along the Thai border. The purpose was to maintain Thai confidence in Chinese guarantees.[28]

Appealing to ASEAN sensibilities, Vietnamese foreign minister Thach in a meeting with his Thai counterpart in June, 1983 stated for the first time that Cambodia should be "independent," "nonaligned," and "neutral." ASEAN officials saw this as a possible diplomatic breakthrough for they had been insisting for several years that a neutralized Kampuchea would end the Chinese threat to Vietnam. Nevertheless, it appears that Hanoi's position may not really have changed. "Solidarity" among Vietnam, Cambodia, and Laos would not be affected by Kampuchea's nonalignment; and it was stated that both Vietnam and Kampuchea would maintain a "special relationship" with the Soviet Union.[29]

In effect, ASEAN and Vietnam are stalemated over the role of China on one side and the Soviet Union on the other. The Vietnamese complain that "the ASEAN countries demand the complete withdrawal of Vietnamese army volunteers from Kampuchea, while saying nothing about China's threat toward the Indochinese countries." The idea put forth at the June, 1983 ASEAN Foreign Ministers' Conference that VPA forces withdraw 30 kms. from the Thai frontier "only serves the policy of the Beijing expansionists . . . to continue using the Pol Pot remnants to oppose the revival of Kampuchea. . . . [S]uch an arrangement cannot ensure security along the Thai-Kampuchean border."[30]

A related problem is the question of which actors are centrally involved in the Kampuchean conflict. The ASEAN position is that the conflict is essentially between China and Vietnam over the future of Cambodia. In this view the ASEAN states constitute a neutral though obviously interested party. While Vietnam does not challenge this interpretation, China does. From Beijing's perspective, the Kampuchean conflict is between the Democratic Kampuchean coalition and Vietnam. It threatens Thailand, therefore involving ASEAN against Vietnam.

Differences between ASEAN and China on Kampuchea are most apparent over the question of dealing with the Khmer Rouge. While China provides all of Pol Pot's military and economic assistance, the ASEAN states refuse to deal with the Khmer Rouge, insisting that ASEAN recognizes only Prince Sihanouk and Prime Minister Son Sann within the Resistance.[31]

Singapore's foreign minister S. Dhanabalan has told Thach that Chinese training of Indochinese subversives is bound to continue the more the Soviets get a foothold in Indochina. The closer Indochinese ties to the Soviet Union, the greater will be the Chinese efforts to subvert the area.[32]

South China Sea Conflicts

There is another realm in which the interests of China and the Soviet Union clash with those of the Southeast Asian states—ownership and control of the small island groups in the South China Sea. Exacerbated by the overlapping claims of 200-mile Exclusive Economic Zones as stipulated in the 1982 Law of the Sea Treaty, the Philippines, Vietnam, China, Taiwan, and Malaysia have lodged overlapping claims to islands in the Spratly group located north of Brunei, west of the Philippines' Palawan island, and east of Vietnam. Additionally, the Paracel islands located south of China's Hainan island and east of Vietnam, though occupied by China in 1974, are still claimed by Hanoi.[33]

The South China Sea, in addition to its strategic location astride the major commercial route to East Asia, is also the military channel to the Indian Ocean/Persian Gulf for both the U.S. Seventh Fleet and the Soviet Pacific Fleet. The area is judged to be rich in undersea petroleum and natural gas resources. Talks on the division of the Tonkin Gulf for oil exploration purposes were held by China and Vietnam in 1974 and 1977 to no avail. Vietnam claims that its sea boundary was settled in the Sino-French Convention (1887). This claim is rejected by China as running too close to Hainan Island to be equitable. China has not proffered an alternative but insists that the division of the Gulf is still unresolved. Nevertheless, beginning in 1982, China offered exploration contracts within the Vietnamese claim area.[34]

This is a highly risky development since the Chinese navy based on Hainan and in Beihai is not sufficient to provide round-the-clock protection to rigs and crews drilling west of Hainan. These latter could be harassed by Vietnamese gunboats. If the Vietnamese ships in turn were challenged by the Chinese navy, then Soviet vessels could be enlisted to redress the balance. If the Soviets chose to become involved on Vietnam's behalf, there would be no local challenge to its naval dominance. While China, Vietnam, and the Philippines have deployed small fast-attack craft in the area, the Soviets have at least ten major military vessels in the South China Sea at any time.[35]

The actual situation may be more stable than the foregoing analysis suggests, however. China tends publicly to lodge maximum territorial claims in the South China Sea while attempting to enforce only its minimal security concerns. The exaggerated claims to areas even under the control of the Philippines and Malaysia, for example, are probably placed on the record only for purposes of subsequent negotiations rather than as a warning to others of China's willingness to use force to obtain them.[36]

U.S. wariness over these conflicting claims, however, has led Washington specifically to exclude them from the joint security responsibilities of the Philippines and the United States. If the Philippines needs to defend its oil exploration activities in the Reed Bank and Macclesfield areas, it will have to do so on its own.[37]

By 1983, Vietnam, the Philippines, Taiwan, and most recently Malaysia had all stationed small numbers of armed forces on islands in the Spratlys. The Hanoi-occupied islands seem to be the best fortified. According to Philippine intelligence reports, they have hardened fortifications and installed antiaircraft batteries and machinegun nests. Spratly Island itself has a runway and control and communications tower capable of accommodating STOL aircraft. These aircraft would have the range to attack the east Malaysian states of Sabah and Sarawak, as well as peninsular Malaysia.[38]

Conclusion

Changes in the Sino-Soviet relationship have had an impact upon the political situation in Southeast Asia. Although the military forces deployed along the Sino-Soviet border have not been reduced, rhetorical insults are at the lowest level in about two decades. Ideological challenges have virtually disappeared in the renewed Sino-Soviet negotiations. Each side realizes that unrestrained competition benefits neither but only permits others (for example, the United States and Japan) to reap political benefits by manipulating the relationship. Both China and the Soviet Union seek to reassure the other at least about medium-term intentions.

The low priority for military modernization in China means that the PRC has no pretensions about challenging Soviet military supremacy. Although Beijing does rely on its ties with newfound friends (again, the United States and Japan) to deter any possible Soviet adventurism, at the same time, through Sino-Soviet talks, China attempts to reassure the Soviet Union of its independent foreign policy. That is, China has no intention of becoming part of a counterencirclement strategy against the Soviet Union. Beijing holds out the prospect of normalization if the Soviets agree to draw down their forces along their common border and persuade the Vietnamese to withdraw their forces from Cambodia—conditions which, over time, might well be met. From China's perspective (as well as ASEAN's) if Vietnam could be removed from the Sino-Soviet conflict, then Beijing's primary *raison d'etat* for supporting the Khmer Rouge would disappear. Then, at least for China and the Soviet Union, the restoration of a truly neutral Cambodia would be a possibility. A Sino-Soviet understanding over Kampuchea might even meet Vietnamese conditions if it were followed by the cessation of Chinese support for the Khmer Resistance in exchange for the withdrawal of Vietnamese forces in Cambodia and the broadening of the Kampuchean government to include some representation from ranks of Son Sann's and Sihanouk's supporters.

Assuming China's goal is not the imposition of its own hegemony over Indochina, but rather the end to any Soviet military threat via Vietnam and a more neutral stance by Hanoi vis-à-vis Moscow and Beijing, accommodation may be possible.[39] If Vietnam were no longer aligned with the Soviet Union, then Laos and Kampuchea would no longer be viewed as a southern threat either. Vietnam's dominance within a *neutral* Indochina would presumably be acceptable to Beijing under these conditions.

These optimistic projections are based on the assumptions that a prolonged stalemate in the region will prove unsatisfactory to Vietnam, China, and the Soviet Union and that all will conclude later in this decade that a *modus vivendi* is preferable to a high level of political tension and the economic drain inherent in military confrontation. If, on the other hand, Vietnam believes it can retain control of Laos and Kampuchea only through indefinite military occupation; that China will sustain military pressure on Vietnam's northern border and continue to supply the Khmer Resistance operating from Thai sanctuaries; and that the Soviet Union views its bases in Indochina as its primary mode of political influence in the region as well as a center for deployments into the Indian Ocean, then prospects for the resolution discussed above are dim. Moreover, as long as China insists that the Khmer Rouge play a role in any future Cambodian government, Vietnam's adamant opposition is assured.

Underlying Vietnam's toughness is the belief that over time it will be able to create a Cambodian regime capable of administering the country under Hanoi's watchful eye and a Cambodian army sufficiently strong to deal with Resistance remnants. This latter hope could be realized if the ASEAN states tire of the confrontation and most VPA troops went home. Vietnam's policy, then, appears to be one of maintaining military control of Kampuchea with Soviet equipment until a Kampuchean government and army can be formed, perhaps around the end of the decade. This does not augur well for reduced Sino-Soviet tensions in Southeast Asia even if Beijing and Moscow are able to reach an understanding on their northern Asian borders.

Notes

1. Harry Harding, "Changes and Continuity in Chinese Foreign Policy," *Problems of Communism*, March-April 1983, p. 16.

2. See the discussion in Donald McMillen's chapter, "The Maintenance of Regional Security in the Southeast Asian Region: China's Interests and Options," in T.B. Millar, ed., *International Security in the Southeast Asian and Southwest Pacific Regions* (St. Lucia: University of Queensland Press, 1983).

3. Harry Harding, *op. cit.*, pp. 13-14.

4. Carol Lee Hamrin, "China Reassesses the Superpowers," *Pacific Affairs* (52,2) Summer 1983, pp. 210-11.

5. See the interview with former PRC Foreign Minister, Huang Hua, in *Al-Akhbar* (Cairo) September 5, 1983, in FBIS, *Daily Report/China*, September 12, 1983. Al.

6. Seweryn Bialer, "The Soviet Union and the West in the 1980s: Detente, Containment, or Confrontation?" *Orbis* (27,1) Spring 1983, p. 52.

7. U.S. Senate, Committee on Foreign Relations, "East-West Relations: Focus on the Pacific," *Hearings* (97th Congress, Second Session, June 10 and 16,

1982,) p. 6, 21, 67. See also, Norman Levin, *The Strategic Security Relations in the 1980s* (Santa Monica: The Rand Corporation, N-1960-FF, March 1983, pp. 3-4.)

8. Paul Dibb, "The Interests of the Soviet Union in Southeast Asia and the Southwest Pacific: Implications for Regional Security," in T.B. Millar, *op. cit.*

9. John McBeth, "Reach for the Sky," *Far Eastern Economic Review*, December 29, 1983, p. 16.

10. Goh Keng Swee, "Vietnam and Big Power Rivalry," in Richard Solomon, ed., *Asian Security in the 1980s* (Santa Monica: The Rand Corporation, 1979, p. 158).

11. Lee Deng-Ker, "Soviet Foreign Policy in Southeast Asia—An Analysis of the Moscow-Hanoi Alliance," *Issues and Studies*, July 1983, p. 56.

12. Chang Pao-min, "Beijing versus Hanoi: The Diplomacy Over Kampuchea," *Asian Survey* (23,5) May 1983, p. 600.

13. *Renmin Ribao*, January 19, 1983, in FBIS, *Daily Report/China,* January 20, 1983, A4.

14. *Far Eastern Economic Review*, June 23, 1983, p. 14.

15. Nayan Chanda, "United We Stand," *Far Eastern Economic Review*, August 11, 1983, p. 25.

16. *Renmin Ribao* Commentator, August 20, 1983, in FBIS, *Daily Report/China*, August 23, 1983, E4.

17. Pei Monong, "China's Future Role in Asia," *Shijie Zhishi* (10) May 16, 1983, in FBIS, *Daily Report/China*, July 22, 1983, A4.

18. Report of the Seventh Indochina Foreign Ministers Conference in Phnom Penh, in FBIS, *Daily Report/Asia Pacific*, July 21, 1983, H4.

19. The following economic assessment is drawn from Carlyle A. Thayer, "Vietnam's Two Strategic Tasks: Building Socialism and Defending the Fatherland" (1983).

20. See footnote 8.

21. Drew Middleton, "Soviet in Asia: Navy Buildup in the Pacific," *New York Times*, December 30, 1982; "Soviet Navy is Said to Make Increased Use of Cam Ranh Bay, *ibid.*, March 13, 1983; and Takashi Oka, "Pacific Commander Sees Fresh, Strategic Focus on the Region," *The Christian Science Monitor*, June 15, 1983.

22. Interview with Vietnamese Foreign Minister Nguyen Co Thach in the *New Straits Times* (Kuala Lumpur) August 9, 1983.

23. Soviet Foreign Minister Andrei Gromyko's address to PRK Foreign Minister Hun Sen as carried by *Tass*, September 20, 1983, in FBIS, *Daily Report/USSR*, September 21, 1983, E2.

24. For an assessment of PRC relations with Asian communist parties that documents the withdrawal of Chinese support, see William Heaton, "China and the Southeast Asian Communist Movements: The Decline of Dual Track Diplomacy," *Asian Survey* (22,8) August 1982.

25. This position was taken by the Secretary-General of the Thai National Security Council in August 1982 as cited in Bernard K. Gordon, "America Redux: East Asian Perspectives on the Superpowers and Asian Security," *Parameters* (13,2) June 1983. p. 37.

26. Chang Pao-min, *op. cit.*, p. 603.

27. See Nguyen Co Thach's news conference in Jakarta as carried by *Agence France Press* (AFP), November 1, 1982, in FBIS, *Daily Report/Asia Pacific*, November 1, 1982, N3.

28. Nayan Chanda, "A Symbolic Offensive," *Far Eastern Economic Review*, May 5, 1983, pp. 42–43.

29. Colin Campbell, "Vietnamese and Thai Officials Meet and Ease Rift on Cambodia," *The New York Times*, June 10, 1983.

30. *Nhan Dan*, June 28, 1983, in FBIS, *Daily Report/Asia Pacific*, June 28, 1983, K3.

31. *The Bangkok Post*, June 29, 1983; and Nayan Chanda, "Seeking the Soft Spots," *Far Eastern Economic Review*, July 21, 1983, pp. 15–17.

32. Nayan Chanda, *ibid*.

33. *The Far Eastern Economic Review*, September 29, 1983, p. 40.

34. A good survey of these issues may be found in Kim Woodard and Alice A. Davenport, "The Security Dimension of China's Offshore Oil Development," *Journal of Northeast Asian Studies* (1,3) September 1982, pp. 3–26.

35. *Ibid.*, pp. 20–21; and *The Christian Science Monitor*, November 8, 1982.

36. Woodard and Davenport, *ibid.*, and Allen S. Whiting, "Sino-American Relations: The Decade Ahead," *Orbis* (26,3) Fall 1982, p. 705.

37. "Manila to Upgrade Navy Because of Sea Law Pact," *The New York Times*, January 9, 1983.

38. Sheilah Ocampo-Kalfors, "Easing Toward Conflict," *Far Eastern Economic Review*, April 28, 1983, p. 38. Also a Malaysian Defense Ministry spokesman as carried by *AFP*, September 6, 1983, in FBIS, *Daily Report/Asia Pacific*, September 7, 1983, 01–02.

39. See the discussion by Martin Stuart-Fox, "Resolving the Kampuchean Problem: The Case For An Alternative Regional Initiative," *Contemporary Southeast Asia* (4,2) September 1982. Especially pp. 213–18. See also the conditions outlined by both China and Vietnam in 1983 for a resolution of the Cambodian conflict. Interestingly, they could be compatible if each followed the other's terms. PRC Foreign Ministry Statement as broadcast by Radio Beijing in Vietnamese March 1, 1983, in FBIS, *Daily Report/China*, March 4, 1983, E1-E2. And the Indochinese Summit Conference statement in *Quan Doi*: *Nhan Dan,* March 1, 1983, in FBIS, *Daily Report/Asia Pacific*, March 25, 1983. K2-K3.

The Taiwan Factor in U.S.-Beijing Relations
6

Winberg Chai and Shao-chuan Leng

For thirty years, from 1949 to 1979, Taiwan was both a reason for Washington's nonrecognition of the Beijing regime and a hindrance to reversing that policy. Despite the retreat of the Republic of China (ROC) government to Taipei in 1950, following the Communist conquest of the Chinese mainland, a number of factors underscored the United States' decision not immediately to switch its diplomatic recognition to the new People's Republic of China (PRC) in Beijing. Some of these factors were of the Communists' own doing, such as their confiscation of U.S. properties and their rough handling and eventual expulsion of the remaining U.S. consular personnel in China. Beijing's intervention in the Korean War after October 1950, directly fighting U.S. forces, confirmed the worst U.S. fears that Communist China was an extension of the Stalinist empire seeking world conquest.

Other factors concerned either U.S. domestic politics or strategic considerations. The Republican campaign to affix the responsibility of "who lost China?" and the McCarthyist witchhunt raised domestic anticommunist sentiments to such a pitch that it was totally impossible to bestow diplomatic recognition on the Chinese Communist regime. To help contain the perceived communist threat in Asia, a new U.S. mutual security network was to be erected, encompassing Japan, South Korea, and Taiwan in East Asia. In the Taiwan Strait, a battle line was drawn, with Taiwan firmly locked in the U.S. camp against the foreboding Beijing-Moscow axis. Taiwan, thus, remained a U.S. ally and a frontline outpost of the United States' defenses in the Asian Pacific.

Both the Sino-Soviet split after 1957 and the Vietnam war in the 1960s compelled a reappraisal and a reversal of U.S. policy toward Beijing. In the 1970s, President Nixon and his senior foreign policy adviser, Henry A. Kissinger, initated a rapprochement with the PRC. The dramatic switch was based on perceived U.S. strategic interests, more especially on the assumption that the Sino-Soviet split was irreversible and therefore China, our adversary's enemy, could be our friend in a common front against the Soviet Union. As Beijing's strategic value increased in Washington's eyes, Taiwan's position correspondingly declined by this reasoning. To encourage Beijing to turn its undivided attention northward toward its Soviet foe, Kissinger wanted to help resolve all China's "southern problems," that is, the Vietnam conflict and the Taiwan question.[1] Through no fault of its own, Taiwan the ally all of a sudden became a stumbling block to Washington's desire to "normalize" relations with Beijing. The Taiwan limbo thus had its beginnings in the Kissingerian power play.

Despite his criticisms of Nixon's foreign policy, President Carter's policy toward China was essentially an extension of the Nixon-Kissingerian initiatives. Carter's senior advisor, Zbigniew Brzezinski, not only inherited Kissinger's assumption regarding the permanence of the Sino-Soviet split and his balancing theory, but turned the Kissingerian "tilting game" into a zealous card game, attempting to involve China in a potential alliance against Moscow. Brzezinski, in fact, embraced the premise of the irreversible Sino-Soviet split with greater piety than Kissinger ever did. If Kissinger would alternately tilt between Moscow and Beijing in order to hold the other at bay, Brzezinski with his deep-rooted Polish hatred for the Soviets made the China tilt permanent. In his devotion to the China card game, Brzezinski overlooked one most important condition for successfully playing the game, namely, China must be kept in the dark that it was being played as a card; otherwise China could play the U.S. card or Soviet card in return.[2] The ensuing developments in Sino-U.S. relations since the derecognition of the ROC on Taiwan and the recognition of the PRC in Beijing could be best described as a game of card playing and counterplaying.[3] Taiwan, the former ally, was thus a pawn to be sacrificed in the process.

Because of Reagan's known pro-Taiwan sentiments, U.S. relations with the PRC, as is noted in Stephen Uhalley's chapter in this volume, faltered in the first two years of the Reagan Administration. It was not until mid-term that a consensus began to emerge within the Administration. Central to the consensus was an understanding that "a good relationship with the PRC was essential to U.S. interests in the context of superpower competition, but that the United States should also maintain as close a relationship as possible with Taiwan for a combination of political, economic and strategic reasons."[4] As a senior U.S. diplomat explained, "we are no longer playing the China card, nor a zero-sum game."[5]

However, regardless of his pro-Taiwan sentiments, Reagan signed the August 17, 1982, communiqué to pacify a Beijing that was bent on tightening the vise on the Taiwan question. Under the new communiqué, Reagan committed the United States to a gradual phasing out of arms sales to

Taiwan, contrary to what the Taiwan Relations Act requires for the defense and security of the island. We shall now turn to a discussion of the Taiwan Relations Act (TRA).

The Taiwan Relations Act

The foundation of U.S.-Taiwan relations since 1979 is the TRA, a unique and unprecedented legislation, authored by the Congress and signed into law by President Carter on April 10, 1979 (Public Law 96-8, 93 Sta. 14).[6] According to Lester L. Wolff, former Chairman of the Asian and Pacific Affairs subcommittee of the U.S. House Foreign Affairs Committee, and one of the architects of the TRA, "the importance of this legislation, now the law of the land, and the intents of its framers cannot be superseded or set aside by reference to any preceding or succeeding communiques [signed by U.S. Presidents]."[7]

The Act clearly and specifically defines United States policy in regard to Taiwan as follows:[8]

(1) To preserve and promote extensive, close, and friendly commercial, cultural, and other relations between the people of the United States and the people on Taiwan, as well as the people on the China mainland and all other peoples of the Western Pacific area;

(2) To declare that peace and stability in the area are in the political, security, and economic interests of the United States, and are matters of international concern;

(3) To make clear that the United States' decision to establish diplomatic relations with the People's Republic of China rests upon the expectation that the future of Taiwan will be determined by peaceful means;

(4) To consider any effort to determine the future of Taiwan by other than peaceful means, including by boycott or embargoes, a threat to the peace and security of the Western Pacific area and of grave concern to the United States;

(5) To provide Taiwan with arms of a defensive character; and

(6) To maintain the capacity of the United States to resist any resort to force or other forms of coercion that would jeopardize the security, or the social or economic system, of the people on Taiwan.

The TRA has worked well generally, in spite of some minor technical and operational problems during the first few months. As one measure of its success, trade between the United States and Taiwan increased by 23 percent in the first year of the TRA's existence; and U.S. investment on the island expanded by about 15 percent. Taiwan is now the United States' sixth largest trading partner, and forecasts are that trade will continue to increase by at least 20 percent a year. At the end of the first year of the TRA's operation, Switzerland's prestigious Bank of International Settlements rated Taiwan as one of the safest investment and lending markets in Asia.[9]

The mechanism established under the TRA to implement U.S.-Taiwan relations has also worked efficiently. The American Institute in Taiwan (AIT), a nonprofit corporation established under the laws of the District of Columbia, has replaced the former American Embassy. Together with its counterpart—Taiwan's Coordination Council for North American Affairs (CCNAA)—the AIT has effectively managed the ' "commercial, cultural, and other relations with Taiwan."[10]

For Taiwan's defense, the TRA authorizes the United States government to "make available to Taiwan such defense articles and defense services in such quantity as may be necessary to enable Taiwan to maintain a sufficient self-defense capability."[11] The Carter Administration did authorize about $600 million in arms sales before leaving office. In December, 1982, the Reagan Administration transferred about $125 million worth of armored personnel carriers and F-104 interceptors to Taiwan. In March, 1983, the Department of State announced that future U.S. arms sales to Taiwan would be indexed to take into account inflation, with 1979 as the base year, which meant that the amount of arms sales would in fact be converted from the 1979 level of $598 million to $830 million in 1983 dollars. The Reagan Administration then designated a "reduced" ceiling of $800 million for arms sales to Taiwan for 1983 and $780 million for 1984. However, as early as January, 1982, Assistant Secretary of State John Holdridge announced in Beijing that the Administration was not going to sell Taiwan FX fighter planes and other advanced equipment it had sought. That did not mute the PRC's objections.

Challenges from Beijing

The arms sales question has been a bone of contention in China's relations with the United States. To these latest measures, the PRC responded with a steady stream of denunciations, accusing Reagan of deliberately violating the August 17 communiqué. Back in 1979, when the TRA was enacted, the conferees who reconciled the two separate versions of the bill passed by the Senate and the House offered an explanatory statement that "the President was required to ensure that the allocation of defense articles and services to Taiwan would be made without regard to the views of the

PRC."[12] The statement, actually, was a response to a prevailing concern in Congress that the President might be under pressure from Beijing to curtail the TRA's commitment to provide defensive arms for the security of Taiwan.[13] The declaration, therefore, was to serve notice that the PRC would have no veto over the maintenance of Taiwan's adequate defensive capabilities.[14]

Initially, after the TRA's enactment, Beijing's objection to the arms-sales clause, among others, was somewhat *pro forma*. Its objection was based on the practical ground that arms sales to Taiwan would have "nullifying" effects on the newly normalized Sino-U.S. relations and would hamper the PRC's peaceful reunification with Taiwan.[15] It, nevertheless, showed a general tolerance for the TRA.

After Reagan became President, Beijing shifted its ground to the question of sovereignty and accused the United States, by its Taiwan arms sales, of interfering in what it claimed to be "China's internal affairs." In the views of an American who participated in many of the events surrounding the Sino-U.S. normalization, in making the claim the PRC was "violating the original deal."[16]

The more recent Chinese claims were repeated in Premier Zhao Ziyang's statements during his visit to the United States in January, 1984. Zhao repeatedly pronounced the Taiwan issue "a main obstacle" to improving relations.[17] In a televised news conference on January 11, 1984, Premier Zhao openly declared that "the Taiwan Relations Act is the essential obstacle to the development of Sino-U.S. relations. This Act must be completely repealed in order to attain steady and sustained development of these relations."[18]

The moral here is that Beijing is not merely opposing our arms sales to Taiwan, but is demanding that we "repeal" a legislation duly enacted by Congress and signed by the President into law.

We can only speculate on the possible reasons for this escalation in Beijing's position. One reason could be that the Taiwan issue is important for China's domestic politics. It is, after all, probably one of the major issues that can rally together different factions behind the Dengist leadership. Another possible reason is Beijing's worries about Reagan's personal amity toward Taiwan, resulting in greater Chinese pressures on the present Administration than ever before. A third conceivable reason is Beijing's realization of Reagan's weakness resulting from his strong desire to cultivate allies to combat the Soviet threat. Beijing thus sees an opportunity to demand more concessions from Washington on Taiwan as a *quid pro quo* for Chinese cooperation.

Finally, there is the element of Chinese nationalism, which sees the return of Taiwan to the motherland as an unfinished mission. Deng Yingchao, widow of the late Premier Zhou Enlai, stated in a recent interview:[19]

> I'd like to remind Mr. Chiang Ching-kuo [leader of Taiwan] and his colleagues that they must see that foreign interference in China's internal affairs will never come to an end so long as peaceful reunification is not realized. . . . Certain people and Congressmen in the United States are prone to interfering in the internal affairs of other countries. The Taiwan issue is a sacred part of Chinese territory. The Taiwan issue is entirely a matter for the Chinese themselves.

Chinese leaders seem to make the Taiwan issue look like the only obstacle in Sino-U.S. relations. The fact is that the two countries have more areas of differences than areas of agreement. In the Middle East, for example, the PRC has espoused an anti-Israel policy and has long supported the radical Arab nations' goal of denying Israel's right of existence. In Latin America, it is not supportive of Reagan's Central American policy in general and opposed the "U.S. invasion of Grenada," in particular. This was reaffirmed by Premier Zhao during his recent visit.[20] In Europe, despite U.S. requests, the PRC refuses to support Reagan's policies toward Poland. In the United Nations, the PRC voted against U.S. positions about 80 percent of the time, even outdoing the Soviet record of voting divergence from the United States. In the fall of 1983, the PRC ignored U.S. pleas and deliberately chose not to vote for the U.S.-sponsored resolution in the Security Council condemning the Soviet downing of a civilian Korean airliner.

In its relations with Moscow, Beijing is gradually breaking away from its earlier anti-Soviet position once described by the Carter people—especially Brzezinski—as "parallel" to that of the United States. Since the 12th Congress of the Chinese Communist Party, China has embarked on a new foreign policy billed as "independent," which translates into "even-handed" toward both Washington and Moscow.[21] Various chapters in this volume have explored the backgrounds and developments of the new Sino-Soviet détente. We shall merely concur here that the détente is an ongoing enterprise and that the PRC is seriously developing a working relationship with the Soviet Union, while simultaneously maintaining its good relations with the United States.[22]

The brief romance with Washington may have brought many advantages to the PRC, such as improved trade, MFN (most favored nation treatment), upgraded technology transfer, arms sales offers, Eximbank credit, and so forth. At the same time, however, there also have been costs involved for the Chinese, as James C. Hsiung has pointed in his chapter on the 3-person game. Most notably, these costs are in the form of continuing Vietnamese intransigence, which has in turn enhanced Hanoi's dependence on Moscow and consequently led to increasing Soviet military presence in Indochina, which defeats the very purpose of the original Chinese policy of befriending the United States. In the Third World, as a whole, too close a relationship with the "U.S. imperialists" has brought on a considerable decline in Chinese influence. Under these circumstances, it is not surprising that the PRC now wants to slow down its relations with Washington, among other reasons, to "preserve its reputation in the Third World as an autonomous international actor,"[23] as Harry Harding put it.

In view of these developments, we cannot fail to note that the original assumption about the irreversibility of the Sino-Soviet split, on which the China-card policy (along with our derecognition of the ROC on Taiwan) was justified, no longer stands up. This, plus the many areas of our disagreement with Beijing beyond the Taiwan issue, as already noted, requires an earnest, conscientious policy review for the good of our own interests.

The Taiwan Card

By contrast, Taiwan remains one of our strongest allies, sharing a common interest in most areas, from bilateral trade to security cooperation. Geographically, Taiwan occupies an important location amid the Western Pacific sealanes. Mideast oil shipments, for example, pass through the Taiwan Strait daily to reach Japan. Should Taiwan's security be threatened or, worse still, should it fall into hostile hands, the security of these sealanes would be severely affected. With its extensive modern airstrips and port facilities, Taiwan could have important strategic value to the United States and the free world.

Taiwan's strategic value to our security interests in the western Pacific has often been glossed over surprisingly even by the Reagan team with its professed affinity to the island. In addition to its importance to the sealanes, 1.5 miles off the east coast of Taiwan, between Hualien and Suao, the seabed sinks precipitously at a 45° angle to a depth of 4 to 5 miles, providing a perfect submarine sanctuary from which SLBMs (submarine-launched ballistic missiles) can be launched against Soviet territories. Who controls the Taiwan Strait during wartime, therefore, would wield a great military advantage.[24]

Although defense analysts may differ in their assessments of the strategic value of Taiwan vis-à-vis mainland China to the United States' global interests, they are virtually unanimous in the view that the fall of Taiwan to Communist hands would not be in our best interests. The United States now holds the key to the future of the island because it can supply the essential defensive weapons Taiwan direly needs and it is Taiwan's largest trading partner. After a real GNP growth of 3.8 percent in 1982, the Taiwan economy, sparked by improved U.S. economy and global recovery, Taiwan was expected to have a 7.14 percent real GNP growth for 1983, with industrial production shooting up to 11.3 percent. The AIT estimated that Taiwan's total foreign trade for 1983 would reach $45.2 billion, producing a favorable balance of $5 billion.[25]

Without U.S. partnership, on the other hand, Taiwan could encounter some difficulties and would be less equipped to cope with a few others, in the next decade or so. The following are among the more serious ones:[26]

(1) Overpopulation. Taiwan already has the second highest population density in the world, approximately 472 persons per square kilometer. It has five times the population density of the PRC and almost 20 times that of the United States. At least 20,000 Chinese in Taiwan emigrate to the United States annually; and hundreds come as students.

(2) Surplus of College Graduates. In 1978–79, Taiwan had 317,188 students in its colleges and universities in an area not larger than Rhode Island and Connecticut combined. Although this can be an asset to Taiwan's economic development, the island cannot absorb the surplus graduates turned out each year by its over 100 colleges and universities. Unemployment as well as underemployment among college graduates can cause serious social and political problems.

(3) Energy Shortage and Environmental Pollution. Taiwan is almost entirely dependent on outside energy supplies, including oil from the Middle East. With an increasing reliance on nuclear power, Taiwan is probably one of the worst polluted nations in the world.

(4) Political Instability. Taiwan's worst fear would be political unrest. Street riots and disruptions in economic development are strong possibilities, should the island be coerced to reunite with mainland China under U.S. pressure. At the present, Taiwan's political process is essentially one toward "routinization" (sometimes known as "Taiwanization"), with Taiwan-born Chinese gaining greater political as well as economic power. This is demonstrated by the 1984 elevation of Dr. Teng-hui Lee, the former Governor of Taiwan, to the position of Vice-President of the Republic. Lee is, in fact, considered a "true" Taiwanese, with a marked difference with Tung-ming Hsieh, the former Vice-President, who was educated on the mainland before its fall to the Communists in 1949.[27] Lee, however, has never been to the mainland. He represents a new generation of Chinese born in Taiwan who have no emotional ties with mainland China.

By keeping Taiwan strong economically, politically, and militarily, the United States will have a faithful ally in the Asian-Pacific region. With Taiwan on its side, the United States could gain important political leverage in its dealings with Beijing, as Robert L. Downen put it, "not unlike the tactical advantage Moscow wields in talks with Beijing through its border weapons and its support for Vietnam."[28] If our strategic sense often suggests the PRC as a possible counterweight to the Soviet Union, isn't it equally strategically sensible that we think about Taiwan as a possible counterweight to the PRC?

Future Policy Options

In terms of U.S. policy in view of the continuing separation of Taiwan and mainland China, we suggest that we consider a few basic elements.

In Regard to the PRC

In spite of its most recent overtures to the Soviet Union, the PRC is moving in the right direction in its domestic program, under the pragmatic leadership of Deng Xiaoping, whose "four modernizations" give high priority to economic and technological development. The full and successful implementation of Deng's program could conceivably transform China into a society that actually tolerates a limited market economy and provides its people with increased political choice and legal protection.

Extensive U.S. economic, educational, and cultural exchanges and cooperation will undoubtedly facilitate China's modernization drive. It is in U.S. national interests to continue its good relations with Beijing, involving it in an inexorable process through which Western democratic ideas and institutions will have a chance of being imported into China along with U.S. technology. Our efforts to promote economic and technological exchanges with the PRC should include the removal of barriers for trade and for high-technology transfer to China, without, of course, violating our national security safeguards. In the educational and cultural spheres, we should have increased exchanges through coordinated planning, to train large numbers of mainland Chinese students and scholars not merely in science and technology, but in other areas of human endeavor as well. We should cultivate a more forward looking, multidimensional China policy that emphasizes genuine, mutually rewarding cooperation rather than merely the containment of Soviet expansionism.

In Regard to Taiwan

We should realize that for both moral and practical reasons it would be wrong for us to wash our hands of Taiwan. Morally, we cannot banish the 18 million Taiwan people to a political fate that they abhor, if that means being engulfed by the Communists from across the Taiwan Strait. In the more practical vein, we should consider the extent of our tangible and intangible investments in Taiwan. Quite deservingly, we share part of the credit for Taiwan's achievement as one of the Asian NICs (newly industrialized countries), whose per capita GNP is eight or nine times that of mainland China. It would be foolish for us to turn our backs on the Taiwan people.

Beijing has repeatedly claimed that Taiwan's ties with the United States are an "obstacle" to furthering U.S.-PRC relations. The fact is that the reverse is also true: An intransigent Beijing is equally an obstacle to the United States' good relations with Taiwan. What is more important, Beijing has its own reasons for wanting to keep a distance with the United States, notably because of its concerns about Third World reactions and its attempt to improve relations with Moscow in order, among other things, to contain the ruthless Vietnamese, as already noted. Hence, it is not true that Taiwan is the only hindrance to better PRC ties with the United States, although Beijing can turn the issue on and off as it wishes at any time.

We have also noted the strategic value of Taiwan, especially as a possible counterweight against the PRC, just as the latter has been perceived as a possible counterweight against the Soviet threat. Even if domestic opinions vary on the extent of Taiwan's strategic value to the United States, there is virtual consensus that Taiwan not be allowed to fall into Communist hands. If we cannot do much to help Taiwan, the least we can do is not to meddle in the delicate matter of Chinese "reunification." We should remain aloof and let the Chinese on both sides of the Taiwan Strait work out a mutually acceptable formula.

In a more positive way, the United States can help by applying a two-pronged policy of (1) helping China develop into a more prosperous, free, and democratic society, which will narrow the gap currently existing between the mainland and Taiwan; and (2) helping sustain the current military balance in the Taiwan Strait, as a transitional measure, pending future outcomes. The latter half of the two-pronged policy is as important as the first; for, if the PRC is militarily superior, it will have less incentive to seek reunification by peaceful means, rather than attempting an invasion. The Reagan government has proffered to supply advanced weapons to the PRC. If that is not coupled with arms sales to upgrade Taiwan's defense capabilities, the military balance in the Taiwan Strait will gradually but surely be altered in Beijing's favor.

If Taiwan is reunified through military conquest, then, Beijing's leaders will have even less incentive to want to allow the Chinese people more freedom and democracy, since the conscious contest with the competing ROC system on Taiwan, as it now exists, will be no more. To prevent all this from happening, therefore, the maintenance of the prevailing military balance in the Taiwan Strait, which depends on continuing U.S. support for Taiwan, including defensive arms sales, will be essential. This lies at the very heart of the Taiwan Relations Act. Precisely because of this, Beijing has been clamoring for the repeal of the Act and the termination of all U.S. arms sales to the island.

In this sense, rather than an obstacle, U.S. defensive arms sales are ultimately conducive to the realization of Beijing's professed goal of a peaceful reunion with Taiwan. Indisputably, only a militarily secure Taiwan can be expected to come to the negotiating table with Beijing to discuss the details of a peaceful reunification. A true test of the PRC leaders' professed peaceful intent, therefore, lies in their attitude toward the U.S. policy so conceived.

The United States has embarked upon helping China complete its four modernizations. It certainly expects to gain much from this endeavor, in terms of expanded trade and investment returns. If the expected gains materialize, they will help offset the perennial huge U.S. trade deficits with Japan. That will be good for us in the short run. We should, however, pause to ponder over the possible long-term consequences from an industrialized China armed with seemingly unlimited manpower. We know of no meaningful futuristic studies yet made of the challenge that China may pose to the United States as a trade competitor. Will China rival or even eclipse Japan as the creator of the largest U.S. trade deficits? While nobody has an answer, one thing is certain: Taiwan, however successful economically, does not have the potential to pose such a threat to the United States. If anything, the Taiwan card, held in U.S. hands, will probably augment our bargaining power vis-à-vis the PRC.

To the basic question raised for this volume—what policy should we pursue beyond the Sino-Soviet détente?—our answer in regard to Taiwan is that the United States and its noncommunist Asian allies should continue to maintain their existing ties with Taiwan and, furthermore, they have all the more reasons not to want to see the existing military balance change drastically in the Taiwan Strait.

Notes

1. James C. Hsiung and Winberg Chai, eds., *Asia and U.S. Foreign Policy* (New York: Praeger, 1981), pp. 121ff.
2. *Ibid.*, p. 125.
3. "Using barbarians against the barbarians" is a well known tradition of Chinese diplomacy. Cf. Mark Mancall, "The Persistence of Tradition in Chinese Foreign Policy," *The Annals* of the American Academy of Political and Social Science, Vol. 340 (September 1963), p. 19.
4. Robert S. Hirschfield, "The Reagan Administration and U.S. Relations with Taiwan and the People's Republic of China," paper delivered at the Conference on U.S. Congressional-Executive Relations and the Taiwan Relations Act, Taipei, Taiwan, January 9-14, 1984, p. 23.
5. Briefing for participants of the Taipei conference mentioned in n. 4 above, by a senior officer of the American Institute in Taiwan (AIT), Taipei, January 14, 1984.

6. Lester L. Wolff and David L. Simon, eds., *Legislative History of the Taiwan Relations Act* (New York: American Association for Chinese Studies, 1982), pp. 288–95.
7. *Ibid.*, p. vii.
8. *Ibid.*, p. 238.
9. *Implementation of the Taiwan Relations Act: The First Year*, A Staff Report to the Committee on Foreign Relations, U.S. Senate, June, 1980. (Washington, D. C.: U.S. Government Printing Office, 1980), p. 6.
10. *Ibid.*, p. 6.
11. Lester Wolff and David Simon, n. 6 above, p. 289.
12. Roy A. Werner, "When a Minuet Becomes a Threesome: The Political and Strategic Factors of the Evolving U.S.-PRC-Taiwan Relations," in Yu-ming Shaw, ed., *ROC-U.S. Relations: A Decade After the Shanghai Communiqué* (Taipei: The Asia and World Institute, 1983), p. 39.
13. *Ibid.*
14. *Ibid.*
15. See remarks made by Deng Xiaoping, in *The New York Times*, April 20, 1979.
16. Roy Werner, n. 12 above, p. 34.
17. *Beijing Review*, January 23, 1984, p. 18.
18. *Ibid.*
19. *Beijing Review*, January 9, 1984, p. 6.
20. *Beijing Review*, January 23, 1984, p. 19.
21. Premier Zhao reiterated the "independent" foreign policy stance in his address to the Canadian Parliament in January, 1980. *Beijing Review*, January 30, 1984, pp. 17–18.
22. Chalmers Johnson, "East Asia: Living Dangerously," *Foreign Affairs*, Vol. 62, No. 3 (1983), p. 735.
23. Harry Harding, "China and the Third World," in Richard Solomon, ed., *The China Factor* (Englewood Cliffs, N.J.: Prentice-Hall, 1981), p. 293.
24. James C. Hsiung, ed., *Asian-U.S. Relations: The National Security Paradox* (New York: Praeger, 1983), p. 1980.
25. Briefing by AIT senior officer, n. 5 above.
26. Hungdah Chiu, "U.S. Recognition of the People's Republic of China and the Future Prospects of Taiwan," paper delivered at a colloquium sponsored by the John Basset Moore Society of International Law, University of Virginia School of Law, October 26–27, 1979, pp. 2–4.
27. *The Free China Journal* (Taipei), February 26, 1984, p. 4.
28. Robert L. Downen, "Reagan, Zhao, and the Taiwan Pawn," *The Asian Wall Street Journal Weekly*, January 2, 1984.

Sino-U.S.-Soviet Relations in a Triadic-Game Perspective

7

James C. Hsiung

As preliminary remarks about methodology, I would like to suggest that we should not indulge in *ad hoc* explanations in our study of international politics, but should bring theory to bear. Theories are generalizations from prior empirical studies that should help explain new situations, *ceteris paribus*. Furthermore, we should not confine ourselves to bilateral relations, but should put them in larger contexts.

In this chapter, I propose to examine Sino-U.S.-Soviet relations in their triadic context, drawing upon some of the theoretical insights from studies of three-person games. In addition, I shall also examine the players' gains and losses in their existing alignments as a relevant variable in speculating about future trends. I hope that in the course of the discussions below the superiority of this three-person-game perspective to that of the habitual "triangle" will become clear.

Here, I shall only offer very brief comments on what I consider to be the inadequacies of the triangular approach. In the first place, the word triangle has become a cliché, often evoking the image of the proverbial romantic triangle, which blinds one to other possible alignment pattens within a triad. Second, the notion of the triangle is too restrictive and is not apt to accommodate the possibility and full complexities of, for example, a 2-against-2 game within a triad. An example of this game would be a situation in which an ambitious United States aligns itself with China in such a way as to treat China both as a partner and as a pawn to be used against the Soviet Union so that in the end both Communist giants will be weakened. Since it involves two partners, the United States and China, and is aimed at two targets, the Soviet Union and China, it is a 2-against-2 triadic game.[1] The triangle metaphor does not square with a game of "2 against 2."

The N-Person Game and the Triad

Although the "n" in the n-person game should be any number, differentiation between dyads and triads, according to Georg Simmel, is much sharper than between triads and tetrads or higher-numbered groups. Indeed, higher-numbered groups can be reduced to triadic forms. Thus, analyses of triadic interactions (or 3-person games) can be a very fruitful enterprise and can form the basis for an expansion to higher-numbered groups (n-person).

Because the use of three-person games in the analysis of Sino-U.S.-Soviet relations is relatively new, it is necessary to mention some of the key characteristics associated with triadic behavior that are relevant to our concerns here.[2]

(a) One is the relative fluidity in alignment patterns in a triad. Although Georg Simmel and others such as Von Neumann and Morgenstern have noted a tendency toward segregation into a pair and an other,[3] this specific line of segregation is only one of the many possible alignments in a triad. But, unfortunately, that appears to be the only pattern that has caught the fancy of the triangular analysts. Furthermore, in triadic game experiments, the third player is found to fare better when facing a conflict than facing a solidary bond between the other two.[4] According to Simmel and others, the weak man (tertius) in a triad that includes two strong players is found to profit, far out of proportion to his real power, by aligning himself with one of the two more powerful members. Furthermore, the weak tertius is found to profit even more handsomely when the two more powerful players are in a logjam of contention.[5] We shall return to this point below, but I merely wish to note here that these findings have enormous significance for forecasting possible future coalition options of our three players—the United States, the People's Republic of China (PRC), and the Soviet Union—if and when they learn their lessons over time.

(b) If the relative strength or power of the three members is known, it is possible to predict the appearance of particular coalitions. On the basis of the relative strengths of the three, Theodore Caplow has constructed eight basic types of triads having different coalitional relations.[6] We shall see below whether the triadic alignments among our three players can be explained accordingly.

(c) There is the basic distinction between "continuous" triadic situations and two short-lived variations. The two variations are: "episodic" situations, which are like one-shot deals such as

Sino-U.S.-Soviet Relations

voting episodes; and "terminal" situations, in which the players are trying to get rid of one another.[7] In a "continuous" situation—of which the Sino-U.S.-Soviet triad is an example—coalitions are formed for a variety of purposes. Although one coalition may be dominant most of the time, the other coalitions are expected to form when appropriate. Those who embrace the triangular model usually look at domestic politics such as leadership changes as reasons for coalition shifts, but rarely at the dynamics within the triad—such as significant changes in the power balance and interactions among the members—as a likewise crucial variable.

(d) Relations within a triad are not merely calculated on the basis of gains for one's own coalition and losses for the adversary, but equally on the basis of one's own gains and losses versus those of one's coalition partner. It is not just how much both partners in a "stable marriage" gain against the common opponent, but equally how much each partner gains vis-à-vis the other partner, that will bear on the partnership itself.

A caveat must be entered before we go any further. While formal game theory is a sophisticated science using mathematic (deductive) reasoning, we are using games as analogies here, to illustrate the dynamics of coalition making and remaking in a triad. Game theory is a rational analysis of optimal strategies based on the calculation of possible outcomes (winning the game), rather than the initial power ratios among the players. The work by Anatol Rapoport, Thomas Schelling, Steven J. Brams, and others is representative of this approach.[8]

The study of how the interactions of participants correspond to their expectations stemming from perceptions (of power ratios) and motives is the concern of social psychologists. This is sometimes called "perception theory," to distinguish it from game theory, although both study relations within a group. Whereas game theory under the inital influence of economics is concerned with what purports to be a player's rational strategy if he is to win the game, perception theory developed by social psychologists and sociologists examines what actually occurs in a group consisting of members confronted with a variety of seeming power relationships to each other. In this study, I shall rely more on the works of Georg Simmel, Theodore Caplow, W. Edgar Vinacke and Abe Arkoff, and Sheldon Stryker and Pasthas than on those of the game theorists.[9]

The Vinacke-Arkoff Experiment

We shall first make use of findings from the Vinacke-Arkoff experiment.[10] In the Vinacke-Arkoff pachisi game involving three players, each player was given a "weight" to reflect uneven power distribution. The game board of pachisi has 67 spaces numbered consecutively; a single die is cast instead of a pair; and at each move the player advances his marker a number of spaces equal to the number thrown times his assigned weight. The game is an instrument for studying the effect of any initial power distribution on the formation of coalitions in triads. The Vinacke-Arkoff game is unusual in that every player moves on every throw of the die.

The predictions to be tested in the Vinacke-Arkoff experiment were drawn from a formulation made by Theodore Caplow which had suggested that under certain conditions the formation of particular coalitions depends upon the initial distribution of power in the triad and may be predicted to some extent when the intitial distribution of power is known.[11]

All together six types of coalitions were predicted on the basis of the assigned weights, as are seen in Figure 7.1.

In the experiment, each group of subjects played 18 games, repeating six power distributions in random sequence. Table 7.1 shows the results obtained by Vinacke and Arkoff when their student subjects played 99 games of each type. In general the results conformed to the theoretical expectations.[12]

Table 7.1. Coalitions Formed in the Six Types of Power Patterns in Triads

Allies	Type 1 (1-1-1)	Type 2 (3-2-2)	Type 3 (1-2-2)	Type 4 (3-1-1)	Type 5 (4-3-2)	Type 6 (4-2-1)
AB	33	13	24	11	9	9
AC	17	12	40	10	20	13
BC	30	64	15	7	59	8
Total	80	89	79	28	88	30
(No Coalition)	10	1	11	62	2	60
P	>.05	<.10	<.01	<.70	<.01	<.50

Source: W. Edgar Vinacke and Abe Arkoff, "An Experimental Study of Coalitions in the Triad," *American Sociological Review*, Vol. 22, No. 4 (August 1957), p. 409.

Type 2, 3, and 5 are of particular interest to us because they seem to help explain the patterns of alignment that have existed in the evolution of Sino-U.S.-Soviet relations. Before we proceed any further, however, a few words of clarification are in order. First, it should be noted that there were exceptions to the predicted outcomes in the Vinacke-Arkoff experiment. In the Type 2 game, for example, with a 3:2:2 ratio, the predicted outcome is a BC coalition. In the experiment, this was borne out in 64 of the 89 games actually played. Although the conformity rate was nearly 72 percent, there

Figure 7.1. The Vinacke-Arkoff Game

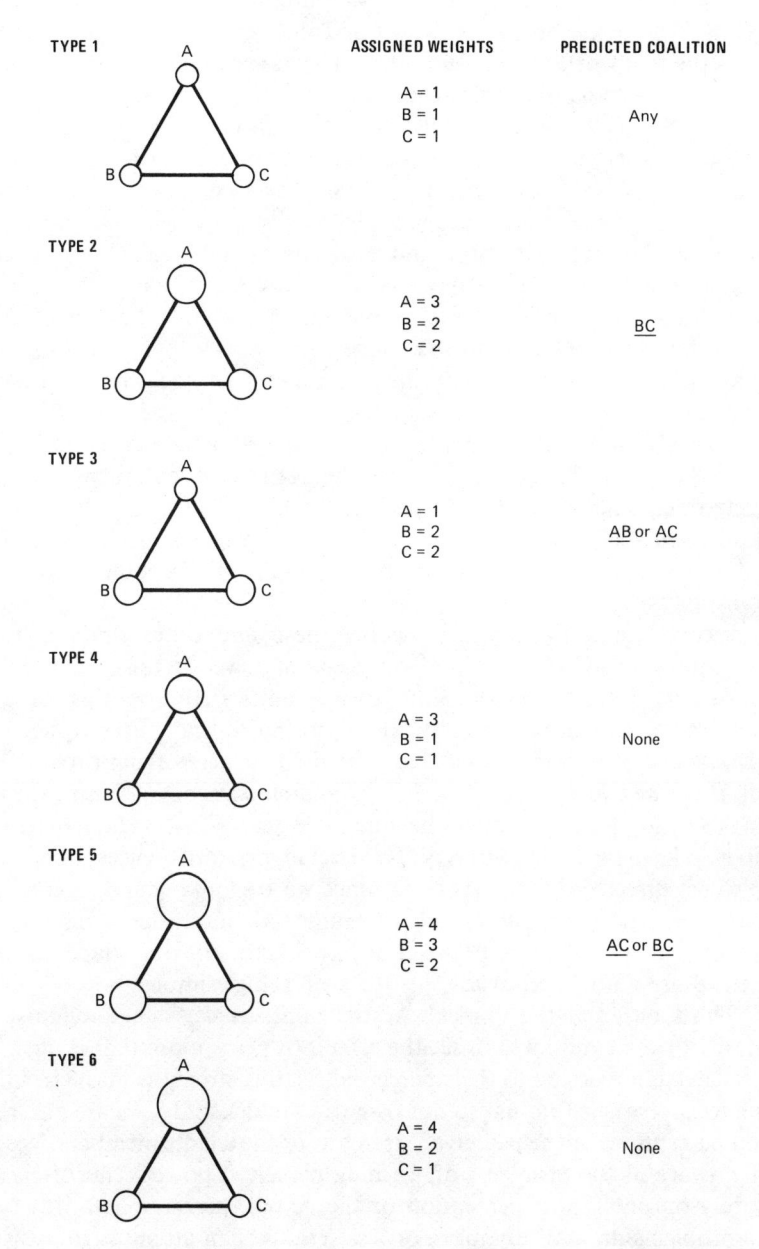

TYPE		ASSIGNED WEIGHTS	PREDICTED COALITION
TYPE 1	△ A,B,C	A = 1 B = 1 C = 1	Any
TYPE 2	△	A = 3 B = 2 C = 2	BC
TYPE 3	△	A = 1 B = 2 C = 2	AB or AC
TYPE 4	△	A = 3 B = 1 C = 1	None
TYPE 5	△	A = 4 B = 3 C = 2	AC or BC
TYPE 6	△	A = 4 B = 2 C = 1	None

Source: Theodore Caplow, *Two Against One: Coalitions in Triads* (Englewood Cliffs, N.J.: Prentice-Hall, 1968), p. 23.

was still a 28 percent deviation (including both the 13 AB and 12 AC bonds as well as 1 no coalition), as is shown in Table 7.1.

In the real world of international politics, exceptions to the predicted outcomes can also be frequently found. For example, although the balance-of-power rules may call for a weak state to align with the lesser of the two powerful members of a triad,[13] actual behavior may be different at times. We need only ponder over the following actual examples from the pre-World War I period: (a) Turkey consistently sided with the strongest member of the triad (Britain, and later Germany) against the second strongest (the Soviet Union); (b) Belgium, as the weakest member of another triad, sought consistently to maintain an equidistance with France and Germany; and (c) Britain, the strongest power then, tried consistently to play off the two weaker continental powers (France and Germany) against each other.

I do wish to point out, however, that exceptions are exceptions. The Vinacke-Arkoff findings do establish high rates of conformity to the predicted outcomes. That should give us some confidence that these findings do have some significant inferential value when applied to the real world, if necessary adjustments are made to take into account extraneous circumstances.

Second, in our attempt to apply these and other findings from perception-theorists' studies of triadic coalitions, we are only dealing with "undirected" dyads within the Sino-Soviet triad. Strictly speaking, because of asymmetry and nonreciprocity, there are more than three dyads in a triad. As Steven J. Brms noted, for a triad constructed from three linked dyads, there are twenty-seven ($3 \times 3 \times 3$) possible ways of combining them.[14] In an AB dyad, besides, A might be much warmer toward B and much more anxious to keep the dyad than B is. To indicate these differences, one would have to use directed dyads. However, since we are looking at past coalition patterns and possible future trends, rather than at the symmetry or reciprocity in the relations between any two actors in our triad, we have chosen to use undirected dyads, just to keep things simple.

Third, although the Vinacke-Arkoff games used assigned weights, the purpose of the exercise was to see the effects of perception, that is, how actors behaved in reaction to their perceived relative strengths in the triad. In trying to apply their findings to our own triad under study, we are also relying on perception, or the perceived strengths of the triadic members. We are highly aware of the problems of defining perceived power (and often one may rely on one's own perception of the actors' perceptions). However, these problems are not any more or less serious than attempts to measure power by any "objective" criteria, as have been done by some more quantitative analysts, or to plot a rational winning strategy on the basis of outcomes defined (i.e., perceived to be rational) by game theorists.

Now back to the Vinacke-Arkoff experiment. We shall now see if its findings can help illuminate the coalition shifts in the Sino-U.S.-Soviet triad. In the 1950s and early 1960s, when there were clearly perceived discrepancies in power distribution, approximating 4:3:2 (for the United States qua A; the Soviet Union qua B; and China qua C), a type 5 alignment would be most probable. This would mean either an AC or BC coalition. However, the strong ideological division at the time made an AC (U.S.-China) coalition out of the question, leaving BC (a Sino-Soviet bond) the only feasible alternative.

In fact, the AC (U.S.-China) alignment was not as improbable as one might assume, now that we know that Mao Zedong and Zhou Enlai had, indeed, in the spring of 1949, approached Washington in an attempt to establish a modus vivendi in anticipation of the establishment of the PRC later that year. It was only after the State Department had rebuffed the offer that the Chinese Communist leaders were left with no other choice than to "lean upon" the Soviet side.

Even if we put aside the ideological factor, the power distribution can explain why adding China's 2 to the Soviet Union's 3 would be more desirable than adding China's 2 to the United States' 4. In a U.S.-China alignment with an aggregate weight of 6, China could easily be engulfed by the United States if the coalition had served its purpose of trouncing the Soviet Union. On the other hand, at a 3:2 ratio, the Soviet Union would treasure the Chinese connection more than the United States would. While the United States could cope with the Soviet Union unaided, given the 4:3 ratio, the Soviet Union would need the Chinese ally to increase the combined weight to 5, just a little over the 4 weight of the United States.[15]

In the late 1960s, however, the United States was saddled with the Vietnam debacle and suffered a decline in power, more especially in the perception of the world. In nuclear weapons, the Soviets probably did not reach a parity with the United States until some time later. If conventional power and perception are added to the equation of power, the Soviet Union was clearly gaining, while U.S. power was on the wane. Domestic protests and reactions including Congressional moves to block another Vietnam-type foreign involvement cast further doubts on the United States' ability to project its power abroad. In these relative terms, the power ratio in the triad approached that in the Type 2 of the Vinacke-Arkoff game, that is, 3:2:2 (Soviet Union = A; United States = B; and China = C). As the predicted coalition in Type 2 is BC, the "normalization" of relations between the United States and China (BC) was therefore not surprising.

In the 1970s and early 1980s, however, there was a parity between the two superpowers, with China lagging behind, approximating the power distribution in Type 3. In the 1:2:2 ratio (China = A; United States = B; and Soviet Union = C), the predicted coalition patterns are either AB or

AC. When applied to our actual situation, an AB (Sino-U.S.) coalition dominated much of the 1970s; and in view of the expanding dialogue between the PRC and the Soviet Union since 1982, an AC coalition is not a too far-fetched development. Many analysts are now beginning to speak about a possible AC bond, although nobody expects a return to the kind of Sino-Soviet alliance of the 1950s.

The Stryker-Psathas Experiment

The dynamics of the Type 3 triads are obviously of enormous interest to those concerned about future developments in Sino-U.S.-Soviet relations in the years ahead, as long as the power ratio approximates 1:2:2.

Stryker and Psathas experimented with a pachisi game involving only Type 3 triads.[16] Among the rules in this game variation is that no ties are permitted. Players who tie are forced to replay the game until the tie is broken. The rule is to make coalitions compulsory. For that reason, the findings from the experiment would be more relevant to our attempts to forecast what is likely to happen to relations in the Sino-U.S.-Soviet triad, given the power ratio noted above.

Figure 7.2. The Stryker-Psathas Game.

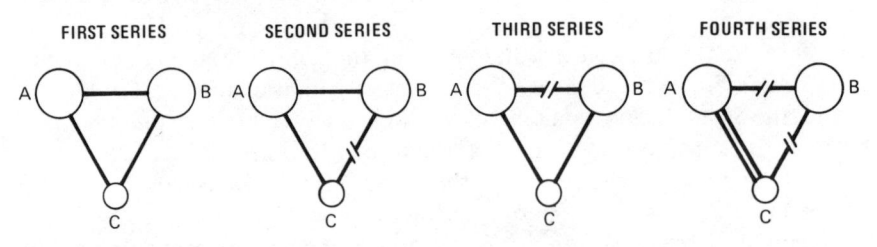

FIRST SERIES	SECOND SERIES	THIRD SERIES	FOURTH SERIES
Condition	*Condition*	*Condition*	*Condition*
Any coalition allowed	BC prohibited	AB prohibited	AB and BC prohibited
Outcome	*Outcome*	*Outcome*	*Outcome*
Equal frequency of AB, BC, and AC coalitions	AC coalition two out of three times	AC and BC coalitions	AC coalition in every game

Source: Theodore Caplow, *Two Against One: Coalitions in Triads* (Englewood Cliffs, N.J.: Prentice-Hall, 1968), p. 28.

As shown in Figure 7.2, certain restrictions on coalitions were imposed. In the first series, all coalitions were allowed. In the second series, player A enjoyed an absolute choice between partners B and C, as the BC coalition was prohibited. In the third series, C was the chooser, as the AB coalition was prohibited. In the fourth series, the AC coalition was compulsory.[17]

If we translate this game into our real-world triadic situation and consider A to be the United States, B to be the Soviet Union, and C to be China, then, we can see the following results:

(a) The Fourth Series seems to be the situation that actually existed during the latter part of the 1970s, when no AB (U.S.-Soviet) or BC (Sino-Soviet) alignment was possible.

(b) The United States will be the winner in a situation similar to the Second Series, as it has the freedom to choose either the Soviet Union or the People's Republic, while a Soviet-Chinese coalition is blocked. This seems to have actually existed during the years of the Nixongerian détente (1969-74).

(c) The Soviet Union, on the other hand, will be the winner in an obverse version of the Second Series, switching roles with the United States (although this is not shown in Figure 7.2), where no AC (U.S.-China) coalition is possible. This was the situation during the 1950s, when a Sino-Soviet alliance existed.

(d) China will be the winner in the Third Series, which rules out an AB (U.S.-Soviet) coalition and which makes China the only player that can freely align itself with either of the other two players.

(e) In view of the above, the only situation in which all players will have equal freedom to make coalitions and benefit from triad-wide stability is the First Series. This situation approaches what Lowell Dittmer calls *ménage à trois*, though it is not exactly the same.[18] In a ménage à trois (harmony among the three), any improved relations between any two players is good for the entire triad and, hence, stabilizing to it. While this is ideal, it is the most difficult to realize because of mutual suspicions and the urge of players to increase their margin of security at the expense of the others. In all the other series (including both variations of the Third Series), as is typical of nation-state behavior in the real world, each player is trying to benefit from blocking the coalition between the other two players and making either of them its own sole coalition partner. As long as this syndrome continues, no ménage à trois is possible. What all this suggests is, nevertheless, that the player that maintains all channels open and retains the freedom of aligning itself with one or the other player in the triad has an edge over one that does not do the same.

Let us now see what the results were in the Stryker-Psathas experiment. In the first series, the two strong players (A and B) chose the weak player (C) twice as often as they chose each other, but only on the basis of the weak player's willingness to accept a lesser share of the prize. In the second series, in which A alone was the chooser, C was again chosen two out of three times on the same terms. C's average share of the prize was 34 percent in the first series and 35 percent in the second series.

In the third series, C was in the strongest position, enjoying an uncontrolled choice of coalition partners. His average share of the prize was 53 percent. In the fourth series, when the coalition AC was in effect made compulsory, most of the C's in the experiment, which included 144 games, negotiated an approximately even division with A.[19]

The results from the Stryker-Psathas experiment suggest an advantage for C, the weakest of the three, that is disproportionate to its power weight in the triad.[20] This merely confirms similar findings by Georg Simmel and by Vinacke and Arkoff.[21] We shall see in the section below whether this is true in the real world of Sino-U.S.-Soviet relations. If it is true, China will have shown to be in the same advantageous position that the weak C enjoyed in the Stryker-Psathas experiment.

Correlations in Shifts Within the Triad

In an ongoing project, I have been attempting to establish some correlations in the changing dyadic relations within the triad that consists of the United States, China, and the Soviet Union. When it is completed, the project will have examined all major shifts in the alignments between each two of the three powers since 1949 and the possible correlations between these dyadic changes. For example, if there was a significant improvement in Sino-U.S. relations in a particular period, was it followed or preceded by a decline in U.S.-Soviet relations, and vice versa?

Although correlations, even if established, do not demonstrate causality, they may indicate some trends and patterns, especially if they are found to be frequent and consistent. Thus far, the project has covered only the years between 1969 (the inauguration of the Nixon Doctrine) and 1980. What I have done is to have three sets of chronologies established, one each for the dyadic relations between the three powers: Sino-U.S., U.S.-Soviet, and Soviet-Chinese. Then the chronologies, after having been verified, were turned over to two coders, each of whom was asked to evaluate the chronologies and to see whether there were any correlations in the ups and downs between any two of the three sets of data. Neither coder knew the work of the other beforehand. One coder did an eye-ball evaluation. The other used a scheme for defining and scaling the ups and downs. The scheme was patterned after but considerably refined from the categories of foreign-policy behavior used in the World Events Interaction Survey (WEIS) established by Charles McClelland.[22]

The scheme divides dyadic interactions into cooperative and conflictual acts, and defines them on a scale of 0 to 10 (cooperation) and 0 to -10 (conflict), thus making it possible to make comparisons and, by adding up the scores, to "measure" the extent of changes. Without going into great detail about the data analyzing process, I shall merely give the bare essentials of the findings thus far. In order to show the diachronic changes, we shall identify certain subperiods based on the changing patterns (i.e., clusterings of ups and downs) in the three sets of dyadic relations. The subperiods are: (a) 1969-1971; (b) 1972-1974; (c) 1975-1977; and (d) 1978-1980. Our data cover only up to 1980.

It may appear desirable to break down the ups and downs of dyadic relations by issue area, since the degrees of conflict and cooperation may vary across issue areas. However, for two reasons we are not doing that. First, each player's strategic concerns still dominate over all others, and mutual adversity has made each cooperative move an adjunct to the larger competitive or conflictual relationship. The United States' opening to the PRC, for example, was a means of keeping the Soviet adversary at bay. In cooperating with the PRC, each U.S. administration was concerned that the assistance Peking received would not be used against the United States. Second, our primary interest is to chart the volatility (ups and downs) within the entire triad as a function of the reciprocal interactions among all three players, not just the changing relations between any two of them per se. The patterns we find below are the results of triad-wide interactions.

1969-1971

(a) The initial effects of the U.S. attempt to "open" to China were seen, beginning with the second quarter of 1969 (the announcement of the Nixon Doctrine) and continuing on through the second quarter of 1970.

(b) As Sino-U.S. relations improved steadily from -10 to a hefty 25 (from the 2nd quarter of 1970 to the 2nd quarter of 1971), U.S.-Soviet relations went up even higher, to 64.

(c) Sino-Soviet relations went up from an all-time low of -34 in early 1969 to an encouraging 11 in the 3rd quarter of 1969, but swiftly dropped to -23 in late 1969 and early 1970. After that, however, slow but steady improvements brought them back to 11 in late 1970.

To sum up, in the 1969-1971 subperiod, Sino-U.S., U.S.-Soviet, and Soviet-Chinese relations all went up. But U.S.-Soviet relations went up more than the other two sets of relations.

Table 7.2. Dimensions of Foreign Policy Behavior

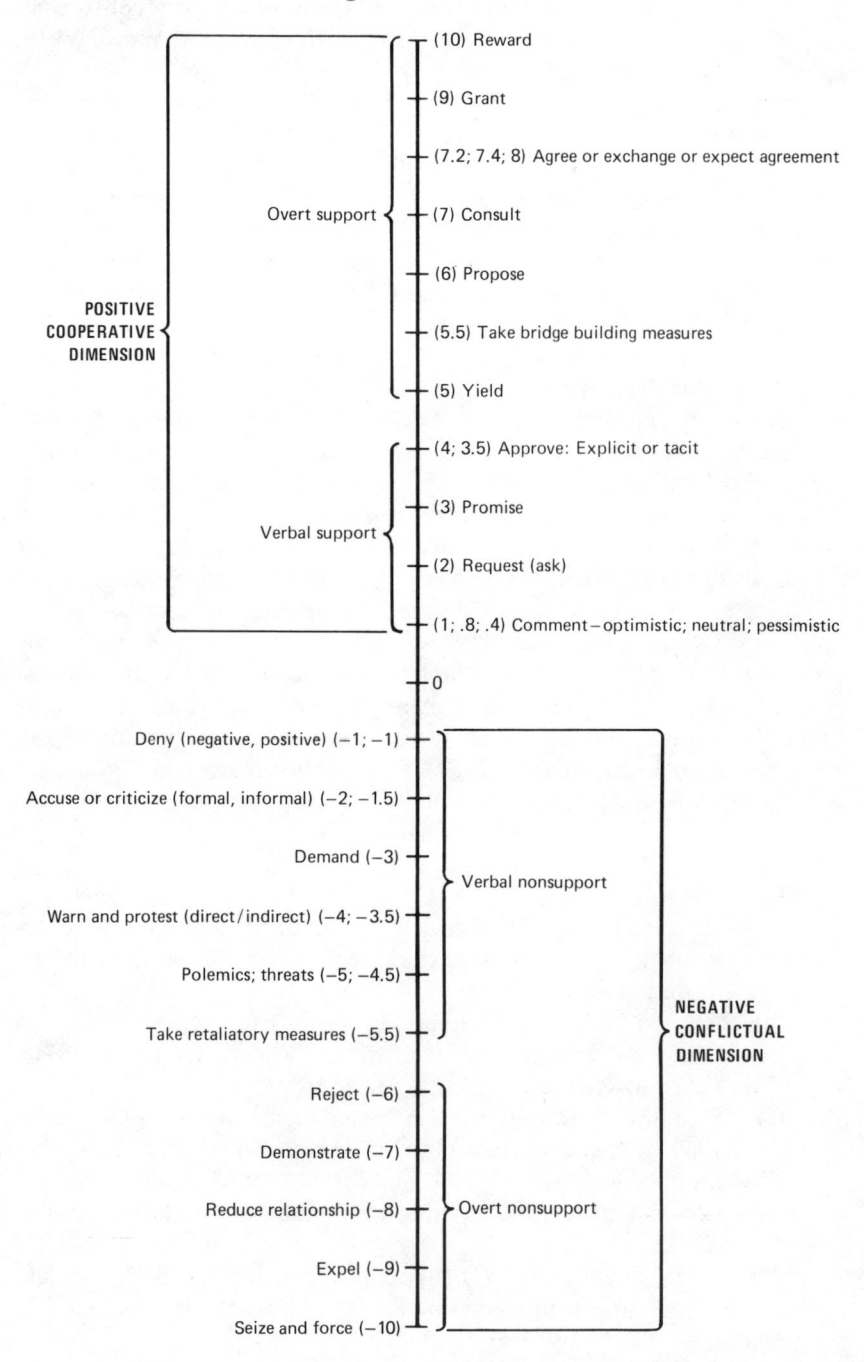

POSITIVE COOPERATIVE DIMENSION

Overt support:
- (10) Reward
- (9) Grant
- (7.2; 7.4; 8) Agree or exchange or expect agreement
- (7) Consult
- (6) Propose
- (5.5) Take bridge building measures
- (5) Yield

Verbal support:
- (4; 3.5) Approve: Explicit or tacit
- (3) Promise
- (2) Request (ask)
- (1; .8; .4) Comment – optimistic; neutral; pessimistic

0

NEGATIVE CONFLICTUAL DIMENSION

Verbal nonsupport:
- Deny (negative, positive) (−1; −1)
- Accuse or criticize (formal, informal) (−2; −1.5)
- Demand (−3)
- Warn and protest (direct/indirect) (−4; −3.5)
- Polemics; threats (−5; −4.5)
- Take retaliatory measures (−5.5)

Overt nonsupport:
- Reject (−6)
- Demonstrate (−7)
- Reduce relationship (−8)
- Expel (−9)
- Seize and force (−10)

118

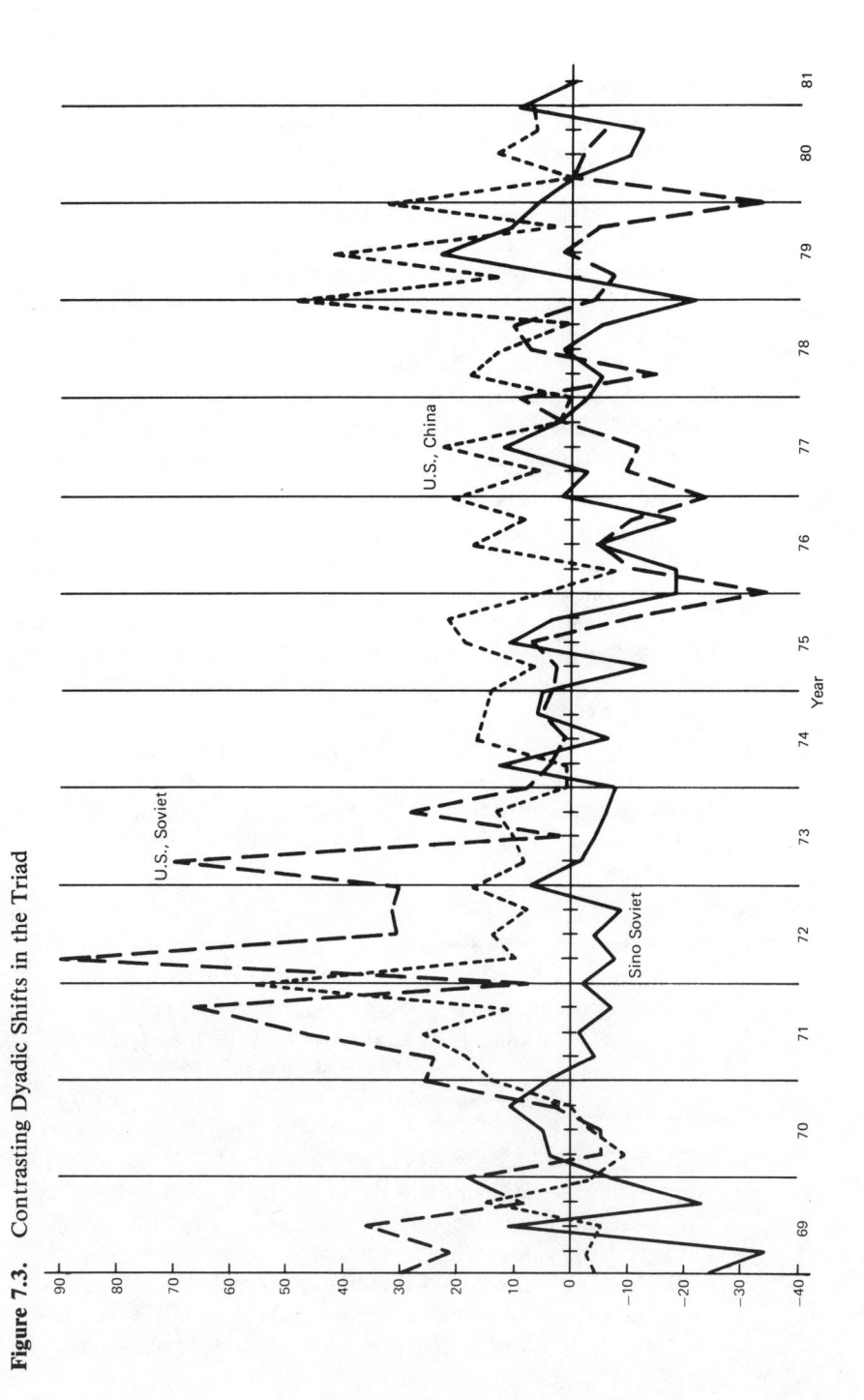

Figure 7.3. Contrasting Dyadic Shifts in the Triad

119

1972-1974
  (a) After a dip to 10 in late 1971 to early 1972, U.S.-Soviet relations leaped to a peak of 87 in the second quarter of 1972, right after the Sino-U.S. courtship reached a phenomenal 54.
  (b) As the U.S.-Chinese courtship cooled off, to a 10, U.S.-Soviet relations moved to another high of 68, at the end of 1973.
  (c) U.S. relations with China steadily declined between the 3rd quarter of 1973 and the 2nd quarter of 1974, hitting below 1 (0.9, to be more exact), but repaired to 16 in the second half of 1974. U.S.-Soviet relations climbed to 27 toward the end of 1973, but were down after that.
  (d) Sino-U.S. relations went down from the 11 reached in late 1970 to below 0, but hovered between 0 and 9 without much change, except that they made an impressive 12 in the spring of 1974.

1975-1977
  (a) U.S.-Soviet relations hit an all-time low (-33.5) in the beginning of 1976 (because of Angola and Soviet electronic interruptions of communication equipment in the U.S. Embassy in Moscow) and remained in the minus (below 0) throughout the 3rd quarter of 1977. Sino-U.S. relations, on the other hand, remained good, hovering in the range of 1-22, with the only exception of the 2nd quarter of 1976, when a -8 was registered.
  (b) As China's relations with the United States remained relatively steady (below 23 but above 0, except briefly in early 1976), Sino-Soviet relations suffered a few setbacks, dipping to -12.5 in mid-1975 and -18 in late 1975 through mid-1966. However, improvement began from the end of 1977 on.

1978-1980
  (a) This is the only period in which a "mirror image" was seen, in which peaks of Sino-U.S. friendship were accompanied by corresponding declines in U.S.-Soviet relations. Compare:
    3 Sino-U.S. peaks: 46 (late 1978-early 1979);
    41.5 (mid-1979);
    2 U.S.-Sov. slumps: -7.5 (2nd quarter, 1979);
    -32.5 (late 1979/mid-1980).
  Although the -32.5 drop was in part a result of U.S. reactions to Afghanistan, it came in the wake of the three consecutive Sino-U.S. peaks, hence reflecting a possible Soviet negative response to the United States' prior abandonment of "even-handedness" in dealing with the two Communist players. (Vice-President Mondale's visit to Peking in August, 1979 is usually considered the official end of the United States' even-handed policy in favor

of a permanent tilt to China.) But, the −32.5 low in U.S.-Soviet relations registered in late 1979 and early 1980 fell a bit short of the −33.5 bottom registered in late 1975-early 1976.
(b) Sino-Soviet relations improved to 11 by mid-1977, but went down to −21.5 by mid-1978. They continued to climb, reaching 22.5 by mid-1979. Following the Soviet invasion of Afghanistan, they steadily fell until they reached a −12 by the end of 1980, but soon climbed back to 8 in early 1981.

Tentative Conclusions. From the above findings, some tentative conclusions can be drawn.

(1) First, the Nixongerian tilt in 1969-74 seems to have accomplished what it purported to do, namely, to get the Soviets to cooperate by manipulating the prospect (as opposed to the reality) of China-card playing. The peaks in U.S.-Soviet détente, reaching 64 in 1971, 87 in 1972, and 68 in 1973, are probably unprecedented. Certainly, they have never been duplicated since, as the China-card playing was no longer a prospect but an ongoing game for real, only to pick up momentum as time went on.

(2) In 1975/mid-1978, the China tilt resulted in a general record of steady cooperation between China and the United States (in the 0-22 range). Simultaneously, however, consistent U.S.-Soviet conflictual oscillations ensued, until an all-time low of −33.5 was reached in late 1975 through early 1976. The original intent of getting the Soviets in line was not achieved as during 1972-74.

(3) From mid-1978 to 1981, the same trend deepened. While Sino-U.S. relations went from moderate peaks to higher peaks between late 1978 and early 1980—although dropping off somewhat after mid-1980—the China-card playing seems to have precipitated greater U.S.-Soviet confrontation. In view of the growing Soviet military presence in Indochina, which was in part a result of the U.S. China-card playing, the policy of using a U.S.-China coalition to constrain the Soviets seems to have failed to achieve its original purpose.

(4) Despite the usual impressions to the contrary, Sino-Soviet relations have witnessed far fewer and less dramatic shifts than have U.S.-Soviet relations. Although they were at an all-time low of −30 in the first half of 1969, Sino-Soviet relations never again went down below −22. By contrast, U.S.-Soviet relations registered both higher climbs in cooperative interactions (peaking to 87 in mid-1972) and more frequent and deeper declines in conflictual interactions (reaching −33.5 in 1976; −24 in 1977; and −22.5 in 1980).

Cumulatively, all these findings indicate that (a) U.S.-Soviet relations were more adversely affected than were Sino-Soviet relations by the improved relations between the United States and China; (b) the Soviet Union did not gain enough from improvements in their relations with China to offset their losses from the deteriorating U.S.-Soviet relations; and (c) China gained considerably from improvements in Sino-U.S. relations, without much definable adverse effects in Chinese-Soviet relations.

The obvious conclusion to draw is that China is the weak player in the triad that has benefited more than either of the other two from the coalitional shifts since 1969. Earlier in discussing the Stryker-Psathas experiment, it was noted that in a 2:2:1 power distribution among players A, B, and C (a Type 3 game in the original Vinacke-Arkoff taxonomy), the weak C is found to have an advantage disproportionate to its power. In the U.S.-Soviet-Chinese triad, which since the late 1970s approximates a 2:2:1 ratio, China seems to enjoy a similar advantage.

However, the C-type advantage which China has been able to enjoy is not necessarily permanent. A number of variables may change that.

In the first place, the power ratio in the triad may change. Second, the two superpowers may learn from past mistakes. If they realize that their disadvantages vis-à-vis China and that their losses were not compensated by their gains, they may act to correct them by not blocking out the possibility of an AB (U.S.-Soviet) coalition or, as in the U.S. case, by not relying too heavily on a coalition with C (China).

Third, although China has been the tertius gaudens (the laughing third) and thus far the gains China has scored from the AC (Sino-U.S.) coalition may surpass the gains by either of the other two players, there are "hidden" costs for China—"hidden" because they are largely outside the triadic relations. We shall address this question in our next discussion on gains and losses as a factor in coalition shifts.

Gains and Losses in the Romantic Triangle

The segregation of the U.S.-China pair and the Soviet Union on two opposing sides in the triad, which has been flaunted by the China-card players as most conducive to the interests of combating the Soviet threat, represents what is usually known as a "romantic triangle." In view of the findings from the above three-person-game studies, neither is this the only coalition pattern within a triad, nor are the gains and losses symmetrically distributed even between the stable-marriage partners. However, the romantic triangle has come down to us as if it was the only pattern of lineup within a triangle. This simplified view is not difficult to understand. In the first place, this lineup is easily comprehensible to most people who generalize from their daily observations of triangular amorous affairs. The assumed merit of the romantic triangle as a strategy to further our "parallel interests" with Peking against the Soviet threat is, therefore, easily acceptable to most people without thinking through the complexities.

There are gains, of course, for both coalition partners in the game; however, there are also costs. The costs include the reactions of the third player calculated to offset or frustrate what the "stable marriage" attempts to do. Each partner's calculations of its own gains and losses relative to those of its partner's, and the efficacy of the two-against-one strategy (i.e., gains and losses relative to the enemy's), will very much determine the future of the Sino-U.S. coalition against the Soviet Union.

I am not suggesting that our triadic players are locked in a zero-sum game in which each gain is canceled out by a loss, or each player's gain is another's loss. Nor am I suggesting the there are no goals that can be shared noncompetitively, such as peace, stability, nuclear deterrence, and other "collective goods" whose benefits are not divisible. What I am suggesting is that (a) there are costs, sometimes even high costs, not set off by the gains in the competition-predominant triad; (b) the costs may not be proportionately distributed across the triad; and (c) the high costs cannot be reduced to "normal" proportions without a prior reduction in the intensity of intratriadic competition.

If nations like individuals can learn lessons from past mistakes, a study of the lessons that can be deduced from the way the three-person game has been played thus far may offer a clue to how things are likely to shape up in the Sino-U.S.-Soviet triad in the future.

The formal beginnings of the U.S.-Chinese coalition were marked by President Carter's acceptance of the anti-hegemony (code word for anti-Soviet) clause, at the insistence of Deputy Premier Deng Xiaoping, in the joint communiqué signed in Washington, on February 2, 1979.[23] If Carter's endorsement was partial and half-hearted then, the Soviet invasion of Afghanistan at the end of the year probably made it complete. The U.S. acceptance of anti-hegemonism has since been reaffirmed many times, including under the Reagan Administration. The reason is simple: Constraining global Soviet expansionism (hegemonism in Chinese parlance) is the identical strategic goal professed by both nations and constitutes, therefore, the cornerstone of the Sino-U.S. coalition.

There are, nevertheless, both gains and costs for both partners; and the common Soviet adversary is not necessarily the only loser. Let's enumerate the gains and losses on the Chinese side first.

Advantages to China: The U.S China tilt has obviously brought many advantages to the Chinese. The tilt began in the summer of 1979. Ever since then, the PRC has been receiving special treatment denied to the Soviets, such as most-favored-nation (MFN) status granted to Chinese imports, Eximbank credits, availability of insurance by the Overseas Private Investment Corporation (OPIC) for U.S. investors in China, increasing instances of technology transfers even in quite sensitive areas (involving possible military use), and so forth.

The U.S. connection has obviously provided the Chinese an added leverage in dealing with Moscow, as they can play the "American card."

The cautious inaction by the Soviets during Peking's "pedagogical war" against their Vietnamese ally in the spring of 1979, following on the heels of Deng's U.S. visit, was a good, early indication that Moscow did not take China's U.S. connection lightly. The relaxation of Soviet rigidity toward China, beginning with the Tashkent speech by President Brezhnev in March, 1982, was a further indication that the Soviets do worry about China's U.S. factor. Since then, five new rounds of talks have taken place, alternately in Peking and Moscow. Soviet congeniality has only increased since Brezhnev's death in November, 1982. Exchanges have increased between the two countries, including visits by high-level officials and scholars. China has more reasons now than before to expect some concessions from the apparent Soviet willingness to be conciliatory.

Costs to China: All this is fine for China. However, there are costs to Peking's playing of the American card.
- (a) In the first place, to play the American card requires the continuation of the Sino-Soviet discord without regard to changing circumstances. Continuation of the Sino-Soviet feud would mean the continuing presence of the 50 Soviet divisions, or one quarter of the total Soviet army and air force, along the border. An armed stalemate would place considerable burdens on Peking's defense budget. The continuing feud with Moscow can only encourage Vietnamese intransigence in their dealings with Peking. Increasing dependency by the Vietnamese on Moscow will only fortify that intransigence, which is bad for the Chinese. A reversal in China's anti-Soviet stand could pave the way for a possible reduction of hostility between Peking and Hanoi, a reduction in Vietnam-Kampuchea conflict, and, above all, a reduction in Vietnamese dependence on the Soviets.[24]
- (b) As long as Peking is known to be unbending on the question of Sino-Soviet rapprochement, North Korea would have a better chance of holding Peking "hostage" to its own radical positions, which may not complement China's interests.
- (c) Increasing Chinese alignment with the industrial North, more especially the United States, runs the risk of alienating Peking from the rest of the Third World, in which there is clear evidence of a decline of Chinese influence in more recent years.[25] To arrest the decline, China has had to distance itself from Washington, starting from late 1981.[26] Although the Taiwan issue has been a very convenient device for doing that, it remains true that Peking's relations with Washington belong to a totally different genre from those of the Maoist era. The U.S. connection cannot but affect Peking's standing in the Third World.

(d) Continuation of the discord with Moscow has one other disadvantage for the Chinese. As Washington is negotiating in earnest with Moscow regarding the removal from the European theater of the Soviet intermediate missiles, including the SS-20s, any agreement cannot but cause fallout in Asia. What assurance is there that an agreed removal of these missiles to the Soviet Far East will not result in their being retargeted against China? In the absence of a dialogue with Moscow, the Chinese would be at a total disadvantage. Peking's recent inclination toward a rapprochement with Moscow, therefore, cannot but be, in part at least, associated with the Chinese concern for its own security in the nuclear balance of terror.[27]

Advantages to the U.S.: The first and foremost strategic gain for the United States is the return of China to its original place on the United States' strategic map. After a three-decade "loss," China is once again back in the eastern "rimland" which, along with Western Europe (as the western rimland) will play a critical role in the common defense against the threat of the "heartland power" (i.e., the Soviet Union). The United States can now fully operationalize this rimland strategy without going through detours, as during the years between 1949 and 1979, and in a manner as anticipated by its original author, Nicholas Spykman back in the early 1940s.[28]

Another significant advantage for the United States is the tying down of 50 divisions of Soviet troops along the Sino-Soviet and Sino-Mongolian borders, alleviating Soviet troop pressures in Europe.

Still another advantage for the United States is the counterweight that China can provide against the Soviet-Vietnamese coalition and in the search for an eventual settlement of the Kampuchea conflict. In the United Nations, an anti-Soviet China could help combat Soviet influence among Third World members. This is still relatively true despite the decline of Peking's standing in the Third World in recent years and the disappointing Chinese abstention on the crucial Security Council vote condemning the Soviet downing of the Korean Airline plane in September, 1983.

Costs to the U.S.: Against these gains, there are also costs for the United States in its pro-Peking tilt.
(a) The resultant termination of U.S. even-handedness toward Moscow and the death of U.S.-Soviet détente has had a tendency to abet Soviet belligerency. The Afghanistan incident may just have been a result of this heightened belligerency as much as a cause for further U.S. hostility.[29]
(b) Another cost is the deterioration of the situation in Indochina, where Soviet military presence has been expanding. The suspension

of the process of normalizing U.S. relations with Hanoi and the continuing U.S. nonchalance has driven the Vietnamese (confronted by a hostile Peking) more and more deeply into Soviet arms. If the original intent of the United States' playing of the China card was to help contain Soviet expansionism in Asia, the increased Soviet military presence in Indochina cannot but be evidence that the U.S. goal has been relentlessly frustrated.

(c) The U.S.-China coalition has served to undercut U.S. leverage in dealing with Moscow directly, such as in the strategic arms control negotiations. Following Deng's visit, for example, Brezhnev refused to go to Washington for the SALT summit as originally expected.[30] President Reagan's offer to supply lethal weapons to Peking, first announced by Secretary Haig in Peking in June, 1981 (albeit not immediately picked up by Peking), only served to deepen the chill in U.S.-Soviet relations.[31]

(d) The China tilt, necessary to win Peking's favor, does not tie the Chinese to a wholly antagonistic policy toward the Soviet Union, as might be expected by Washington. Indeed, the contrary may hold, as Jonathan D. Pollack laments: "By placing ourselves so unequivocally in a posture of total hostility toward the USSR, we would leave the PRC free to deal however it pleased with the USSR, secure in the knowledge that the United States and its allies had reduced their room for maneuvering to dangerously low levels."[32] Mortgaging Washington's maneuverability to Peking is another cost incumbent upon the United States in its current preoccupation with the U.S.-China coalition.

Soviet Gains and Costs: Since by and large Soviet gains and losses are already reflected in those of the other two triadic players mentioned above, we need not be long in this enumeration.

The gains for Moscow in continuing the Sino-Soviet feud are that it would (a) relax NATO's vigilance, (b) alleviate U.S. fears, (c) help perpetuate Soviet influence in Indochina, and so on. The losses from the Sino-Soviet split are, on the other hand: (a) the immobility of at least 50 divisions of troops along the Sino-Soviet borders; (b) impediments to greater trade with China, including Soviet imports of Chinese agricultural produce to relieve pressures on the current supply-lines from the European half of the Soviet Union to Siberia; (c) enabling the United States to continue playing the China card, and so forth. Even for the Soviet gains in Indochina, Moscow has had to pay for them, in the order of about $5,000,000 a day at one point, as the aid was badly needed to prop up its Hanoi client so that the latter could continue the operations in Kampuchea.

Vis-à-vis the United States, Moscow has little to gain from the perpetuation of the Sino-Soviet feud, as it would only help drive the Chinese and the Americans closer to each other. With the Chinese partner on its side, the U.S. would only be more intransigent in dealing with Moscow, on matters such as the strategic and INF (intermediate nuclear force) arms-control negotiations.

Concluding Remarks

In view of the above enumeration of gains and losses in the existing romantic triangle, one immediate question is: Are the gains enough to offset the losses, or are the gains worth the costs? If not, then what would be the justification for continuing the current "romantic triangle" that pits the United States and the PRC aligned against the Soviet Union? Within the U.S.-Chinese coalition, and between each of the two adversaries, too, the same question may be asked. If the costs outweigh the benefits, what would be the justification for continuing the coalition?

Once questions about gains and costs are raised in this fashion, then there is no reason to assume that any of the dyadic relationships within the triad will be perpetual. It becomes so apparent that despite the assumption about the irreversibility of the Sino-Soviet feud, on which the U.S.-PRC bond is based, the Chinese and the Soviets appear now, in the early 1980s, to be moving together again, however slow the pace may be at the present stage.

Both the teachings about the dynamics of three-person games, noted in an earlier section, and the calculations about gains and losses by each player combine to indicate at least two things:

(a) There is no permanence in any of the coalition patterns, as all depend on the prevailing power balance and the kind of cost-gain calculations just suggested. There are no gains without costs, and, as we have seen, the costs could be formidable. The power balance, too, cannot be expected to be permanent. Shifting coalitions, therefore, should not be surprising. If one coalition happens to be in existence at the moment, it does not mean that other coalitions will not form in other times.

(b) There is no permanent tertius gaudens (the laughing third that benefits from the conflict between the other two) in the triad. Not only that, there are costs for the tertius guadens, too. China, very much like the Player C in the Stryker-Psathas game, may have an advantage disproportionate to its relative power, thus approximating a tertius guadens. Nevertheless, as we have seen, China has not escaped the cost dilemma.

If all three players will learn their lessons, eventually they will probably come to the realization that ménage à trois (triadic harmony) will be in the best interests of them all. However, this is difficult to materialize in the foreseeable future, because of mutual distrust, the newness of the idea of triadic harmony (unlike a romantic triangle, which to most people seems to be the only logical thing to happen), and the requirement that short-range interests of the players be submerged under their long-term interests.[33]

The next best thing to a ménage à trois is a willingness on the part of each player to adopt an even-handed policy toward the other two. In the 3-person game language used before, this means that each player should maintain the freedom of entering into coalitions with either of the other two. It is as though all three players were playing the First Series in the Stryker-Psathas game.

China seems to be doing just that in its current effort to develop a rapprochement with Moscow, without foresaking its bond with the United States. Whether the other two players will be doing the same remains to be seen. However, the advantages of playing the role of a "pivot," which maintains good relations with both wing players and has the capacity to mediate between them, are understandably great.

For the good of its national interests, the United States should not be left behind in the quest for the pivot's role. Although rational choice (calculating the gains and losses and in view of the power balance) on the part of our decision-makers will probably bring the United States eventually to playing the role of a pivot, certain rules are worth being heeded by Washington. There are three such rules discovered by Gerald Segal in a study of the U.S.-Soviet-Chinese relations.[34] They are as follows:

(a) The pivot stands to gain from some "common ground" that exists between the two wings in the triad. In other words, there has to be a certain amount of normal contacts, or modus vivendi, between B and C, before the pivot A can play off B and C.

(b) The pivot's leverage depends on both wing players' concerns lest a coalition, or stable marriage, develop between the pivot and one of them. (In fact, I might add, this is consistent with usual behavior in all triadic relations. Theodore Caplow notes, for example, that each power in the triad is restrained from attacking another by the expectation that his attack would provoke the other two powers into a winning coalition against him. The feared possibility of an opposing coalition, not the actual existence of the coalition itself, nor a symmetric power distribution, is the more effective source of deterrent, hence stability, in the triadic balance of power.[35])

(c) The pivot's leverage depends on the competition of the other two players for its friendship. The pivot cannot play one off against the other if either or both of the wing players cease to vie for the pivot's amity.

The rules deduced from Gerald Segal's empirical studies merely confirm the value of the Stryker-Psathas experiments and the results from my own study of the triadic shifts noted above. Those who play what is the First Series in the Stryker-Psathas game are better off than playing the other series. The most important practical implication here, to reiterate, is that those who maintain the freedom of entering into coalitions with either of the other two triadic players have great advantages. In view of the fact that these various findings reinforce one another, I am more confident about the following possible future developments:

(a) The Sino-Soviet split will gradually give way to a more normal working relationship.

(b) U.S.-Soviet hostility will wear down over the long haul, in favor of more pragmatic interchanges.

(c) The U.S.-China romance will eventually enter into a period of more realistic (hence, more "normal") give-and-takes, less tinged by the anti-Soviet emotionalism that has colored it from the very inception.

I am not so starry-eyed as to expect that all these will happen in the next two or three years. But they are expected to be the trends for the intermediate future. Nor do I expect all these trends to advance at the same pace. Nevertheless, my expectations are, to reiterate, based on the lessons that can be drawn from three-person-game studies, a conviction that decision-makers do learn from past mistakes if given long enough time, and my own observation of cumultive changes within the Sino-U.S.-Soviet triad.

Notes

1. The idea of a 2-against-2 game was developed in Peter Yu, "A Strategic Model of Chinese Checkers: Power and Exchange in Beijing's Foreign Policy" (dissertation completed in the Department of Politics, New York University, October, 1983).

2. For a discussion of the characteristics of triadic behavior, see Theodore Caplow, *Two Against One; Coalitions in Triads* (Englewood Cliffs, N.J.: Prentice-Hall, 1968).

3. Kurt H. Wolff (trans. and ed.), *The Sociology of Georg Simmel* (Glencoe, Ill.: The Free Press, 1950), chs. 2, 3, and 4; John Von Neumann and Oskar Morgenstern, *Theory of Games and Economic Behavior* (Princeton, N.J.: Princeton University Press, 1944), ch. 5; Theodore M. Mills, "Power Relations in Three-Person Groups," *American Sociological Review*, Vol. 18, No. 4 (August, 1953), pp. 351ff.

4. Mills, "Power Relations," *ibid.*, p. 352.

5. Kurt H. Wolff (trans. and ed.), *The Sociology of Georg Simmel*, n. 3 above, p. 157.

6. Caplow, *Two Against One*, n. 2 above, p. 23.

7. *Ibid.*, p. 5.

8. Cf. Anatol Rapaport, *N-Person Game Theory Concepts and Applications* (Ann Arbor, Mich.: University of Michigan Press, 1970); Thomas Schelling, *The Strategy of Conflict* (New York: Oxford University Press [Galaxy Books], 1963); and Steven J. Brams, *Game Theory and Politics* (New York: Free Press, 1975).

9. See works cited in notes 5, 10, 11, and 12.

10. W. Edgar Vinacke and Abe Arkoff, "An Experimental Study of Coalitions in the Triad," *American Sociological Review*, Vol. 22, No. 4 (August, 1957), pp. 406-414.

11. Theodore Caplow, "A Theory of Coalitions in the Triad," *American Sociological Review*, Vol. 21, No. 4 (August, 1956), pp. 489-93; also idem, *Two Against One*, n. 2 above, p. 22.

12. W. Edgar Vinacke and Abe Arkoff, n. 10 above; and Caplow, *Two Against One*, pp. 21-27.

13. Kenneth N. Waltz makes the same point ("Because power is a means and not an end, states prefer to join the weaker of two coalitions."), in *Theory of International Politics* (Reading, Mass.: Addison-Wesley, 1979, p. 126.

14. Steven J. Brams, "The Search for Structural Order in the International System: Some Models and Preliminary Results," *International Studies Quarterly*, Vol. 13, No. 3 (September, 1969), p. 256.

15. Cf. discussion above at reference for n. 13.

16. Sheldon Stryker and George Psathas, "Research on Coalitions in the Triad: Findings, Problems, and Strategy," *Sociometry*, Vol. 23, No. 3 (Sept., 1960), pp. 217-30.

17. *Ibid.*; Caplow, *Two Against One*, p. 27.

18. Lowell Dittmer, "The Strategic Triangle: An Elementary Game-Theoretical Analysis," *World Politics*, Vol. 33, No. 4 (July, 1981), pp. 485-515.

19. Stryker and Psathas, "Research on Coalitions," n. 16 above, p. 229.

20. *Ibid.*, pp. 219; 229.

21. Vinacke and Arkoff, "An Experimental Study," n. 10 above, pp. 408; 413; Simmel, n. 5 above; Caplow, n. 2 above, p. 29.

22. Charles McClelland, "The Acute International Crisis," in Knaus Knorr, ed., *The International System* (Princeton, N.J.: Princeton University Press, 1961), pp. 182-204. Also C. McClelland, *Theory and the International System* (New York: Macmillan, 1966).

23. *The New York Times*, Feb. 2, 1979, p. 9.

24. Gerald Segal, "China and the Great Power Triangle," *China Quarterly*, No. 83 (September 1980), p. 501.

25. Decline in Chinese influence in the Third World can be seen (a) in the lack of support for Peking when it was denounced by Castro during the 1979 Havana summit conference of the nonaligned nations; and (b) in the way China lost out in the United Nations General Assembly's debate on the resolution on controlling "hegemonism" in the fall of 1974. See discussion in Samual S. Kim, "Whither Post-Mao Chinese Global Policy?" *International Organization*, Vol. 35, No. 3 (Summer, 1981), p. 439.

26. Starting in late 1981, Peking appeared to be making an effort to put distance between it and Washington. Officials from Premier Zhao Ziyang (while

visiting North Korea in December, 1981) to Foreign Minister Huang Hua (during visits to Nigeria and Ghana in November the same year) began to characterize the United States as being just as bad a superpower as the Soviet Union. Such unkind language is reminiscent of earlier portrayals during the reign of the Radicals before Mao's death. Christopher Wren, "China Attacks the Foreign Policy of the U.S.," *The New York Times*, December 28, 1981. In an attempt to regain China's good will in the Third World, Premier Zhao Ziyang embarked upon an eleven-nation tour of Africa, December 10, 1982 through January 17, 1983. *Beijing Review*, Nos. 1, 2, 3, and 4 (January 3, 10, 17, and 24, 1983).

27. For the Chinese view on the question of Soviet SS-20s, see *Renmin Ribao* (People's Daily) editorial, September 17, 1983, p. 3.

28. For a fuller discussion on the rimland strategy and U.S. strategic thinking since Spykman, see James C. Hsiung, *U.S.-Asian Relations: The National Security Paradox* (New York: Praeger, 1983), ch. 1.

29. For a list of Soviet grievances against the United States long before Afghanistan, see Robert Legvold, "Caging the Bear: Containment Without Confrontation," *Foreign Policy* (Fall, 1980), p. 78.

30. *The New York Times*, June 17, 1981, p. 1.

31. Hedrick Smith, "Deepening U.S.-Soviet Chill," *The New York Times*, June 18, 1981. See also John Bryan Starr, "U.S.-China Relations in 1980," briefing packet distributed by the China Council of the Asia Society, Washington, D. C. (March, 1981).

32. Jonathan Pollack, in Douglas T. Stuart and William Tow, eds., *China, the Soviet Union, and the West* (Boulder, Colorado: Westview, 1982). p. 290.

33. Dittmer, "The Strategic Triangle," n. 18 above, p. 513.

34. Segal, "China and the Great Power Triangle," n. 24 above, pp. 499-505.

35. Caplow, *Two Against One*, n. 2 above, pp. 5-7.

China's Foreign Policy: Domestic-International Linkages

8

Gavin Boyd

The major changes in the Chinese Communist regime since the death of Mao Zedong in 1976 have affected its foreign relations. External policy has been reoriented from a highly conflictual statecraft to one that stresses the expansion of economic exchanges with the major industrialized democracies and the absorption of their technology. With this change the connections between the domestic and external sources of foreign policy have been altered, in ways that have introduced more instrumental rationality into the management of foreign relations.

The evolution of the post-Mao regime has been a process of intraelite conflict in which a new ruling group has established its authority while promoting technocratic modernization. This has had deradicalizing effects because it has entailed rejecting Mao Zedong's revolutionary idealism, which had proved to be dysfunctional, and because it has been oriented toward a form of market socialism, with a private sector, rather than toward the continued building of an egalitarian and self-reliant command economy. A new political culture, based on concepts to state power fostering entrepreneurial activity, with reduced party involvement in the government structure and in the lives of citizens, but rejecting the decadent features of Western cultures, is gradually being established. Acceptance of this political culture, however, is being opposed by officials with Maoist outlooks, large numbers of whom remain in the party and the government departments.

The reorientation of foreign policy toward management of the tasks of dependent modernization has tended to make the direction of external relations a somewhat more pluralistic process. Many specialized agencies in the economic bureaucracy have become involved, the perspectives of large numbers of officials have been influenced by frequent interactions with representatives of foreign enterprises and governments, rivalries and conflicts of interest appear to have increased between government agencies with active concerns about external commerce, and the scope for legitimate representations of such concerns has increased. The substantive content of foreign economic policy, of course, has greatly expanded and appears to have been separated to a greater degree than previously from external security policy.

In the new and more constructive foreign policy processes domestic inputs relating to trade expansion and the attraction of foreign direct investment are necessarily sensitive to and are conditioned by the behavior of firms based in the industrialized democracies and the trade, investment, technology, and monetary policies of their governments. In the security and political areas of foreign relations, however, domestic inputs into the policy processes seem to be less influenced by international factors and follow operational principles that include conflictual as well as cooperative elements. Habits of relatively pragmatic bargaining and adaptation in foreign economic relations evidently tend to influence high level approaches to security and political issues, but conflictual attitudes in those areas of external policy can also be expressed in the management of major questions of foreign commerce.

Analysis

The Chinese Communist regime is still basically a closed and overmanaged system.[1] Little political liberalization has accompanied the trend toward economic liberalization. Deng Xiao-ping's group evidently wish to construct, in the long term, a system in which there will be some dispersal of power, in the interests of efficiency, between high level government and party structures, and in which there will be less active party involvement in government affairs. This group's need to consolidate its authority and remove the large number of Maoists from government and party positions, however, necessitates the maintenance of strong central control, and that has to be made effective through the utilization of supportive factions and clientelist networks.[2]

Closed and overmanaged systems depend heavily on internal information processing, and their political discipline together with their centralization of power tend to cause much bureaucratic inertia. The political discipline imposed on officials affects their capacities to assess information, especially by tending to obligate acceptance of leadership views. The discipline moreover obliges officials to act with caution and to seek opportunities to diffuse responsibility by inventing complex procedures and adding staff. Strong task orientation at the leadership level can impose pressure on officials to improve performance, but such task orientation and the competence it needs tend to be lacking in the ruling elites of closed and overmanaged systems. Such elites comprise authoritarian personalities, more concerned with generating and maintaining power than with using it to implement policy. Fears of losing elements of power and status through the acceptance of informal accountability associated with close task engagement cause leaderships of this kind to restrict themselves to general directiveness, pushing operational responsibilities onto government and party bureaucrats. Gaps thus widen between leadership knowledge and secondary elite expertise, and these affect the quality of decisional interaction. Officials in the secondary elite tend to be inhibited by fears of challenging leadership views, and the leadership can be inclined to assert its authority without an adequate grasp of the issues to be decided.[3]

A closed system has to be maintained by sustaining the logic of closure in its political culture, with emphasis on dangers of external penetration that can destroy vital elements of that culture. This can be quite feasible if there is stress on self-reliant development, but if great importance is given to acquiring foreign technology and skills it can be difficult to absorb these while rejecting all the values of the cultures in which they have developed. Innovative use of what is absorbed can be increased in a relatively liberal setting but can be discouraged if strong political discipline threatens inventive borrowing from the foreign cultures. Tension between the requirements of system maintenance and the requirements of system development can be serious because of the vital importance of the values in this polarity. Deep intraelite divisions can result and can be difficult to resolve because they will be inseparable from issues of regime control, which have to be settled through contests for power rather than through institutionalized methods of elite choice.[4]

System maintenance in a closed regime necessitates authoritative use of political symbols for the generation of consensus in support of the official belief system. The intrusion of potentially challenging foreign concepts, causal notions, and values must be restricted. Although this becomes difficult when interactions and exchanges with other states are increasing, it can certainly be effective, and its costs, apart from the inhibiting effects on entrepreneurial use of the foreign technology, include inadequate capabilities for communication with foreign governments and peoples. There is a tendency to use domestic communication methods, employing the regime's own political language, thus limiting identification with foreign perspectives and concerns.

Deradicalization has affected China's characteristics as a closed and overmanaged system. Several of the attributes of an *estalished one party state* have been assumed.[5] The ideology has been to a considerable extent relativized by a critical rejection of much of the Maoist philosophy and by the reorientation of domestic and external policies, as well as by continuing intraelite conflicts. The emphasis on technocratic modernization has enhanced the role of the government structure, while tending to weaken that of the Communist Party. Institutional interest groups, by articulating their views and demands, have begun to introduce bargaining into the policy processes, and this is likely to increase as state enterprises assume greater autonomy and function within a more liberalized economy.[6]

The concept of an *established one party state* has been a representation of the Soviet system, but China has undergone a more profound process of deradicalization, involving protracted intraelite strife, and the post-Mao policies that have contributed most to this process have been much more "revisionist" than those introduced in the post-Stalin regime. Functionally, the principal implication is that the task orientations that have been assumed for technocratic modernization will tend to lead to even more "revisionist" policies, in order to promote the dynamic growth that is desired in the system of market socialism, and, thus, to demonstrate the logic of opting for this program of economic growth.

The foreign policy consequences of change to an *established one party state* with strongly "revisionist" orientations mainly concern imperatives for productive exchanges with the international community. For China, underdevelopment makes such exchanges necessary, and makes necessary efforts to reduce their asymmetries through bargaining for better terms of trade, the development of manufacturing for export, the financing of technology transfers, and the utilization of foreign direct investment for resource extraction and for production in special export zones.[7] External political and security objectives have to be related to the foreign economic imperatives, while those imperatives are served through vast numbers of professional inputs from the working levels in the government departments concerned with foreign trade, industrial growth, investment, and technology. The links between the major areas of external relations, however, are complicated by the deep cleavage between the technocrats and the Maoists which makes the Chinese system quite distinctive. There are, of course, no comparative studies that can illuminate the dynamics of this type of intraelite conflict, but it is clear that the status of the technocrats and their capacity to consolidate their authority depend in large measure on the progress that is being made under their modernization program, and that this progress requires effective utilization of the opportunities to secure foreign technology and administrative skills. Politically, this high priority requirement necessitates the development of very friendly relations with the industrialized democracies, and moderation of support for revolutionary struggles in the Third World and for the efforts of Third World states to negotiate a restructuring of the international economy. In external security policy the principal implications appear to be that China must now draw intense hostility from the Soviet Union—the major adversary—and must somehow shift to other states the burden of "containing" the Soviet Union, at least until the long process of building an advanced form of market socialism is completed.

Structures and Processes: Foreign Economic Policy

Domestic and international inputs into China's foreign policy process appear to interact, in different ways, at leadership, secondary elite, and staff levels, and more in external economic relations than in the less complex and substantively smaller areas of international security and political affairs. In external economic relations the inputs from foreign sources tend to draw the regime into forms of international behavior that can facilitate export-led growth like that attained by more advanced Third World states, including South Korea and Taiwan. Political leverage based on China's significance as a major adversary of the Soviet Union can serve the growth strategy by extracting moderate concessions on trade and developmental financing issues from the major industrialized democracies, especially the United States.

The functional requirements of managing the greatly expanded area of foreign economic relations appear to have forced some diffusion of authority through the structures dealing with external trade, technology transfers, foreign direct investment, energy, transportation, monetary affairs, and international organizations. Leadership direction seems to have been limited, in the main, to setting general principles, while exerting pressure on the secondary elite and the staffs to restrict bureaucratic expansion and to promote higher organizational efficiency. The staffs are most exposed to information, assessments, proposals, forecasts, enquiries, and advice from foreign firms and governments, as well as international agencies. Pressure from the less exposed leadership and secondary elite requires staffs to learn from and utilize effectively these external inputs, but there are problems of organizational performance that evidently tend to be aggravated by the antagonisms between the technocrats and the Maoists.[8]

The problems of organizational performance have been identified in recent studies of the Chinese economic bureaucracy. They tend to hinder productive use of the opportunities for interaction and cooperation with the sources of external inputs into foreign economic policy. The most basic problem is a lack of coherence in the pattern of structures, which gives rise to numerous conflicts of jurisdiction and interest, which have to be settled at the State Council level, and which necessitate extensive and protracted attempts at coordination.[9]

Since 1982 the management of foreign economic relations has been the responsibility of the Ministry of Foreign Economic Relations and Trade, which was formed by combining the former Ministries of Foreign Trade and Economic Relations with Foreign Countries and merging them with the former Foreign Investment Control Commission and the former Import-Export Commission. The new ministry was formed with one-third less staff than the organizations that were combined to form it, and two-thirds fewer departments, some regional, some functional. Among the functional departments are one for Foreign Trade and another for Foreign Investment, but outside the Ministry, under its supervision, is the China Council for the Promotion of International Trade (CCPIT) and the China International Trust and Investment Corporation (CITIC). The Ministry collaborates with the State Planning Commission in drawing up foreign trade plans, and it controls foreign trade corporations that each have monopolies over specific groups of commodities. At the national level, however, several production ministries operate their own export and import corporations to conduct foreign trade independently, in light industrial products, electronics, general industrial equipment, precision machinery, scientific instruments, mining equipment and materials, and aircraft. Moreover, several provincial and municipal governments have been given authority to set up and operate their own foreign trade corporations, but under planning and budgetary supervision of the national foreign trade corporations, which still manage the bulk of the regime's external commerce.[10]

Reviews of the structures involved in foreign economic relations and of the economic bureaucracy as a whole indicate that the development of specialized functions and organizations has not been altogether orderly, that attempts at decentralization—aimed at greater efficiency—have multiplied the problems of coordination and planning, that indecision about issues of further economic liberalization has tended to have negative effects on the work of government agencies and the various national and local trading enterprises, and that party involvement in the branches of the administration adds to the problems of overall management. Confronted with all these difficulties, and reckoning with the possibilities of change in the current policies, officials seek to maximize personal security by following instructions closely, diffusing responsibility through extensive procedures, and identifying with personalized networks attached to high and middle level patrons.[11] Leadership capacities to impose rationalization are limited because of inadequate expertise at the highest levels, and efforts at those levels to promote collaboration between all the branches of the economic bureaucracy are severely hindered by the narrow departmental perspectives of officials, most of whom spend their entire careers in the structures that they first joined. Many of these officials, moreover, are quite old, and the large number who gained office during the late Maoist period lack competence.

Foreign businessmen, although attracted by China's economic opportunities, tend to be discouraged by the regime's bureaucratic inertia and the difficulties of coordination between its government agencies and enterprises, as well as by the dangers of arbitrary shifts in policy that may upset carefully negotiated agreements. The most serious problems have been evident in the regime's attempts to manage large scale technology transfers. These have revealed grave deficiencies in planning for infrastructure development, financing, and the integration of new technologies into the national economy. Following several cancellations of major contracts in 1980/81 a policy of industrial reorganization has come into effect, and it is unclear whether there will be further contracts for the establishment of large scale industrial complexes by foreign firms.[12]

All the organizational difficulties appear to affect staff and secondary elite responses to the functional requirements of implementing the strategy of export-led growth and relating to the interests of foreign enterprises. Leadership pressures for overall performance through trade expansion and the utilization of foreign direct investment tend to promote a new management culture throughout the system, but it is clear that vast numbers of officials have vital interests in operating within the established formal and informal frameworks, especially to maximize their personal security, in the light of future uncertainties.

Leadership decisions on foreign economic relations appear to be made by a small group within the Chinese Communist Party's Politbureau and a Standing Committee of the State Council. The key figures include Premier Zhao Ziyang and Party Chairman Hu Yaobang.[13] The State Planning Commission and State Economic Commission heads, who appear to be involved, are probably sources of emphases on centralization, and this may also be true, on balance, of the Ministry of Foreign Economic Relations and Trade. Government representation in decision making at this high level is evidently greater than party involvement, in line with a trend toward stronger government participation in the Central Committee of the party. Government figures comprise nearly 50 percent of the membership of the Central Committee appointed at the 12th party Congress in 1982, and State Council members number about 22 percent of the full members of that committee. These proportions reflect major increases of those in the 11th Central Committee appointed in 1979.[14] Increasing governmental rather than party involvement in the shaping of foreign economic policy is to be expected, but with differences on the governmental side regarding the issues of centralization, enterprise autonomy, and the maintenance or reduction of administrative pricing, which affects the operations of enterprises manufacturing for export.

It must be stressed that, making foreign economic policy, leadership dependence on the expertise of the secondary elite and the staffs has become heavy and is increasing. Hence there is probably direct leadership responsiveness only to the most salient international factors that relate to foreign commerce and the attraction of foreign direct investment, and this responsiveness is no doubt geared to professional assessments at the lower decision-making levels. The difficulties of rational choice at those levels, however, call for strong leadership in policy formulation, as well as for structural reform, or else for the development of much greater middle level autonomy, in line with the Japanese model of bureaucratic policy making.

The established policy of export oriented industrialization necessitates responding to international market opportunities by allocating resources for manufacturing in areas where comparative advantages have been attained or are anticipated; the development of international marketing mechanisms; and aggressive bargaining on trade issues with the major industrialized democracies. The still very extensively administered pricing and the rigidities of the partially liberalized command economy, however, are serious hindrances to realistic central strategic planning and to the establishment of effective external marketing structures. In these respects China is disadvantaged, by comparison with the high growth developing market economy states such as South Korea and Taiwan, which are exploiting major comparative advantages gained in manufacturing for export, and in assessing new opportunities in foreign markets.[15] A bias against exporting tends to persist in the Chinese system insofar as it maintains many of the characteristics of a command economy, but it is not clear to what extent this functional problem is understood by the regime's leadership. Aggressive bargaining for entry into the markets of the industrialized democracies is possible, it must be reiterated, because of the international significance of the Chinese market and China's strategic importance, but this cannot sufficiently compensate for the basic difficulties in gaining comparative advantages within appropriate areas of manufacturing for export. The high growth developing market economy states have overcome technology barriers and have already secured important comparative advantages in relatively capital intensive export items.[16]

The policy of attracting direct foreign investment into export manufacturing within special zones entails competition against the attractions of investment opportunities in the high growth market economy developing East Asian states, where the environments for operating are more orderly and more stable, the levels of administrative performance are higher, and the economic infrastructures are more developed. Considerable negative feedback has been received from foreign firms about the conditions of entry and operation in China, but sensitivity to this appears to have been only moderate at all levels. International business interest in the Chinese investment opportunities has been lukewarm for several years because of the difficulties of negotiating with the Chinese bureaucracy, the limited utility of the concessions offered, currency problems, the disadvantages of operating in what is still to a considerable extent a command economy, and the uncertainties about future Chinese policies.[17]

The attraction of direct foreign investment into resource extraction, including especially offshore oil, has been hindered by the problems that have tended to discourage investment in manufacturing, but awareness of technological and administrative deficiencies appears to have caused the Chinese authorities to grant larger concessions for entry. The prospects of revenue from oil exports, possibly on a scale sufficient to finance very large increases in technology imports, have presumably encouraged this generosity. In the longer term oil production for export, moreover, will greatly enhance the prospects for developing a broader and less asymmetric economic relationship with Japan because of that country's heavy dependence on external sources of energy.

The expansion of the major areas of foreign economic relations and the emergence of major issues in those areas, with domestic ramifications, has clearly absorbed much leadership attention, and must be tending to demand even more attention, especially because the principal problems affecting the implementation of current policies call for high level decisions. The established practice is to move toward such decisions cautiously and experimentally, with extensive consultations in which it seems to be possible for government agencies to hinder consensus by intransigent articulations of their own interests. Over time, unless there is a considerable development of leadership administrative capabilities, the difficulties of working toward resolution of the basic issue affecting foreign economic relations will tend to increase, because of the expansion of international economic interactions and exchanges and the effects of the current partial liberalization, especially insofar as it has stimulated entrepreneurial assertiveness in the national and provincial foreign trade enterprises.

Structures and Processes:
Political and Security Affairs

External political and security issues have received less consideration, it seems, at the leadership level, and certainly appear to have demanded less attention at the secondary elite and staff levels. The Ministries of Foreign Affairs and Defense have not undergone functional expansion to cope with a multiplication of their international activities, the ranges of issues confronting them have not been enlarged to any major extent by inputs from external sources, and the decision processes in these areas of foreign relations have evidently remained strongly hierarchical. The requirements for performance on political and security issues, of course, are less clear and less demanding and normally are not matters on which evaluations by foreign sources can affect leadership status. The ruling elite's confidence in its own expertise relating to these areas is undoubtedly higher than it is on matters of foreign economic policy. On questions of military modernization there have been numerous professional inputs from foreign governments, firms, and research institutes, but the leadership's domestic standing does not seem to have been affected by the very slow utilization of such inputs and by the evidence of indecision and procrastination in the implementation of measures for upgrading the very low technological levels of the armed forces.[18]

The responsibilities of the Foreign and Defense Ministries clearly overlap, and this may be a source of conflict, especially because there have been indications of tension between the military establishment and the dominant technocratic group in the regime's leadership. Influential figures within the higher defense machinery have been expressing strong opposition to the penetration of "bourgeois" cultural values that has accompanied the expansion of economic bonds with the advanced capitalist states, and there have been indications of upper level military dissatisfaction with current restraints on defense spending that reflect the high priority given to the development of industrial capacity for export.[19] Numerous rotations of regional and district army commanders, moreover, which have probably weakened loyalty systems within the armed forces, have no doubt been resented, although the regime's leadership has clearly been obliged to cope with a longstanding problem of inadequate cooperation between the regional commands and with resistance to central authority by well entrenched senior officers within those commands.

The technocratic group in the regime's leadership evidently depends on the support of some key military figures, at the center and in the regional commands, but apparently wishes to limit the overall influence of the military establishment. This establishment's status in the regime tends to be lowered somewhat by the emphasis on economic modernization, especially insofar as this directs public attention to the opportunities opening up in industry and agriculture. With the gradual improvement of Sino-Soviet relations, moreover, following détente with the United States, the significance of the armed forces for external security has been to some extent reduced. Leaders of the military establishment may accordingly see a need for a foreign policy that will produce an atmosphere of vigilance against external threats.

On the question of opposition to the penetration of "bourgeois" cultural influence there appears to be an affinity of interests between the concerned elements in the military leadership and high level party officials. While the party's role in shaping the political culture has been somewhat weakened by the new economic policies and by the emphasis on professional performance in the government structures, this seems to have roused serious concerns among segments of the leadership identified with the party apparatus. Hu Yaobang's speech at the 12th Party Congress in September, 1982 stressed the party's responsibilities for shaping policy and directing the work of the administration.[20] The development of strong task orientations by officials in the economic ministries will of course tend to produce pressures for reduced party involvement in the administration, especially because of the extent to which officials in the government departments will be influenced by their dealings with foreign businessmen, bureaucrats, and consultants.

In the political issue area, which is primarily the responsibility of the Ministry of Foreign Affairs, the chief concerns appear to be strengthening China's autonomy and status, weakening Taiwan's international position, establishment of a zone of influence in Southeast Asia, and manipulation of the relationship with the United States. The principal external influences, clearly, are the United States' active interest in aiding China's evolution as an independent power, the Soviet mix of threatening and cooperative behavior, and the adversary role assumed by Vietnam. With respect to political issues the leadership is probably much more inclined to rely on its own judgment than it is with respect to foreign economic relations. The views of the Ministry of Foreign Affairs undoubtedly have a strong influence on the perspectives of the secondary elite and the staffs, and its status within the higher levels of the regime is strongly affected by events that reflect positively or negatively on stands that it has taken.

The strengthening of China's autonomy and status is clearly seen to require visibly assertive "arms' length" dealings with the United States, involving cooperation without apparent dependence, and a moderate improvement in relations with the Soviet Union that will facilitate exploitation of the U.S. administration's interest in a closer relationship. The domestic sources of this policy are basic nationalist concerns, and it must be implemented with regard for indications of change and continuity in U.S. attitudes. Excessive assertiveness will tend to reduce U.S. interest in the connection, while indications of a strong desire to collaborate will encourage U.S. manipulation and harder U.S. bargaining on matters of necessary cooperation.[21]

A special consideration is the gradual extraction of concessions from the United States regarding Taiwan. Political opposition to the continuation of U.S. military and other links with the Taiwan administration has to be appropriately combined with the development of Sino-U.S. economic cooperation and with manifestations of interest in Sino-U.S. military and possibly political cooperation, as well as with demonstrations of intent to maintain a high degree of independence and of capacity to acquire a strong position in world affairs.[22] All this can involve some choices about favoring or not favoring the political interests of prominent U.S. figures in the light of their attitudes toward the problems of containing the Soviet Union. A U.S. administration committed to a strongly anti-Soviet policy but rather unyielding on the Taiwan question may well be preferred to one less firmly opposed to the Soviet Union but more accommodating on the Taiwan problem.

On the Taiwan issue especially, and on the larger issue of managing the connection with the United States, the management of policy in the light of U.S. responses is no doubt very much a process of leadership directiveness. The status of the new ruling group must be heavily dependent on its handling of these matters, and there is clearly no accepted basis for anticipating a substantial growth of staff expertise in these policy areas like that which is recognized to be taking place in foreign economic relations. There may indeed be some leadership vigilance to ensure that the foreign ministry staffs will not permit their professional development to be strongly influenced by instrumental concerns that have become more sophisticated through dealings with Western governments and business groups. Party involvement in the Ministry of Foreign Affairs, moreover, is probably more extensive and more active than in the functionally oriented economic ministries, and the resultant political discipline is presumably much more conducive to the acceptance of leadership direction on policy issues.

The establishment of a zone of influence in Southeast Asia appears to be a longstanding objective, shared by leadership figures since the foundation of the regime, and given more importance since the break with the Soviet Union in the 1960s, and especially since the 1978 Vietnamese decision to align with the Soviet Union. There has been a considerable commitment of the present ruling group's status to the current policy of pressuring Vietnam to withdraw its forces from Cambodia and terminate its collaboration with the Soviet Union. Lack of success with this policy has necessitated continuation of a Chinese diplomacy that seeks friendship with the ASEAN members, especially Thailand. Negative external inputs into this policy come from Indonesia and Malaysia, as these states view China as a long-term threat to Southeast Asia and oppose the Chinese policy of hostility to Vietnam.[23] It seems highly probable that responsiveness to Vietnamese, ASEAN, Soviet and U.S. behavior in the Southeast Asian context is very much determined by leadership direction, because of the ruling group's confidence in its capacity for judgment in this area, and staff caution in view of the gravity of the issues, the numerous uncertainties posed in this context, and the possibility of change in the ruling group's own perspectives.

Leadership attentiveness to relations with the United States, it must be stressed, is no doubt very active. Swift high level decisions were evidently responsible for the deletion of sensitive items from Chinese media coverage of remarks by President Reagan during his 1984 visit to China. These items included comments about the Soviet Union, democracy, and religion. High level decisions were probably also associated with Premier Zhao Ziyang's criticisms of the Reagan administration's Central American, Middle East, European, and Taiwan policies during that visit. Several of these criticisms reflected an interest in improving relations with the Soviet Union by taking stands relatively favorable to the Soviet Union on issues outside East Asia.[24] On such vitally important matters leadership involvement in policy is probably close and constant, shaping reactions to external events very much in line with the ruling group's own perspectives. The active leadership concern with exerting pressures, directly and indirectly, relating to the Taiwan issue, has clearly involved high level assessments about how far the United States can be pushed on this and on issues in other parts of the world. Relatively optimistic evaluations have presumably been encouraged by the U.S. administration's eagerness to export advanced technology to China, including nuclear technology, which was made evident by the signing of a nuclear cooperation agreement during Reagan's visit. In August, 1982 pressures that the Chinese had applied over U.S. arms sales to Taiwan had resulted in a U.S. commitment to reduce these arms sales, and during his stay in China President Reagan, placed in a defensive position by Chinese questioning, had asserted that the Taiwan question was an "internal" Chinese affair in which the the United States would not become involved.[25]

All the regime's major external political concerns are linked with international security issues, and the most salient of these relate to the Soviet Union. Responsiveness to Soviet behavior is almost certainly determined at the highest levels of the Chinese system, and staff assessments of that behavior are undoubtedly influenced very strongly by leadership views. In this area of external policy the Chinese ruling group appears to have recognized the increasing strength of the Soviet Union, as compared with that of the United States in the global and regional strategic balances, and the domestic constraints as well as international difficulties that hinder the U.S. administration's efforts to develop adequate military power and to cope with Soviet supported revolutionary violence in Third World countries.[26] Improvement of China's relations with the Soviet Union has evidently seemed necessary in view of the prospect of further likely changes in the global balance of forces and because of the regime's need to increase its leverage against the United States. There may well be divisions within the military elite on this policy, especially because it is doubtful whether China could negotiate a settlement that would substantially reduce the threatening Soviet presence in Vietnam, Mongolia, and along the common northern border, but it is likely to remain a matter for high level decision making, with little scope for independent professional inputs from defense and foreign ministry staffs.

Input Linkages

The interactions between domestic and international inputs in China's foreign policy processes appear to follow a pattern that is determined mainly by functional considerations, in foreign economic relations, and by leadership outlooks and preferences on major political and security matters. Factional rivalries and the interests of government and party structures evidently affect the pattern, especially with respect to lines of policy to which leadership status has been committed.

The very numerous and diversified constructive international inputs from foreign enterprises and governments into external economic policy tend to reinforce and encourage domestic inputs, especially at the staff levels, that are oriented toward economic liberalization and entrepreneurial development, with emphasis on utilizing approaches to growth strategy in the advanced capitalist states. The influence of these international inputs is to a significant extent supplemented by liberally oriented research publications from Chinese social science institutes,[27] but is opposed by figures within the military establishment and, evidently with more effect, by elements in the party apparatus that seek to maintain the basic features of the command economy, with greater self-reliance in growth policy.

Slow responsiveness to the initiatives of foreign firms and governments is a major consequence of the linkage dynamics in external economic policy. The principal reasons appear to be inadequate scope for decision making at the staff levels, leadership overload and managerial deficiencies, the problems of coordinating agencies with overlapping interests, the uncertainties produced by high level indecision as leaderships resort to experimental incrementalism, and the bureaucratic inertia resulting from political discipline, overmanagement, and the noncooperation of Maoist officials.[28] How all these factors will continue to operate is likely to depend very much on the policy choices made at the leadership level, which of course will be related to trends in the ongoing intraelite rivalries.

The most cooperative international inputs come from Japanese firms and government agencies, and in general express intent to consolidate Japan's position as the regime's main supplier of technology. China has relatively favorable access to the Japanese market, receives very considerate treatment in financing technology imports, and is clearly favored over the Soviet Union in Japanese foreign economic policy. In general, less consideration is received from the United States, and U.S. governmental initiatives reflect relatively less business interest, as well as less responsiveness to Chinese concerns. The U.S. administration's attitude is based mainly on political and strategic considerations, and, while these motivate efforts to stimulate U.S. business interest in the Chinese market, such interest is much less influenced by government policy than in Japan, and is sensitive to the attractions of more developed and more accessible foreign markets.

The Chinese capacity to bargain for better access to the U.S. and West European markets is quite limited. Trade with these states is normally in deficit—$3,600 million in 1982—because the products exported lack competitiveness and encounter import restrictions of the kind directed by advanced states against most Third World exports. Chinese opposition to the discriminatory trade practices is moderate, and this may well reflect the pragmatism of officials in the foreign trade structures, who have been given some basis for optimism by steady increases in Chinese sales to the United States and to the industrialized democracies as a group.[29] An option for the regime is to develop a new role as an aggressive Third World state agitating for a New International Economic Order, but there are no indications that such a response to China's trade problems is under consideration. China remains apart from the Group of 77, although expressing moderate solidarity with them, and on the whole avoids antagonizing the major industrialized democracies on issues of North-South relations.[30] One of the apparent benefits has been rather considerate treatment of Chinese developmental needs by the World Bank, attributable partially to U.S. influence in that organization.

The domestic-international linkages operative in foreign economic policy, it must be reiterated, evidently tend to increase awareness, especially among the staffs in government organizations, of the basic needs for change in the national economy that will facilitate technological, managerial, and marketing advances for export oriented industrialization. The obstacles to such change deriving from ideology, structural deficiencies, administrative inadequacies, factional rivalries, vested organizational interests, and the presence of numerous Maoists are clearly very large, especially in relation to the influence of officials and research economists who have a grasp of the issues. Many of the most exacting requirements now visible concern problems of technological advancement, and in relation to these leadership and secondary elite competence has been seriously lacking.[31]

The effects of international inputs in the external political and security policy areas, being determined largely by leadership views because of the importance of the major issues and the greater political discipline imposed on the staffs, are ambiguously functional. Performance in these areas has to be measured against criteria set by leadership outlooks and decisions, which can be changed at will and which do not have to be related to elite views that have been shaped by public social science research literature: there is no significant development of theorizing by the regime's scholars in this area that would necessitate substantial rationales for leadership decisions to make shifts in policy on any of the larger external political or security problems. The current improvement of relations with the Soviet Union, for example, has not been justified with reference to any open Chinese theoretical discussions of policy toward the superpowers.

The significance of international happenings and situations in relation to the domestic sources of policy on external political and security issues has to be defined in terms of ideology and nationalist concerns, which are primarily matters of leadership responsibility and which have to be settled according to operational principles that emphasize mixes of struggle and cooperation. Opportunities for leadership learning experiences are open mainly in relations with the United States, in which blends of each type of behavior have been utilized with considerable net advantages. The United States has been induced to offer advanced technologies for China's economic growth and to moderate its support for Taiwan's interests, at a time of improvement in Sino-Soviet relations, and despite considerable Chinese criticism of U.S. policies directed against the Soviet Union. On the Chinese side a tacit linkage has been manipulated, as manifestations of basic friendship have been useful for the U.S. administration's domestic political interests.

High volume feedback is a feature of the relationship with the United States, enabling the Chinese leadership and staffs to assess the utility of the manipulative strategies in use. In dealings with the Soviet Union, however, there are much smaller and less reliable information flows, and, while this increases the importance of expertise in the staffs of the foreign and defense ministries, it also allows more scope for leadership idiosyncratic evaluation and decision making, while necessitating much caution by the staffs in providing their policy inputs. Moreover, intraelite divisions more serious than those affecting policy toward the United States may well be having complex effects on the management of responses to Soviet behavior, thus making staff caution even more necessary.

In the regime's Third World relations, limited results from the cultivation of friendly states and the development of a more instrumental approach based on high priority economic concerns have been responsible for moderation of the political support given to revolutionary movements and lower allocations for economic diplomacy aimed at noncommunist administrations. With these responses to an unencouraging environment there have been signs of a contraction of Chinese interests to nearby areas of more immediate strategic significance. Most of the regime's Third World trade is with East Asian states, including several of the high growth ones, and important surpluses in this commerce help to offset the unfavorable balances in trade with the industrialized democracies. The prevention of Soviet intrusions into more distant Third World areas, however, remains a basic Chinese interest, and increasing Soviet involvement in those areas, especially Africa, represents a serious challenge. The Chinese desire to expand economic cooperation with the advanced capitalist states prevents active competition against the Soviet Union in the export of revolution, and China's much weaker economic and military capabilities hinder effective rivalry against Soviet diplomacy aimed at "bourgeois" Third World governments.[32]

Altogether, the linkages between domestic and international inputs into China's foreign policy that can be managed most effectively are those in Sino-U.S. relations, where major advantages are derived from the strong U.S. interest in China as an adversary of the Soviet Union. That interest can be exploited to secure technology, exert pressures against the Soviet Union, maintain status in world affairs, and gradually weaken Taiwan's position. Changes in the mix of conflictual and cooperative behavior toward the United States can evidently be evaluated without difficulty from the multiple U.S. feedback by decision makers at all levels in the Chinese foreign policy structures, and the consensual quality of the U.S. policy processes facilitates Chinese predictions.

In the interactions with the Soviet Union, which mainly concern security issues, the management of responses to Soviet behavior and the adjustment of Chinese objectives and strategy, while much more difficult because of the adversary relationship and the resultant information problems, is probably hindered also by the more severe effects of political discipline on the staffs and by the leadership's reliance on its own competence. These problems may be reduced somewhat by the current improvement in Sino-Soviet relations, but that improvement will probably be limited because of the Soviet Union's interest in utilizing its strong bargaining position and China's interest in retaining the major benefits of its ties with the United States.

Issues and Prospects

The various issues in the domestic-international linkages of Chinese foreign policy raise questions about leadership and staff capacities to assess and engage with these questions of statecraft. Leadership attention to these issues is no doubt limited by the distractions of factional politics, but is probably influenced by compulsions to utilize foreign relations for the advancement of personal interests in factional contests. The scope for rational leadership-staff exchanges on foreign policy choices is evidently affected by the strong element of authority in these relationships, as well as by cognitive factors associated with the official political language, despite the reduced importance of ideology under the new leadership. The more productive and objective considerations clearly relate to foreign economic policy, whereas in political and international security affairs the more hierarchical character of the policy process must have restrictive effects on searches for rational solutions.

It is uncertain whether the increased instrumental rationality in foreign economic policy will spread to political and security affairs, but there appears to be a well established elite consensus that economic and military strength must be gained over the long term, through comprehensive modernization, in order to assert national status and advance the regime's interests effectively. This would appear to be the main result of current experiences in managing relations with the advanced capitalist states, the Soviet Union, and the Third World. The principal issues, then, presumably concern the adjustment of short and intermediate term interests in relation to the long-term aim of transforming China into a powerful modern state.

The choices involving short, intermediate and long-term concerns link economic with political and security considerations, which of course relate to the management of functional connections between external factors and the domestic sources of foreign policy. In the perspective of the regime's revised ideological outlook, short and intermediate term political and security interests are being subordinated in certain respects to the long-term policy of export led growth within the framework of the international economic system dominated by the advanced capitalist states. This, it must be reiterated, evidently tends to provoke intraelite controversies, involving party and military interests, and awareness of the high level differences must tend to have inhibiting effects on staff contributions to policy planning. The intraelite cleavages, moreover, concern domestic as well as external policy, and the major issues are the highly salient ones of economic liberalization and the evolution of the political culture.

The views of groups within the leadership on the management of the regime's interests over different time periods will no doubt be very much influenced by perceptions of progress or failure in the policy of substantially dependent modernization. Achievements and setbacks in the implementation of this policy, however, will be attributable in large measure to the quality of the efforts made to promote efficiency in the partially liberalized command economy. On present indications, these efforts, over the intermediate term, are likely to have only moderately successful results, especially because of leadership indecision and the persistence of administrative problems in the economic bureaucracy.

The management of responses to international factors while sustaining commitments to the modernization policy is likely to be subjected to increasing strain, over the intermediate term, by Soviet gains in the Third World and further projections of Soviet power in the immediate environment. Advocacy of renewed emphasis on revolutionary ideals to inspire greater national unity and to influence radical forces in the Third World may then seem imperative to frustrated party and military figures who are concerned about the domestic and external effects of the relativization of the ideology that is associated with the modernization program. Improvement in the regime's capacity to cope with issues in the domestic-international linkages of its foreign relations will require reductions in intraelite conflict, the development of stronger leadership task orientation and expertise, and comprehensive organizational reform in the bureaucracy. These needs will probably be difficult to meet while Deng Xiaoping moves into retirement because this will tend to intensify high level rivalries. Constructive behavior by other states, especially the United States, may thus be of crucial significance for the stability of the Chinese leadership and the quality of its statecraft.

Notes

1. See discussion of overmanaged systems in Amitai Etzioni, *The Active Society* (New York, N.Y.: Free Press, 1968). See also E. Feit, "Political Groups under Severe Pressure: a Comparative Study based on the Communication Control Model," *General Systems Yearbook, 1964*, 265-82.

2. See Lowell Dittmer, "Ideology and Organization in Post-Mao China," *Asian Survey*, XXIV, 3, March 1984, 349-69; Michel Oksenberg, "Economic Policy Making in China: Summer 1981," *China Quarterly*, 90, June 1982, 165-94; Kenneth Lieberthal, "Political Reform," *China Business Review*, 10, 6, Nov-Dec 1983, 10-11; Gordon White, "Socialist Planning and Industrial Management: Chinese Economic Reforms in the Post-Mao Era," *Development and Change*, 14, 4, Oct 1983, 483-514; Robert F. Dernberger, "The Chinese Search for the Path of Self-Sustained Growth in the 1980s: an Assessment," in *China under the Four Modernizations*, Part 1, Selected Papers, Joint Economic Committee, Congress of the United States, August 13, 1982, 19-76; John P. Burns, "Reforming China's Bureaucracy," *Asian Survey*, XXIII, 6, June 1983, 692-722; and Dorothy J. Solinger, "The Fifth National Peoples Congress and the Process of Policy Making: Reform, Readjustment, and the Opposition," *Asian Survey*, XXII, 12, Dec 1982, 1238-75.

3. See comments on leadership competence in Erik Baark, "China's Technological Economics," *Asian Survey*, XXI, 9, Sept 1981, 977-1000.

4. See references to intraelite rivalries in Dorothy J. Solinger, cited.

5. See discussion of this concept in Samuel P. Huntington, "Social and Institutional Dyanmics of One Party Systems," in Samuel P. Huntington and Clement H. Moore (eds.) *Authoritarian Politics in Modern Society* (New York, N.Y.: Basic Books, 1970), 3-47.

6. See Kenneth Lieberthal, cited, and Lowell Dittmer, cited.

7. See Robert F. Dernberger, cited.

8. See John P. Burns, cited, and Victor C. Falkenheim, "Organizational Politics and Policy Cycles: a Perspective on Post-Mao Reforms," *Hong Kong Journal of Public Administration*, 2, 1, June 1980, 21-33.

9. See Michel Oksenberg, cited.

10. See Nicholas H. Ludlow, "China's New Foreign Trade Structure," *China Business Review*, 9, 3, May-June 1982, 30-31.

Domestic-Foreign Policy Linkage 151

11. See comments by Michel Oksenber, cited.
12. See Erik Baark, cited.
13. See Michel Oksenberg, "China's Economic Bureaucracy", *China Business Review*, 9, 3, May-June 1982, 22-29.
14. See Hong Yung Lee, "China's 12th Central Committee: Rehabilitated Cadres and Technocrats," *Asian Survey*, XXIII, 6, June 1983, 673-91.
15. See Alexander Yeats, "China's Recent Export Performance: Some Basic Features and Policy Implications," *Development and Change*, 15, 1, Jan 1984, 1-22.
16. *Ibid.*
17. See Jeanne Chiang, "Investment Problems," *China Business Review*, 10, 5, Sept-Oct 1983, 26-29.
18. See review of party and army relations in Ellis Joffe, "Party and Military in China: Professionalism in Command?" *Problems of Communism*, XXXII, 5, Sept-Oct 1983, 48-63.
19. See Kenneth Lieberthal, "China in 1982," *Asian Survey*, XXIII, 1, Jan 1983, 26-37.
20. *Ibid.*
21. See discussions of the dynamics of this relationship in Robert A. Scalapino, "Uncertainties in Future Sino-US Relations" and Allen S. Whiting, "Sino-American Relations: the Decade Ahead," *Orbis*, 26, 3, Fall 1982, 681-97, 697-720, and in John W. Garver, "Arms Sales, the Taiwan Question, and Sino-US Relations," *Orbis*, 26, 4, Winter 1983, 999-1036.
22. *Ibid.*, and see John Quansheng Zhao, "An Analysis of Unification: the PRC Perspective," *Asian Survey*, XXIII, 10, Oct 1983, 1095-1114.
23. See Gavin Boyd, "Peking and the Third World," *The American Asian Review*, 1, 2, Summer 1983, 47-82.
24. See "Hot and Cold Shoulder," *Far Eastern Economic Review*, 124, 19, May 10, 1984, 14-16.
25. *Facts on File*, 44, 2268, May 4, 1984.
26. See predictions in Seweryn Bialer, "The Soviet Union and the West in the 1980s: Detente, Containment, or Confrontation?," *Orbis*, 27, 1, Spring 1983, 35-58.
27. See Cyril Chihren Lin, "The Reinstatement of Economics in China Today," *China Quarterly*, 85, March 1981, 1-48; but see also Suzanne Pepper, "China's Universities: New Experiments in Socialist Democracy and Administrative Reform—a Research Report," *Modern China*, 8, 2, April 1982, 147-204.
28. See reviews of problems of industrial development in Richard Conroy, "Technological Innovation in China's Recent Industrialization," *China Quarterly*, 97, March 1984, 1-23, and in Richard Baum, "Science and Culture in Contemporary China: the Roots of Retarded Modernization," *Asian Survey*, XXII, 12, December 1982, 1166-86, as well as in Erik Baark, cited.
29. *Direction of Trade Statistics, 1983 Yearbook*, International Monetary Fund. See also *China: Socialist Economic Development*, Vol II, World Bank, August 1983, Annex G.
30. See Gavin Boyd, "Peking and the Third World," cited.
31. See Richard Conroy, cited, and Erik Baark, cited.
32. See Gavin Boyd, "Peking and the Third World," cited.

Some Propositions on U.S. Credos About Sino-American Relations
—— 9 ——

Steve Chan

A major concern of the present volume is the reconceptualization of Chinese foreign policy in general and of Sino-American relations in particular. In this chapter, I present and discuss two perhaps self-evident and yet crucial points. The first point is that the product of any effort at conceptualizing or reconceptualizing the foreign policy of a government is shaped by the investigator's analytic repertoire. Therefore, an introspective examination of the validity and appropriateness of this analytic repertoire—including one's assumptions, logics of interpretation, rules of evidence, and agenda of important empirical and policy questions—represents a first and critical step for engaging in this endeavor. My second point is that the foreign policy of any government (be it that of China, of the United States, or of any other country) cannot be understood in isolation. No country is an island unto itself. Whether the leaders of a country choose to pursue one policy course as opposed to another is obviously influenced by the actions (or inaction) undertaken by other governments toward their country. Accordingly, any serious attempts at reconceptualizing any bilateral relations (say, that between the People's Republic of China and the United States) must deal with the analytic apparatuses that are used to investigate the motivations and behaviour of *both* governments. As these attempts are actually carried out in practice, they often focus disproportionately on only one party in a relationship (e.g., China) and pay much less attention to the other party (e.g., the United States). In other words, we—by which I mean Americans, scholars, officials as well as laypeople—have by and large treated the twin elements of the injunction to "know thyself" and "know thy enemy" in a disjointed fashion, when in fact the crucial point is to attend to their *joint* effects. As a consequence, we often fail to grasp—not to mention, to cope with—the critical implications deriving from the discrepant views that we hold of ourselves and of our foreign adversaries and allies.

Psychological research has shown rather convincingly that people tend to make different causal attributions, depending on whether they are explaining their own behavior or that of others. Egocentrism, ethnocentrism, and uninformed parochialism are not the only causes of this phenomenon. We all know that people (even, and sometimes especially, expert observers) tend to treat foreign cultures (whether that of Indian tribes, of Pacific islanders, or of the "celestial empire") as objects of curiosity and as somehow quaint, special, and exotic, if not downright strange and bizarre. This is common knowledge and hardly requires belaboring. Suffice it to say that the attribution of unique or unusual qualities to others is not independent of career or disciplinary motivations. Which anthropologist or area specialist would want to admit that the subject of his lifelong study is mundane or commonplace (generally taken to mean somehow lacking intrinsic importance or interest)? Conversely, uniqueness is equated with importance and, of course, with the need for expert judgment and specialist training.

We sometimes possess rather strong evidence indicating that the perceived differences between ourselves and others are exaggerated or quite baseless. Yet, we often persist in our old beliefs and intellectual habits and insist on treating many differences in degree as if they were differences in kind. Furthermore, we invoke different assumptions, logics of inquiry, data, and emotive characterizations in our analyses, depending on whether we are examining our own behavior or that of others. We are often quite willing to resort to certain kinds of evidence and rules of interpretation when we are inferring, describing, or explaining the motives, character, or actions of others. However, we are generally not prepared to accept the same sorts of evidence and rules of interpretation when the object of the analysis is own our motives, character, or actions.

Let me illustrate my point through some examples that must be familiar to Western scholars on China. They have often used fragments of the Chinese language to make substantive inferences about the Chinese people and culture. For instance, the Chinese word for China (chung-kuo) has been translated into "Middle Kingdom" and interpreted as a sign of Chinese ethnocentrism and cultural chauvinism. Now, if I were to point to the phenomenon that the people of the United States routinely appropriate for themselves the name of a continent (calling themselves *Americans*) and to use this observation to argue the existence of inflated national ego or messianism, I suppose my argument would not be taken very seriously. Similarly, few (if any) Americans are likely to accept the proposition that they defer to authority figures (an attribution that Sinologists have had no trouble in assigning to the Chinese), simply because they have named cities, schools, and national holidays after political notables (e.g., Washington, Jefferson, Madison, King). As a further example, some Sinologists have suggested the epistemology of the Chinese world for crisis (*wei-ji*) means that the Chinese people tend to see both danger (*wei*) and opportunity (*ji*) in such situations. I doubt that these same scholars will agree with the inference that speakers of English are religious because they call their first meal of the day *break fast*, or with the inference that they think of governance primarily in terms of regulations because of the epistemology of the word *rule*.

Just as scholars sometimes present national characters as something *only* other people have, officials frequently treat national security as something *only* their country has a right to be concerned about. Thus, the sort of discrepant analytic treatment mentioned above is not restricted to the Sinology or, for that matter, academic community. To cite just another example, recall the U.S. reactions to Charles de Gaulle's decision to develop an independent *force de frappe*, to Mao Tse-tung's assertion that nuclear weapons are "paper tigers," and to Ali Bhutto's statement that his people would rather eat grass than to give up their effort to build an atomic bomb. At best, the treatment of these leaders by the U.S. press and government suggested that they were being unreasonable. At worst, they were simply out of their minds. It is a common human tendency that when others do not behave as we expect or wish them to behave, we do not try to see the problem or situation as they see it. Instead, we are apt to challenge their motives or denigrate their mental capacity. Consequently, although the United States possesses a huge nuclear arsenal and is still worried about a "window of vulnerability," Americans commonly depict the nuclear aspirations of other countries as somehow the product of paranoia, of xenophobia, of a false sense of grandeur, of the irresponsible pursuit of narrow national interests without regard for the collective good of the global community or, at best, of fuzzy-headed thinking about national economic and political priorities.

Discrepant analytic treatments such as those just mentioned usually go unnoticed and unchallenged because they rely on widely shared credos about ourselves and about the objects of our analysis. The Webster dictionary defines credo as "a set of fundamental beliefs." Credos may have a great deal of or very little empirical support. They may also have had a kernel of truth at one time but may have subsequently become outdated and thus invalid. My favorite examples of unwarranted but popular credos (though hardly of the stature of fundamental beliefs) include the following:

° Giant alligators thrive in the sewer systems of major cities as a consequence of people buying baby alligators in Florida, eventually getting tired of these animals and flushing them down the toilets.

° If a nine-year old boy digs a hole deep enough in his backyard, he will eventually emerge in the outskirts of Peking.

° The Japanese can drink infinitely more sake, Russians and Poles more vodka, and Mexicans more tequila, than Americans can—and still stay sober.

U.S. Credos

°Sir Isaac Newton was beaned by an apple, which enabled him to wrap up the laws of gravity.

°Adolf Hitler was a paperhanger, or housepainter, before he became Germany's leader.[1]

The critical thing about credos is that they are *believed* by many people, and that people act on the basis of their beliefs. A credo's credibility does not necessarily depend on the holder's awareness or understanding of its reasons ("eat that spinach, it's good for you"). The very popularity of credos means that one need not probe deeply about their validity. Instead, credos are usually employed as shorthand assertions of conventional wisdom, or as self-evident truths that require no further investigation of their factual basis. We all rely on implicit credos in our discussions or analyses, so that we need not bother with tedious explanations or justifications to clarify or defend our premises. We assume that because our listeners or readers share our credos, such explanation or justification would be unnecessary. This assumption is usually correct. As a result, many critical elements that prop up our diagnosis (such as our assumptions, rules of inference, and criteria for admissible evidence) are hidden from view and taken for granted rather than critically examined. Thus, although credos provide useful shortcuts in engaging in discourse, they can also become blinkers that distort our perception if we are not watchful.

I suggest below several propositions on U.S. credos about Sino-American relations. To avoid any possible misunderstanding, I do not affirm or deny the validity of any particular U.S. credo in some absolute sense. My intention is rather to observe, juxtapose, and contrast some quite striking differences between our self-image and our image of others. In other words, in this chapter I am more interested in identifying some major discrepancies between these two sets of views than in arguing about the inherent validity of their individual components. I leave for another occasion the empirical verification of my hypotheses and the assessment of their policy implications.

I also realize that the perceptual differences suggested below vary according to analysts, problems, and context. Moreover, they are matters of relative emphasis rather than strict dichotomies. That is, these differences should be understood in "more or less" terms instead of in "either-or" terms. Additionally, since my propositions refer only to central tendencies, they do not deny the existence of some major exceptions to the rule.

I should also point out that the individual credos need not be logically consistent or substantively coherent. In fact, people often invoke different and even incompatible credos at different times or under different circumstances. As another caveat, I do not suggest that any culture or political system has a monopoly on the use of unwarranted credos. Nor do I exclude my own previous work from the criticisms of biases or exaggerations discussed below.

In addition, I do not imply that one's public self-image is necessarily believed by oneself. As will be noted shortly, regimes often have a vested interest in presenting and perpetuating a particular image of itself to domestic as well as foreign audiences (not the least of whom are officials and scholars whose metier is to analyze their policies). For instance, Peking has propagated and cultivated the belief—both at home and abroad—that it must be reckoned with as a major force in international affairs. Naturally, this does not mean either that the Chinese leaders actually believe in China's self-proclaimed importance, or that China should objectively (in terms of its actual or foreseeable military, economic, or political capabilities) loom so large in other countries' foreign policies. Parenthetically, the Sinologists' general inclination to attribute much importance to China and their apparent willingness to subscribe to a Sinocentric view of international relations (a book such as this one is typically organized along the lines of PRC relations with X, with Y, and so on) raise interesting and significant questions about how disciplinary incentives can possible affect the management of the image of the object of one's analysis.

Finally, even though I have drawn most examples from Sino-American relations, I have couched my propositions in general terms. I believe that these propositions have broad relevance for U.S. relations with other governments, especially those of the authoritarian or totalitarian genre. Indeed, some of the propositions, being derived from experimental research in psychology, are applicable to international as well as interpersonal relations in general.

Proposition 1. We tend to explain others' behavior according to our perception of their motives and to see our own behavior as a result of environmental conditions. Psychological research has produced strong evidence for this proposition.[2] In the words of one analyst, China is frequently viewed by Americans as a ship "plowing its way single-mindedly through the oceans of international affairs, relatively uninfluenced by the waves and storms around it."[3] Thus, we are inclined to treat China's foreign policy as relatively unhindered by environmental constraints and as primarily determined by such factors as Mao's thought, the communist ideology, and strategic calculations. Conversely, we are apt to depict U.S. foreign policy as the outcome of bureaucratic bargaining, congressional pressure, interest group politics, voter attitudes, and various political or economic imperatives (e.g., to seek reelection, to secure foreign oil, or to maintain alliance cohesion). One significant consequence of these divergent attributions is that when the Chinese fail to behave as Americans wish them to, we assume that it is because they are unwilling to. But when we do not do something that they want us to (e.g., stop selling weapons to Taiwan), it is because we are unable to. Since we view their behavior as calculated, we are prone to interpret any harm caused by them to our interests as deliberate. On the other hand, since we are all too aware of the constraints on our policy process ("our hands are tied!") and since we perceive ourselves as benign, we assume that they will naturally appreciate our decision dilemma as well as our reasonable intentions. We take for granted that what is evident to us must also be obvious to them, and that they will understand any "unhelpful" actions on our part result from necessity rather than malevolence. Of course, if both sides of a relationship hold these views, a stalemate or, worse still, an escalation of conflict, becomes more likely. On the eve of World War I, the European leaders on both sides felt that the situation left them with no choice but to prepare for war and that, if war were to be avoided, the other side must make the necessary concessions.

Proposition 2. We tend to adopt a rational-actor model in explaining others' behavior, but are inclined to employ the bureaucratic politics and the organizational-processes models in accounting for our own behavior. Obviously, this proclivity to use the divergent perspectives discussed by Allison[4] is closely related to Proposition 1. It is also related to the availability of different kinds of data. Information pertinent to the rational-actor model (e.g., official statements explaining policy issues, public political thought of leading cadres) is more abundant and easily accessible than information about Chinese organizational processes and bureaucratic politics. While the reasons for our tendency to adopt different analytic perspectives are perhaps understandable, its consequences remain. We are more ready to portray Chinese (and Soviet) leaders as bureaucratic supermen. They are often seen as somehow possessing a unique source of wisdom; not only are they allegedly capable of anticipating every twist and turn of international developments and of making meticulous preparation to deal with the expected events, but they are also able to carry out their planned policy with remarkable dispatch and effectiveness. Everything they do fits into a coherent and well-coordinated master plan. Nothing they do can be attributed to accident, inadvertence, impulse, or blunder. In comparison, U.S. officials come through these descriptions as dense, pig-headed, or absent-minded (e.g., Dulles's speech on the U.S. defense perimeter before the outbreak of the Korean War), and our policy processes as frequently mired in ego clashes, interservice rivalry, and bureaucratic insubordination. The left hand of the U.S. government never seems to know what the right hand is doing. U.S. officials have to be constantly reminded of important lessons of history (be they Vietnam, Korea, Munich, or some other favorite topic of the writer). Naturally, the Chinese have particularly long memory (dating back to at least the Ch'in dynasty, if not earlier), and can be trusted to draw the proper conclusions from these lessons. Such attribution conforms well with our self-image as a passive and, in some ways, incompetent giant that eschews tedious planning and prefers business as usual, but one that has the will and capability to rise bravely to the occasion whenever a foreign foe threatens us or our allies (e.g., in World Wars I and II and Korea). It also reflects our image of communists as dangerous adversaries, who are endowed wth particular cunning and guile. All contradictory behavior of the Chinese can be explained. If they are belligerent, this behavior confirms their aggressiveness. If they are conciliatory, they must be trying to embarrass, trap, or exploit us (e.g., to play the "U.S. card" against the Soviets). In response to such attribution of cleverness, Ko Mo-jo reportedly confessed that "we Chinese just cannot live up to Mr. Nixon's aspirations for us."[5]

Proposition 3. We are apt to assume the other's policy processes as highly monolithic and centralized and our own policy processes as highly diffused. This proposition is obviously related to our proclivity to explain others' behavior according to our perception of their motives and calculations (Proposition 1). It is also congruent with our penchant for employing the rational-actor model to account for others' behavior (Proposition 2). We often assume—almost automatically—that whatever the Chinese government does, it must be because of the wishes of its top leaders (principally Mao and, now, T'eng). This assumption has persisted even after the Cultural Revolution and subsequent events have shown its serious flaws, and despite occasional warnings by informed observers.[6] Although some analysts do attend to personal rivalries, bureaucratic factions, interest group politics, and popular pressures (e.g., consumer demand)[7] in their discussion of Chinese foreign policy, these factors receive decidedly less emphasis than "top man" theories (e.g., what Mao thought, saw, or wanted). This tendency to adopt a unitary perspective in describing and explaining our adversaries' policies is in contrast to an inclination to depict our own policy processes as diffused and pluralistic. We attribute any real, imagined, or contrived differences of policy opinion expressed by U.S. officials to our democratic and decentralized political system. Thus, if the Chinese happened to be more concerned about Douglas MacArthur's threats to invade their country than Harry Truman's reassurances to the contrary, it is because of their failure to appreciate our pluralistic politics. Similarly, if the Chinese complain about Ronald Reagan's policy toward Taiwan, it is because they do not understand his need to deal with congressional opposition and to appease the feelings of his conservative supporters. By the same token, the Chinese have to be educated that delays in licensing U.S. technology exports to China are attributable to the inevitable bureaucratic red tape and departmental squabbles in Washington, that the adjudication of the claims asset issues has to be decided by the courts which are independent in our system of government, that special interest groups and voter sentiments would not permit greater trade concessions to Peking (e.g., Chinese textile exports to the United States), and that our government has no authority to dictate the commercial policies of private companies (e.g., Pan Am's decision to resume flights to Taiwan). In short, the President and his top associates should not be blamed for policy slipups, delays, or nonperformance, because they do not have unilateral control over the formulation or implementation of U.S. foreign policy. We sometimes employ this characteristic of our political system to deflect others' criticisms of complaints, when it may not be unreasonable for them to suspect that we are actually unwilling rather than unable to meet their demands. In reality, if a President wants something badly enough and is willing to expend resources to acquire it, he will almost always get it. Congress is usually inclined to follow presidential leadership in foreign affairs, and the U.S. voters are remarkably "permissive" in their political attitudes. Moreover, arguments of free trade and of private commercial interests have rarely stopped an administration from taking decisive actions when it wants to (e.g., trade embargo against various communist countries, including China, during an earlier era, and most recently, the embargo of grain and pipeline equipment to the Soviet Union). Nevertheless, political pluralism is featured prominently as a limit on U.S. officials' decision-making freedom in our description of our own policy environment. We expect others to understand and accept this description, but are at the same time often unwilling or unable to acknowledge the existence of similar constraints for them (especially when we are dealing with regimes that we perceive to be authoritarian or totalitarian). Thus, if Peking were to speak with different voices or take seemingly incompatible positions on international issues, we are more likely to interpret these divergent signals as a devious ploy rather than as a sign of contending interest groups or lack of policy coordination.[8] They must have intended to deceive or confuse us. Similarly, if Peking were to fail to live up to its treaty or contract commitments, we are apt to perceive this behavior as indicating its inherent bad faith or untrustworthiness.

Proposition 4. When others behave according to our wishes, we tend to overestimate the impact of our actions on them; conversely, when we behave according to others' wishes, we tend to underestimate the impact of their actions on us. Most of us are addicted to a simple-minded stimulus-response approach to interpreting events; "we tend to take it for granted that people's actions depend on nothing but the momentary stimuli they receive, stimuli that we, the manipulators, can control at will."[9] We thus often ignore other possible sources that influence people's behavior. Concomitantly, we exaggerate the influence that we have had on others' behavior, because after all we are most familiar with our own desires and prior actions. This tendency is most noticeable when our attempt to influence others is apparently successful; that is, when others behave as we wish them to. We are likely to interpret their behavior as a consequence of our previous influence attempt rather than as a consequence of the others' prior motivations or internal circumstances. Accordingly, for many years U.S. officials and scholars have tended to treat Chinese restraint and caution in international conflicts as evidence of a successful U.S. containment policy rather than as a sign that the attribution of aggressive intentions to Peking needs to be reexamined.[10] The opposite side of these observations is that we tend to minimize others' influence on our behavior in nonconflict situations. We are especially likely to rationalize our behavior by readjusting our perceived interests and goals to conform to it, if this behavior signals a major break from long established policy. Thus, the normalization of Sino-American relations is more apt to be explained in terms of Washington's newly discovered strategic and commercial interests (e.g., to play "the China card" against the Soviets, to open the Chinese market to U.S. companies) than in terms of Peking's prior actions (e.g., the Sino-Soviet dispute, the overture to invite U.S. ping-pong players to China).

Proposition 5. In situations laden with clashes of interest or will, we prefer to see others as always acting and ourselves as always reacting to their initiatives. Again, this proposition is obviously related to Propositions 1 and 2 and applies to situations in which the other party is acting hostilely or uncooperatively (we tend to invoke Proposition 4 only when explaining our policy successes or changes). It reflects the view that the communists are always seeking easy targets of opportunity. This propostion is also hardly surprising given our self-image as guardian of international tranquility and defender of the status quo. Naturally, the recognition that the United States is capable of initiating hostile policies to which our adversaries are subsequently forced to respond would tarnish this self-image. Scant consideration is therefore given to the possibility that the other's belligerence is in fact a response to our own prior hostility. We and our allies are cast in the role of the aggrieved party. Thus, never mind that the United States had supported Chiang Kai-shek in the Chinese civil war, that it had used its fleet to prevent a communist attack on Taiwan, and that its army was converging on the Yalu (or what Ronald Reagan would do, if a Chinese army were to march toward Rio Grande), the Chinese intervention in the Korean War was for many years taken as indisputable proof of Peking's aggressiveness and hostility.

Proposition 6. We tend to portray the practice of "linkage politics" (i.e., trade-offs) by others as somehow unfair, illegitimate, and beyond the normal rules of the game, whereas we are quite willing to accept and defend the same practice by ourselves. Thus, we usually express a sense of dismay, disapproval, and sometimes even anger and shock, when others try to shift a contest from one arena (whether geographic area, substantive issue, or international forum or actor) to another arena, or to link the two arenas. The Arab oil embargo in the aftermath of the Yom Kippur War was customarily presented in at least the public discussions with these overtones. As another example, recent Chinese attempts to link the negotiation of textile exports to the United States with the purchase of U.S. grain met expressions of chagrin, misgiving, and concern. At best, such attempts are viewed as regrettable intrusions that complicate bilateral negotiations and expand areas of mutual disagreement. At worst, they are signs of the other's manipulativeness and deviousness, and indicate their propensity to exploit one's vulnerabilities. Such sentiments are less often heard in connection with the U.S. grain embargo against the Soviet Union and the boycott of the Moscow Olympics in retaliation against the Soviet invasion of Afghanistan, with Washington's efforts to tie trade and mutual defense arrangements in negotiating with its allies, or with Truman's order to interpose the Seventh Fleet in the Taiwan straits immediately after the outbreak of the Korean War. This kind of discrepant treatment also manifests itself in the phenomenon that while U.S. scholars and officials talk rather openly and matter-of-factly about the "playing of the China card" (although often disagreeing about the wisdom or effectiveness of such a policy in dealing with the Soviets), they are at the same time preoccupied with and fascinated by the prospect that Peking may somehow take advantage of us by "playing the U.S. card" against Moscow. Yet, it would be a bizarre world of international relations, if the theoretical possibility (as opposed to the actual possibility which is a matter for empirical analysis) of employing a bilateral tie as a lever to influence the behavior of third parties were evident or available to only one of the two sides of a relationship.

Proposition 7. We are inclined to depict ourselves as particularly naive in subscribing to a static view of international relations, and to describe others as particularly adept in coping with changing circumstances. In line with the self-deprecating image mentioned in connection with Proposition 2, we often attribute to our culture and our leaders a lack of sophistication and nimbleness in conducting foreign policy. For example, it has frequently been suggested that the U.S. people and government tend to dichotomize friends and foes, that they tend to assume stasis rather than change in international relations, and that they tend to treat détente as an end state or a set outcome rather than as a fluid process that is vulnerable to reversals. As a result, it is alleged that we are often caught flat-footed by events (because we tend assume permanent enemies and friends), that we miss policy opportunities and leverage (because we fail to anticipate, notice, or exploit changing conditions such as the Sino-Soviet split), that our policies are not sufficiently discriminating or finely tuned (because we often adopt a posture of either all-out conflict or all-out cooperation, without mixing "carrots" and "sticks" judiciously), and that our mistaken optimism (e.g., détente with Moscow, the "China market") frequently leads to nasty surprises and bitter disappointments. In contrast to this self-image of remarkable naivete, clumsiness, and ineptitude, we are apt to attribute to our adversaries great agility and flexibility in engaging in diplomatic maneuvers (e.g., in organizing united fronts), substantial skill in coordinating conciliatory ("tactical retreat") and coercive ("strategic advance") moves, considerable ability in anticipating and exploiting oncoming events, and a superior understanding of history which is always in flux. As elsewhere, I am not denying in some absolute sense the accuracy of these individual components of our self-image and of our image of our adversaries, but am rather questioning whether the alleged differences between us and others are sometimes overdrawn. Unwarranted attribution of expertise and decision-making ability to others can divert our attention from the past policy disappointments, surprises, and setbacks experienced by Peking (and Moscow), and the sharp swings and breaks that have taken place in both its domestic and foreign policies. It should also be noted that in painting a wily image of the Chinese (and Soviet) leaders such as the one suggested here, we set aside temporarily other contradictory characterizations of them (e.g., doctrinaire, rigid, xenophobic, "peasant mentality," belief in Marxist historical determinism, dichotomous treatment of class supporters and enemies), which we invoke when we want to impugn their motives or denigrate their mental capacity.[11] Thus, Sinologists (and Kremlinologists) sometimes "shuttle" images of the object of their analysis to suit particular occasions. Such a tendency is, for example, quite noticeable in the endless debates about the "'Chineseness' and 'communistness'" of Peking's leaders and about the "stability and change" of their policies. The images of "revolutionary change" and "cultural continuity," of leadership "stability" and "turmoil," and of the persistence of ideology and of abrupt switches in policy lines are often alternately presented in the same discussion.

Proposition 8. We tend to view Chinese behavior as being determined by long-term visions, whereas our own behavior as being influenced primarily by short-term concerns. Again, this proposition is obviously connected with the preceding discussion, particularly in regard to our self-perception as a nation that prefers to arouse itself to confront imminent dangers rather than to engage in plodding long-range planning and in regard to the imperatives of campaign politics and the personnel and policy changes associated with election cycles. It is also not difficult to imagine why the Chinese would want to foster and perpetuate an image that attributes to them qualities of patience, stamina, and perseverance. As a nation that possesssses few current resources that would enable it to attain its ambitious goals in international as well as domestic arenas in the immediate future, an emphasis on the long-term offers a useful psychological and political mechanism for coping with the incongruity between present reality and aspirations. However, we should not automatically accept this self-attribution by the Chinese, because no empirical study—to my knowledge—has been undertaken to actually investigate its validity systematically. As just alluded to, instead of being an inherent cultural trait or dogma of the regime, the alleged extended nature of the Chinese time horizon may simply reflect their past and current circumstances; namely, the harsh reality that permits them no option but to postpone the immediate gratification of their cherished goals. The same reasoning would suggest that the alleged short-range concerns of Americans may be less innate than circumstantial. Until recently, as the representatives of the most powerful military and economic country in the world, U.S. officials could afford to eschew long-range planning and to devote most of their attention to the satisfaction of immediate goals. It is also not clear to me what exact inferences about policy behavior can be drawn from the alleged differences in Chinese and U.S. time horizon. At the very least, a longer time horizon has not necessarily meant more stable policies. We are all aware that there have been frequent and sharp breaks or discontinuities in Peking's foreign and domestic policies (e.g., alignment and subsequent dispute with the Soviet Union, confrontation and then détente with the United States, the recurrent policy swings between stressing redness and expertise).

Proposition 9. We are apt to view others, especially our communist adversaries, as "tough-minded" and to see ourselves as being "sentimental." "Tough-mindedness" usually translates to mean ruthlessness. This perception is associated with other credos such as the Chinese have low respect for human life, they lack individual personality ("they all look alike," "armies of blue ants") and they are seemingly able to keep their "cool" (i.e., control their emotions, especially fear, anger, and pity) under almost all circumstances. The opposite of these images is our self-attribution of sentimentalism, which is usually meant to suggest humaneness and a concern with moral or ethical considerations in foreign policy conduct. It is, of course, gratifying to see the policy of one's government in the latter light, even if one disagrees with this policy for other reasons. Thus, Reagan's refusal to "abandon" Taiwan is more apt to be explained on sentimental or moral grounds than on the grounds of crass *realpolitik* motives. Although this sort of self-characterization makes one feel good (i.e., self-righteous), it strains our credulity. Rather than being considered a vice, "toughness" has been actively sought and projected by various high U.S. officials as a leadership quality by their own accounts (especially the Kennedys). Nor can the description of the U.S. bombing of North Vietnam as an "orchestration that should be mainly violins, but with periodic touches of brass"[12] be easily construed as an expression of excessive sentimentality or faintheartedness.

It is not difficult to comprehend why the various credos discussed above exist. They present a generally, though not always, positive image of ourselves and at the same time put our opponents in a negative light. Although at least some aspects of our self-image and of our image of others undoubtedly have substantial empirical validity, we all too often tend to exaggerate the differences between ourselves and others and to erect false dichotomies in our attempts to diagnose and manage foreign affairs.

The danger of misunderstanding is especially great when both sides of an adversarial relationship hold similar views of the other's motivations and intentions (i.e., mirror images of hostility and suspicion). They tend thus to heighten the risk of perpetuating cycles of self-fulfilling prophecies (if we act as if others were hostile, they would eventually behave antagonistically toward us). Moreover, we know that wishful-thinking and misperception can occur even between close allies such as the United States and the United Kingdom.[13] Naturally, the difficulties of engaging in accurate signaling and the danger of miscommunication are increased when we must overcome the barriers imposed by cultural, ideological, and political differences that are far greater than those existing between the United States and Britain. In other words, if countries as familiar to each other and as culturally and politically similar as these two nations are prone to misperceive each other's intentions and behavior, then the chances for misunderstanding are presumably much higher between countries such as the United States and China.

In conclusion, I repeat the obvious disclaimer that Americans do not have a monopoly on perceptual distortions. Self-righteousness, overestimation of one's own importance, and attributions of negative qualities to one's adversaries reflect common psychological biases that are not limited to any particular culture or political system. Given their responsibility for national security, it is also understandable that foreign policy officials sometimes seem to be excessively suspicious about others' motives and intentions. They are inclined to make "worst case" assumptions about these matters in order to "play it safe." Finally, these officials are usually unfamiliar or only vaguely familiar with the details of others' policy processes, and can only see the finished products of these processes. They therefore often find it easier to explain others' behavior according to the rational-actor perspective, even though they are aware that this perspective cannot adequately explain their own policies.[14] Nevertheless, the recognition that common psychological biases, bureaucratic pressures, and disciplinary "ideologies" can create and sustain distorted images should not cause us to dismiss them as simply the natural and thus somehow unavoidable consequences of human fallibility. If anything, this observation suggests that their effects are especially pernicious and likely to go unnoticed and unchallenged. If we are serious about developing valid concepts, models, and theories about the reality of international relations, we must begin by examining critically the analytic and not-so-analytic "baggage" that we bring with us to this undertaking. As the well-known "Chinese proverb" (popularized by Americans) tells us, "a journey of a hundred miles begins with a single step."

Notes

1. These examples are taken from excerpts of a book by Paul Dickson, and Joseph C. Gouden (entitled: *There Are Alligators in Our Sewers and Other American Credos*), as reported in a six-part series in *The Houston Chronicle*, August 23-September 2, 1983.

2. See, for example, Richard E. Nisbett, and Leo D. Ross, *Human Inferences: Strategies and Shortcomings of Social Judgment* (Englewood Cliffs, N.J.: Prentice-Hall, 1980).

3. Harry Harding, "Linkage Between Chinese Domestic and Foreign Policy," paper presented at the Workshop on Chinese Foreign Policy. Ann Arbor, Mich., August 12-14, 1976.

4. Graham T. Allison, *Essence of Decision: Explaining the Cuban Missile Crisis* (Boston: Little, Brown, 1971).

5. Quoted in A. Chalfont, "Reluctant Giant," *Guardian Weekly*, October 7, 1972, p. 5.

6. Michel Oksenberg, "The Dynamics of Sino-American Relationship," in *The China Factor: Sino-American Relations and the Global Scene*, ed. by Richard H. Solomon (Englewood Cliffs, N.J.: Prentice-Hall, 1981), pp. 48-80; Lucian Pye, *Chinese Commercial Negotiating Style* (Santa Monica, Calif: Rand Corp., 1982) (R-2837-AF).

7. For an example of research on the effects of consumer pressure on East European budgetary process, see Valeri Bunce, *Do New Leaders Make a Difference? Executive Succession and Public Policy under Capitalism and Socialism* (Princeton, N.J.: Princeton University Press, 1981).

8. There is, of course, the danger of committing the opposite mistake of constructing any subjectively determined nuances in the "esoteric communications" of the Chinese media as evidence of factional differences or strife.

9. Kecskemeti quoted in Robert Jervis, *Perception and Misperception in International Politics* (Princeton, N.J.: Princeton University Press, 1976), p. 349.

10. Davis B. Bobrow, Steve Chan, and John A. Kringen, *Understanding Foreign Policy Decisions: The Chinese Case* (New York: Free Press, 1979), p. 22.

11. Although seemingly contradictory, such divergent images can serve important psychological and policy purposes (e.g., "respect the enemy strategically, but despise him tactically"). For a discussion of bimodal Chinese attitudes, see Bobrow, Chan, and Kringen, *ibid.*, pp. 56-57; 64-67.

12. James C. Thomson, "How Could Vietnam Happen? An Autopsy," in *Readings in American Foreign Policy: A Bureaucratic Perspective*, ed. by Morton H. Halperin, and Arnold Kanter (Boston: Little, Brown, 1973), p. 106.

13. Richard Neustadt, *Alliance Politics* (New York: Columbia University Press, 1970).

14. Robert Jervis, "Hypotheses on Misperception," in *Readings*, n. 12 above, pp. 113-38.

Challenge of China's Independent Foreign Policy
——10——
James C. Hsiung

It is clear from the preceding chapters that China's "independent foreign policy" is pointing to an eventual "normalization" of relations with the Soviet Union. The process may be long and drawn-out; and a return to the honeymoon of the 1950s is not in the cards. But the process is unmistakably continuing. The Chinese have modified their demands for improving relations with Moscow (see Berton's Chapter 2). They have even revised downward their assessment of the Soviet threat in Indochina, as a signal to both the Soviet and domestic audiences (see Simon's Chapter 5). The momentum, as Premier Zhao Ziyang assured the National People's Congress on May 15, 1984, is not going to be reversed by such temporary setbacks as the postponement of Soviet First Deputy Premier Ivan Arkhipov's visit to China.

The Chinese deletion of Ronald Reagan's anti-Soviet remarks during his visit in April 1984 may have come as a surprise to the President, who was hoping to get Chinese endorsement of his crusade against the Soviets. Obviously, he was not sensitive enough to a growing Chinese concern that the United States under Reagan might in effect turn the "China card" into the "China pawn," in the event of a bisuperpower showdown. That concern was best depicted in Deng Xiaoping's often-repeated remark: "We do not want you Americans to stand on our shoulders to fight the Russians."

Why China's New Posture Toward Moscow?

During the Carter Administration, the idea of a U.S.-PRC military alliance seemed very much alive. China, which was then promoting a global united front against Soviet hegemonism, also seemed receptive. Now, in 1984, the Chinese are unabashedly seeking an accommodation with the

Soviets, and Premier Zhao told Mr. Reagan so in Beijing. Prolonged tension and confrontation between China and the Soviet Union, Zhao said, was detrimental to both nations and did no good for world peace and stability. "Therefore," he told Reagan, "we stand for normalizing relations under the five principles of peaceful coexistence."[1]

But, why this turnabout in China's position on the Soviet question? There can be at least three possible explanations. First is the proposition that Reagan's China policy has been adversely affected by his pro-Taiwan bent, which allegedly has alienated Beijing's leaders and impelled them to resort to playing the "Soviet card." A second explanation is tied to the domestic leadership shakeup in Beijing consummated in June, 1981, which has in turn brought about vital policy revisions, including the "independent" foreign policy. A third possible explanation is that the new posture results from a combination of external strategic considerations, including China's (a) reactions to its own cumulative gains and losses within the Sino-U.S.-Soviet triad, and (b) response to its immediate security needs vis-à-vis the Soviet Union. We shall take up these points separately.

Reagan's China Policy

We have to examine the Reagan record to determine whether his pro-Taiwan reputation had interfered with the state of U.S.-PRC relations. Only then can we answer whether that had anything to do with China's shift toward an "independent" foreign policy. Stephen Uhalley's chapter (Chapter 3) deals with this question. It concludes that if there were any negative effects they were confined to the initial two years of the Reagan presidency and that a distinct Reagan "turnaround" with respect to the PRC was made after May, 1983.

The temporary eclipse of Sino-U.S. relations until mid-1983 does not seem to be plausibly related to China's decision to seek a détente with Moscow, which by all indications was an independent policy decision. Even before the so-called turnaround, Reagan was quite accommodating to Beijing, despite his 1980 campaign pledge to upgrade U.S. relations with the Republic of China (ROC) on Taiwan. Alarmed by the Reagan pledge, Beijing lost no time in pressing its demands with respect to Taiwan as soon as the new administration was installed in January, 1981. Without going into great detail, I shall list these demands:

(a) That the two communiqués (the Shanghai communiqué of 1972 and the normalization communiqué of December 15, 1978) have precedence over the Taiwan Relations Act (TRA);

(b) That Reagan not reinstitute the six Taiwan consular offices closed down at the time of U.S. derecognition, as he had pledged to do during his 1980 campaign;

(c) That arms sales to Taiwan be terminated;

(d) That the Reagan Administration explicitly recognize and in action respect the PRC's sovereignty over Taiwan; and

(e) That the TRA be abolished or at least revised.

Subsequent Chinese demands included the ouster of Taiwan from the Asian Development Bank (ADB); a disavowal by Reagan of the two Congressional measures adopted in November, 1983, that Beijing considered an interference into China's "domestic affair."[2]

Contrary to what one might expect, the Reagan government conceded to most of these demands quite promptly. By early March, 1981, the State Department in effect had tacitly accepted the PRC's view on the two communiqués vis-à-vis the TRA. It was also made known that relations with Taiwan would not be upgraded after all.[3] Except for the Boston office of the Coordinating Council for North American Affairs (Taiwan's "unofficial" representation in the United States), which was allowed to reopen after some delay in August, 1982, none of the other five previous ROC consular offices were reopened.

Arms sales to Taiwan were also to be curtailed. In January, 1982, Assistant Secretary of State John Holdridge announced in Beijing that the Administration was not going to sell Taiwan the FX fighter planes and other advanced equipment it had sought. The most accommodating step Reagan took in this respect was a new communiqué signed with Beijing on August 17, 1982. In that document, the United States undertook "gradually to reduce its sale of arms to Taiwan, leading, over a period of time, to a final solution."

As to the PRC's claim of sovereignty over Taiwan, Reagan responded favorably in his April 5, 1982 letters, hand-delivered by Vice-President George Bush, to the three top leaders in Beijing (Deng Xiaoping, Hu Yaobang, and Zhao Ziyang). In his letter to Deng, for example, Reagan wrote: "There is only one China. We will not permit the unofficial relations between the American people and the people of Taiwan to weaken our commitment to this principle." Reagan also spoke of a U.S. "abiding interest in the peaceful resolution of the Taiwan question." In this vein, a favorable reference was made to the nine-point proposal Beijing had advanced on September 30, 1981 for the peaceful annexation of the island. In the August 17, 1982 communiqué, the U.S. side went even further on this point, as it declared unequivocally:

> The United States Government attaches great importance to its relations with China, and reiterates that it has no intention of infringing on Chinese sovereign and territorial integrity, or interfering in China's internal affairs, or pursuing a policy of "two Chinas" or "one China, one Taiwan."[4]

Only on the abolition or revision of the Taiwan Relations Act, Beijing has not received similar compliance from the Reagan Administration. On November 26, 1983, Hu Yaobang, General Secretary of the Chinese Communist Party, during his visit in Tokyo, threatened to cancel the forthcoming exchange of visits between Premier Zhao Ziyang (to the United States in January, 1984) and President Reagan (to China, in April, 1984). The source of the Chinese ire was the two measures on Taiwan that Congress had entertained in the same month. Within two days, Reagan publicly dissociated himself from the two disputed Congressional measures as being contrary to Administration policy.[5]

In addition, as Uhalley suggests, the Reagan government has taken other positive steps, some on its own initiative, to placate the Chinese. At least twice, it offered to sell arms to them, first during Secretary of State Alexander Haig's trip to Beijing in June, 1981, and then through Caspar Weinberger, Secretary of Defense, who visited in September, 1983. The Reagan offer went beyond President Carter's authorization of sales of only nonlethal ("dual purpose") equipment on a case-by-case basis.

In resolving the textiles quota problem, the Reagan government allowed a growth in Chinese textiles imports of between 2 and 3 percent a year, higher than what is accorded to other Asian suppliers. It has adopted a congenial position that would allow Beijing off the hook in the suit brought by American claimants over the Huguang Railway bonds. It has liberalized restrictions on U.S. exports of sophisticated technology to China.[6] For the purposes of the U.S. Export Administration Act, the PRC was first removed from the Y group (Communist states, such as the Soviet Union) and placed in the intermediate P group in 1981, and then elevated in May, 1983 to the V group of friendly countries (among the ranks of the NATO allies).

While in China, Reagan signed four agreements and protocols (including one on avoiding double taxation and one on cultural exchanges) and initialed one more agreement on nuclear energy cooperation. By his own admission, the trip had raised Sino-U.S. relations to "a new level of understanding."[7] China was gratified also, as the New China News Agency proclaimed:[8]

> In a word, President Reagan's trip to China and his reiteration here of his commitment to abide by the Chinese-U.S. communiqués represented a significant step forward.

Following the trip, Reagan admitted that his past view on "Red China" as an implacable foe of the United States was wrong. Dramatically shifting his language, he asserted that the United States could get along "with this so-called Communist China" since it was not an expansionist power and since it wanted U.S. investment.[9]

Despite Reagan's long list of accommodations and the "maturing" of U.S.-China ties following his successful visit,[10] Beijing's course of normalizing relations with Moscow is unswerving. In his report to the Second Session of the 6th National People's Congress, on May 15, 1984, Premier Zhao reiterated that policy: "We sincerely desire the normalization of Sino-Soviet relations and are ready to develop economic, technological and cultural exchanges with the Soviet Union."[11] Although the policy was codified at the 12th Party Congress in 1982, the timing of the reiteration suggests that true to its "independent" label, China's new posture toward the Soviet Union would not change despite the Reagan visit and the recharged euphoria in its wake.

The answer to the question whether Reagan's Taiwan tilt had anything to do with Beijing's shift in regard to Moscow is, therefore, that: Reagan's accommodations to Beijing were in no way hampered by his publicized friendship for Taiwan. Seeking a détente with the Soviet Union is, therefore, a set Chinese policy course not likely to be affected by anything the United States might or might not do.

Domestic Politics and China's New Soviet Policy

Various chapters above, especially Boyd's, have dealt with this aspect. I shall be very brief. In post-Mao China, the domestic political process can be properly called one of "Dengization," in terms of both personnel and policy changes. The process took a number of identifiable steps: (a) Removal of the "Whateverists" (i.e., Maoists like Wang Dongxing, who believed that whatever Mao had said or done was correct), which began in the summer of 1979; (b) downgrading of the "Petroleum Faction" in late 1979 to early 1980, which was than in league with Hua Guofeng, Mao's successor; (c) trial of the "Gang of Four," consummated at the end of 1980; (d) removal of Hua Guofeng as Premier in the fall of 1980; and (e) Hua's ouster as head of the Party and his replacement by a Deng protégé, Hu Yaobang, at the 6th plenum of the 11th Party Congress, in June, 1981. In the latest shake-up, some of the key Petroleum Faction members were brought back into the new Dengist coalition.

It is important to note that the new Chinese efforts to carve out an "independent" course and to accent China's renewed interest in the Third World emerged after the 6th plenum. Starting in late 1981, Beijing was deliberately putting distance between itself and Washington.[12] The fact that this conspicuous shift began nearly one year after Reagan took office is sufficient to dispel any lingering doubt that his pro-Taiwan stand was the reason for China's "independent" foreign policy.

At the 12th Party Congress, in 1982, three fundamental doctrinal changes bearing on foreign policy, were made more particularly on Sino-Soviet relations:

First, the Maoist "three-world theory," which had been used to justify a global united front against the Soviet Union, was shelved. China, nevertheless, continues to adhere to the importance of the Third World.

Second, the Maoist doctrine of the "inevitability of war" (i.e., with the imperialists and socialist imperialists) was abandoned. Since this had been an area of severe disagreement with Moscow ever since the days of Khrushchev, the change removed a huge hurdle for eventual reconciliation between the two Communist parties which have had no contacts since 1963.

Third, China now subscribes to the view that it is possible for China to have conflictual relations with socialist countries, just as it is possible to have cooperative relations with capitalist nations. This shift anticipates China's readiness to re-recognize the Soviet Union as a socialist (as opposed to revisionist) nation. It also anticipates cooperation as well as conflict with the Soviet Union in the time ahead.[13]

These fundamental changes followed the final removal of the remnant Maoist elements and the consolidation of power by the Dengists. They no doubt paved the way for an uninhibited Chinese attempt to upgrade their relations with the Soviet Union for the sake of mutual benefits. Thus, the internal-politics thesis—or what is billed in Gavin Boyd's chapter as the "domestic international linkage"—proves more plausible than the first thesis (Reagan's pro-Taiwan bias) in explaining China's détente course with the Soviets.

Combination of External Strategic Desiderata

In Chapter 7, we have seen the intratriadic dynamics at work, a game of coalition making and remaking largely keyed to two factors: (a) the power configuration across the Sino-U.S.-Soviet triad, and (b) the relative gains and losses calculated not only between adversaries but between partners as well. In the U.S.-PRC alignment against the Soviet Union in the 1970s, China was found to have scored better than either of the other two more powerful players. Although this confirmed the "tertius gaudens" thesis (the laughing, weak third player), it was also shown that continuing the same game would have its undesirable costs for Beijing, too. For example, the expanding Soviet influence in Indochina, the continuing Vietnamese intransigence bolstered by Soviet support, and the decline in Chinese influence in the Third World, were among the direct costs arising from too close a Chinese alignment with Washington in the latter half of the 1970s. Distancing itself somewhat from the United States was a logical move if Beijing was not to perpetuate its past mistakes.

This appears to be precisely what the PRC is doing under its "independent" foreign policy, which has three interrelated parts: (a) distancing itself somewhat from Washington, (b) cultivating a rapprochement with

Moscow, and (c) reorienting itself toward the Third World.[14] Within the Sino-U.S.-Soviet triad, China is obviously moving toward an even-handed stance toward the other two players, while encouraging normal contacts between them. This means that China is as though playing a First Series Stryker-Psathas Game (i.e., maintaining channels open to both the other two, as discussed in Chapter 7).

Gavin Boyd considers the Chinese shift to be a natural result from its failures to rally an all-out united front against the Soviet Union (Chapter 8). When China is playing a First Series Stryker-Psathas, however, she no longer plays by the earlier strategy of being adversary to one and friend to the other. Instead, she is seeking advantages from the role of a "pivot," having access to both Washington and Moscow. She seems to be acting *as if* she were aware of Gerald Segal's three cardinal rules for the pivot (discussed in Chapter 7). One indication of this is the fact that China now considers normal relations between the other two players to be essential for her ability to play one against the other.[15]

Two dictums seem to guide the PRC's policy toward the two superpowers. One is to avoid a confrontation with both at the same time, and the other is to maintain a working relationship with both, circumstances permitting. From 1949 to 1963, under conditions of U.S. hostility, the PRC entered into a coalition with the Soviet Union. It was playing a 2-against-1 game aimed at Washington. From 1963 to 1968, especially during the initial period of the Cultural Revolution, Beijing was driven by both domestic and external forces to a stance of simultaneous hostility toward both Washington and Moscow. By the spring of 1969, at the time of the border war with the Soviets, all factions in Beijing realized that it was dangerous to continue the 1-against-2 game, which could risk a war on two fronts.

From 1969 on, China resorted to a one-to-one dialogue with the United States, which by then was cultivating an "opening" to China under the Nixon doctrine. From 1972 to about 1981, the Chinese were experimenting with a variant of the 2-against-1 game, this time directed against Moscow. However, from 1982 on, after Brezhnev's Tashkent speech, which anticipated a new round of Sino-Soviet talks, Beijing turned to playing a one-to-two dialogue.[16]

By the early 1980s, in other words, there was a convergence of Chinese and Soviet desires to try to move their stalemated relations off dead center. By this time, China's relations with the United States had gone a long way from flirtation to normalization to mature partnership. The Chinese found their first opportunity to develop better ties with the Soviet Union, as the second dictum calls for, without the fear of jeopardizing their good relations with the United States.

Chapters 2 and 7 have discussed why both China and the Soviet Union are willing to seek a conciliation. In addition, Boyd in Chapter 8 argues that

China, for its own security, is now willing to seek accommodations with a Soviet Union that is fast moving ahead as a military power. I would add that, as they entered into the 1980s, the Chinese did not feel secure in a structure inherited from the latter half of the 1970s, wherein they found themselves in an anti-Soviet league with the United States but neither partner has a working relationship with Moscow. This is different from the situation prevailing in the early 1970s, when the United States was having a détente with Moscow while simultaneously seeking an "opening" with the PRC. While Reagan's unrelenting stand vis-à-vis the Soviets may be reassuring, the Chinese paradoxically began to feel insecure as long as the U.S.-Soviet war of nerves continued while the Sino-Soviet tensions were also unmitigated.

There are at least two sources of the Soviet threat for the Chinese: One is the Soviet encirclement, as perceived from Beijing, that stretches from Vladivostok to Indochina through a Soviet-occupied Afghanistan and an India allied with Moscow. Thus, Soviet involvements in Kampuchea and Afghanistan were named among the obstacles to improving relations with China.[17] The other source is the Soviet missile threat, notably that posed by the SS-20s. In addition to the estimated 140 SS-20s stationed in Asia, part or all of the 243 additional ones targeted toward Western Europe could easily be retargeted toward Asia (which reads China and Japan). This is the reason that during Japanese Premier Yasuhiro Nakasone's visit in Beijing, on March 24, 1984, Premier Zhao Ziyang declared the Soviet Union to be a greater threat than was the West to China.

From the Chinese point of view, neither the continuance of the unbridled nuclear arms race nor an INF (intermediate nuclear force) reduction agreement between the two superpowers would be desirable. In the first instance, an increasing number of Soviet SS-20s will be deployed in Asia as well as in Europe. In the event of a U.S.-Soviet INF reduction agreement, China fears, the Soviets may simply retarget their SS-20s from Europe to Asia. While that move may satisfy the United States, it would pose an inordinate threat to China (and Japan). These security concerns, therefore, underline the present Chinese attempt to contain their differences with Moscow, to cautiously calibrate their good relations with the United States, and to encourage the two superpowers to ease their mutual tensions and resume their nuclear arms talks.

Along with the domestic political factor, these strategic considerations (i.e., reactions to lessons learned from within the triad, and national security concerns) provide an equally important explanation for China's new independent foreign policy. Of the three possible theses presented, it is plain, the first (Reagan's personal pro-Taiwan bias) is the least plausible.

Lagging U.S. Perceptions

Despite the weighty evidence discussed in this volume that the Sino-Soviet dialogue is a continuing process, it is apparent that perceptions, especially in Washington, lag behind the changing reality.

Earlier, we noted that Reagan was insensitive to Beijing's growing fear lest it be pushed against Moscow as a U.S. "pawn." The insensitivity, in part, bespeaks the failures of his aides and advisors who briefed him for the China journey. Mr. Reagan and his advisors will most probably continue to operate *as if* nothing is going to change despite the Chinese insistence that they are seeking a normalization with Moscow and greater autonomy in their relations with both superpowers. Despite mounting evidence, many in the United States, including some China experts, will refuse to believe that China's professed intention to redress the Sino-Soviet anomaly is real. Our question is: Why? Why do they refuse to accept a fact as a fact?

The answer probably lies in what Steve Chan calls "credos" that guide our understanding or misunderstanding of China's foreign policy (Chapter 9).

The first such credo is the premise that the Sino-Soviet split is irreversible (see more on this below). The policy flowing from this premise has sought to play China against the Soviets. It was not foreseen at the inception of the China-card policy that the Chinese and the Soviets may one day agree that perpetuating the split serves neither one's interests (as Premier Zhao told Reagan in Beijing) and that it makes sense to bury the hatchet despite their differences. Since the China-card playing has been so deeply imbedded in U.S. foreign policy, a revision of its first premise would run the risk of unraveling the policy per se. In view of bureaucratic inertia and the vested interests of so many groups, both in and out of government, it would be a long, long time before perception catches up with the empirical changes.

Steven Chan notes, in his Proposition 1, that we in the United States tend to explain other nations' behavior according to our perception of their motives, and to see our own behavior as a result of environmental conditions. This may explain why so many of our experts and lay people alike, who share a fixation on China's hostility toward the Soviets, find it difficult to conjecture that she would really seek a reconciliation. Besides, despite the new policy, the Chinese have never ceased to vocalize their objections to Soviet hegemonism. What these observers seem to neglect is that, consistent with its doctrinal changes since the 12th Party Congress, noted before, Beijing now believes that simultaneous conflicts and cooperation are possible within the Communist world, just as outside it.

Steve Chan's Propositions 4 and 6 suggest that Americans tend to exaggerate their ability to effect desired changes in other nations' policy course and to underestimate the latter's ability to do similar maneuverings in return. In the U.S.-PRC-Soviet tangle, it seems, many Americans refuse to believe that the Chinese would want to have any dealings with Moscow if they already have such good ties with the United States. In other words, they would not believe that this country would "lose" the China card, especially if we have done so much to help the Chinese for our mutual interests. As long as their convictions lead them on in this fashion, these people will not be ready to accept what they see.

We have noted China's security concerns as a factor behind her new independent foreign policy. Despite its paramount importance, this point does not seem to have been taken seriously by many of our experts. A possible reason for this negligence is provided by Steve Chan, who sees a discrepant analytic treatment in the U.S. credo that sees national security almost an exclusive concern of the United States, not of other nations.

I would add one adjunct comment on this point. Most of our China experts (as area specialists) are trained to watch what is going on *within* China, immediately *surrounding* China, and *between* China and the United States. The kind of Chinese security concerns, emanating from the threat posed by the Soviet encirclement and the retargetable SS-20s requires a much broader perspective than the habitual Sinocentric world affords. Our arms controllers, who are keen on security matters and the START and INF negotiations, on the other hand, are too preoccupied with their immediate concern of removing the Soviet missile threat from Western Europe to be mindful of possible Chinese reactions on the other side of the globe. If this observation is correct, few of our China experts and arms controllers would readily appreciate that China's own security concerns are a factor in her recent conciliatory posture toward Moscow.

As long as these various problems remain, perceptions will continue to lag behind changing events because many of our analysts, in and out of government, will continue to judge Sino-Soviet relations of the 1980s by the imageries of the 1960s and 1970s.

Impact of a Sino-Soviet Détente

If relations between China and the Soviet Union are going to normalize, there are bound to be far-reaching effects beyond the Sino-Soviet dyad. In the first place, so many of the policies or alignments that were premised on the continuance of the Sino-Soviet split would be subject to review. These include the U.S.-PRC coalition, the Sino-Japanese amity, the Sino-North Korean bond, the Soviet-Vietnam alliance, the Vietnam-PRC impasse, and the Taiwan limbo, to name a few. If the Sino-Soviet normalization is going to stay, it will undoubtedly foreshadow future realignments in totally different ways from those of the last decade or so.

We shall first ascertain the more immediate possible effects, incorporating the major findings from the preceding chapters. In the ensuing section, we shall then discuss what conceptual and theoretical challenges the Sino-Soviet normalization will pose and what policy response the United States should be contemplating.

We have noted that, under its professed "independent" foreign policy, China now acts *as if* she is (a) playing the role of the "pivot" in the triad, and (b) beginning to see the value of a ménage à trois. To be a pivot, China has to have open channels to both wing players so that they will vie for her friendship; and she must encourage some "common ground" between the latter two. That means enhanced three-way communication flows. As noted, China does not believe that a sensible solution to the Soviet missile threat lies in the transfer or retargeting of the existing SS-20s either from Europe to Asia or vice versa. It would require instead commitments by both superpowers to reduce drastically their existing missile forces, which could only result from a prior improvement of their bilateral relations. On this point, the Chinese leadership under Deng differs with Reagan, who is hanging on to an inflexible, tough position vis-à-vis an equally angry and unyielding Moscow.

Playing pivot, China is urging that the two superpowers end their deadlock and resume their arms control talks. She has also expressed a willingness to join belatedly in the search for arms-control solutions. Premier Zhao has been expounding this dual theme both to Reagan in person (during the President's China visit) and through U.S. allies in Western Europe (where Zhao visited in early June, 1984).

Over the long haul, moreover, as the weakest player in the triad, China can benefit more from both superpowers if there is triad-wide harmony. For, only then can China receive aid, for her gargantuan modernization needs, from both the United States and the Soviet Union without their mutual jealousy. Otherwise, jealousy may alternately close out one or the other of the two possible sources of help.

Consequence of China's Playing the Pivot

The most likely consequence from the Chinese playing of the pivot's role is that the Sino-U.S. bond against the Soviet Union of the late 1970s will undergo a qualitative change. In its place will come a more even-keeled mode of relationship in both dyads: There will be neither the same euphoria in Sino-U.S. relations, nor the same strident feuds between Beijing and Moscow. For the United States, it means that the value of the China card would ultimately need a realistic reappraisal. Many other vital issues would also have to be reexamined, including the United States' alliance structure, especially in Asia. It would mean that the role of Japan and other traditional allies would have more value to Washington than before.

However, that is not going to be as disastrous as it might sound. In the first place, the much touted U.S.-PRC alliance was never more than a U.S. conceptual game plan, as Peter Berton points out in Chapter 1. Zbigniew Brzezinski, President Carter's national security advisor, and others like him, were simply carried away by the succession of events such as the formalized Sino-U.S. and Sino-Japanese relations in 1978 and the Soviet invasion of Afghanistan in 1979. The notion of a quasi-alliance among the United States, China, and Japan (plus Western Europe) was not clearly thought through when it was floated. The proposal for military cooperation was earnestly put to the Chinese by Secretary of Defense Harold Brown in Beijing, in January, 1980. Washington was eager to give the impression of a rapidly developing alliance with the PRC, as part of U.S. reactions to the Soviet invasion of Afghanistan. The Chinese were never more than nominally receptive to the idea. The return visit in May that year by Brown's Chinese counterpart, Geng Biao, which had been expected to flesh out the details of the U.S. proposed military cooperation, produced no more than a public speculation by Mr. Geng that China might buy U.S. arms "in the future." Although the Pentagon released a list of equipment that would be freed of export restraints, the Chinese did not follow up with action.[18]

It should be remembered that all this happened during the Carter Administration. The Chinese cautiousness not to be physically drawn into a U.S. crusade against Moscow, therefore, went back at least to the Carter years. This is one more evidence that the Chinese resistance to an alliance with the United States was not caused by Reagan's alleged personal Taiwan bias. Although the PRC's lukewarm responses were habitually brushed off by many of our China-card players as a result of its displeasure with Washington's Taiwan policy, that interpretation should be somberly reassessed in light of the latest developments. Particularly noteworthy was the discrepant characterization in Washington and in Beijing of Defense Minister Zhang Aiping's visit in the United States in June, 1984. While the Pentagon saw the mission as crucial for a "strategic dialogue" and developing a "lasting defense relationship," in Beijing the event was deliberately played down. The official press ostensibly declared that the visit would not lead to a threat to any "third party."[19] To Washington's surprise, Zhang left without signing any arms purchase agreement.

Second, the vanishing of the China card also frees the United States from certain restrictions inherent in the card playing. For example, the United States would be under less constraint in dealing with Beijing on issues that have divided them, such as the Middle East, Southern Africa, Central America, and so forth. Furthermore, Washington would be better able to carry out its policy of not abandoning Taiwan as a price for having good relations with the PRC (see Chapter 6 by Chai and Leng).

Third, the relaxation of tensions between the two Communist nations may bring stability to the larger international system, which would be beneficial to all parties in the long run. Within the triad, the stability would make things easier for the United States, which would no longer have to see a Soviet Union being so resentful to an alleged U.S.-China collusion. Nor would the United States be haunted by the fear of "losing" China for anything it might or might not have done.

George Totten, in Chapter 4, foresees auspicious implications for Japan, if tensions are reduced between China and the Soviet Union. Under the new circumstances, Beijing would devote less attention to its arms buildup and concentrate more on its own economic development. That would mean more business for Japan, whose trade and technology China needs. Besides, if changing Chinese relations with the Soviets could help scuttle the chances of any European-based SS-20s being transferred to Asia, Japan would also benefit from the result.

Thus, Japan could be a beneficiary from a Sino-Soviet détente. An earlier analogy of this is the effects for Japan of U.S. normalization with China, which mollified the anti-U.S. sentiments held by many Japanese who had never shared the same U.S. fear of "Red China" and felt that their desire to expand economic and other ties with Beijing had been throttled by Washington's policy. The change in U.S. relations with China helped reduce the criticisms by the opposition parties in Japan of the U.S.-Japan Security Treaty and of a stronger Japanese defense, so notes Totten. The improved U.S.-Chinese relations actually brought the United States and Japan closer and made it easier for the ruling Liberal Democratic Party to sell a more expensive defense program to the opposition leaders, which the United States has been urging upon Japan. This seems to confirm the rippling effect in a menage à trois game, in the sense that amelioration in any one dyad is beneficial to the other two dyads, hence stabilizing for the entire triad.

Extension of the Auspicious Rippling Effect

Actually, the auspicious rippling effect is forecast by nearly all the contributors to this volume. Besides Japan, Indochina may also see a similar spill-over from a Sino-Soviet détente. As Sheldon Simon (Chapter 5) sees it, a Sino-Soviet understanding holds the remote possibility of a solution to the Kampuchea question. With prior commitments between Moscow and Beijing, the likelihood of a cessation of Chinese support for the Khmer Resistance, in exchange for the withdrawal of Vietnamese forces in Kampuchea, would be heightened. So would the possibility of the so-called "tripartite coalition" solution. That means broadening the Kampuchea regime—now dominated by the Hanoi-installed Heng Samrin—to include some representation from the ranks of Son Sann's and Sihanouk's supporters.

If such a solution indeed arrives, Moscow would no longer be strapped with financing Hanoi's operations to the tune of $5,000,000 a day, as it is reportedly doing. China would no longer have to combat what she calls Hanoi's regional hegemonism and shoulder the burden of sustaining the insurgents in the Kampuchean conflict. Vietnam, too, would find the outcome acceptable. A coalition government in Kampuchea acceptable to Hanoi could come about only if prior guarantees are worked out with and between Beijing and Moscow. When the Kampuchea question is resolved, the proud Vietnamese would begin to have hopes of reducing their subservient dependency on the Soviet patron. If they prefer, they could become a recipient of aid from a wide consortium of donors, such as has been suggested by the ASEAN states (Thailand, Phillippines, Indonesia, Malaysia, Singapore, and Brunei), to lift itself up from its dismal economy sapped by the Kampuchea war.[20] Wider choice would beget greater freedom and respectability for Hanoi. The Socialist Republic of Vietnam would "return" to the world community. If the Indochina impasse was tied to the Sino-Soviet conflict,[21] then an ease-up of the latter would also augur well for the chances of a solution for the former.

The ASEAN states, too, would breathe easier when a Kampuchea solution is made possible by a Sino-Soviet détente and the consequential reduction of tensions between China and Vietnam. The Indochina impasse has tended to divide the ASEAN: while Thailand and Singapore consider the Soviet-Vietnam alliance the main threat to peace in the region, others in the group, especially Indonesia and Malaysia, believe that China is the problem and that the United States must avoid arms sales to the Chinese (Chapter 5). The phasing out of big-power meddling in the Indochina imbroglio would end this internal difference of opinion within the ASEAN. It would mean that the establishment of a ZOPFAN (Zone of Peace, Freedom, and Neutrality), favored by the ASEAN nations, would have a much better chance of acceptance. ASEAN's relations with Hanoi, Beijing, and Moscow would be cast in a better light.

As for the Korean peninsula, a similar effect might be felt, too. With its relations with Moscow normalized, China would no longer find its policy options mortgaged to the whims of the North Koreans, as the latter would no longer have a credible Soviet card to play. The Soviets would not have to worry as much about North Korea being too closely aligned with Beijing at their expense. North Korea, on the other hand, would be able to maintain good relations with both of its Communist "big brothers." It would be in a position to play the same "pivot" role to Beijing and Moscow that China is seeking to play in the Sino-U.S.-Soviet triad. When the North Koreans can no longer "blackmail" the Chinese with a potential Soviet card,[22] the chances of a solution to the Korean peninsula question through negotiations, rather than war, would be much greater. That would be good news for South Korea and its U.S. ally and Japan.

The same reasoning could go on and on. But the above is enough to show the likely auspicious effects that could spin off from a steady Sino-Soviet détente. Before we leave the subject, however, I wish to point out that the suggestions just made are only meant to illustrate the kind of gain-and-loss recalculations that will be forced upon decision makers in the wake of a Sino-Soviet détente. I also wish to reiterate that while all the suggested possible spill-over effects depend on a reliable Sino-Soviet détente, there is no telling how long that détente process is going to take. Most possibly, it will take a long time, perhaps longer than the normalization of U.S.-China relations. There will probably be no spectaculars like the Nixon visit to China of 1972. The Sino-Soviet disputes have long roots, and neither country is given to "quick fixes." Even when relations between the two communist nations are normalized, there may be a long interregnum before some of the auspicious effects are felt, especially in Indochina. There may also be intervening variables that one cannot foresee.

After having said that, it is probably equally true, on the other hand, that following its initial fits and starts the détente process may gain momentum later on. What is more important is that when there is a strong desire on both sides to make progress, many of the known obstacles may find a solution in time. Of the three Chinese conditions for conciliation with Moscow, for example, Soviet aid to Hanoi in the latter's occupation of Kampuchea is no less serious than either the Afghanistan question or Soviet troops along Chinese borders. But, as we have seen, even on the Kampuchea problem, China's position is much more fluid now than before. The Chinese have begun to play down the Soviet threat in Indochina, arguing that the Soviets have no fighter aircraft stationed in Vietnam and that the Soviet navy is still no match, in its fighting capabilities, to the United States navy in the area (Chapter 5).

Although China's future in the short- and middle-range lies with the West (the United States and Japan, especially), as Berton reminds us in Chapter 2, its long-range interests call for an equidistance with the United States and the Soviet Union. As the title of this volume suggests, we are looking into the long-range possibilities, *beyond* the more immediate future. While the shape of things to come is not so clear yet, one thing is certain: China is seriously pursuing a foreign policy aimed at gaining greater freedom and status vis-à-vis the two superpowers, which cannot but have enormous and far-reaching effects.

Theoretical and Policy Implications

The inadequacy of the habitual "triangular" analysis, as applied to the U.S.-PRC-Soviet tangle, has been brought up in both Berton's Chapter 1 and Hsiung's Chapter 7 in this volume. I shall not belabor the point any further, except to reiterate that we should appreciate the value of an "n-person game" paradigm. This way, we would not be straightjacketed into three fixed corners in a triangle; and the number of actors could be expanded to allow for a fourth player such as Japan or additional players like Vietnam, North Korea, and Taiwan, and so forth.

The "triad" concept often mentioned here is a "3-person game," or a variant of the "n-person game." Just to mention one advantage, a triad does not invoke the usual imagery of a "romantic triangle," which could subconsciously predispose one to a fixed type of alignment that may not tally with the actual situation and may therefore inhibit our ability to cope with it. Unlike its "triangular" counterpart, the triadic (3-person) paradigm does not convey the static imagery of a fixed game with fixed corners. We have already noted how our experts, accustomed to the triangular mode of analysis, are ill at ease with the changing reality of the 1980s, which can no longer be comprehended by the "romantic triangle" of the 1970s. A 3-person game perspective, on the other hand, keeps us attuned to the fluidity of alignments and realignments, as the changes in power configuration and circumstances may warrant over time.

The worst outcome from adopting a "triangular" outlook, moreover, is that it is often associated with the notion that conflict is going to perpetuate. It does not seem to be keen on the possibility that nations might learn over their mistakes that conflicts, especially certain types of them, do not pay in the long run. A "3-person game" outlook, on the other hand, is much more flexible and open on this point.

In the paragraphs below, we shall concentrate on the conceptual foundation (or a complex of fundamental premises) underlining the United States' China policy since 1969 and assess its adequacy in light of the new Chinese "independent" posture.

The Conceptual Foundation of U.S. China Card Policy Revisited

In previous writings, I have discussed this subject at some length.[23] But, in view of the more recent march of events, as discussed in the present volume, it is time to take another look and offer an updated review of the major premises underpinning our post-1969 China policy. To simplify things, I shall list these premises in the most succinct form:

(1) First and foremost was the assumed irreversibility of the Sino-Soviet split. (This has been embraced by all administrations at least since Nixon.)

(2) A related premise was that China was strong enough to be a counterweight to the Soviet Union but not strong enough to threaten the United States (Kissingerian in origin).

(3) If China was to be encouraged to direct its undivided attention northward, to deal with the Soviet threat, all its "southern" problems (i.e., the Vietnam conflict and the Taiwan question) must be resolved once and for all (Kissingerian in origin).

(4) China's preoccupation with its internal Four Modernizations at home would make it dependent on U.S. and Japanese goodwill and technological assistance (popularized during the Carter presidency by Brzezinski).

(5) A China made strong enough to stand up to the Soviets would remain in the U.S. camp (a premise most earnestly cultivated by Brzezinski).[24]

Under the original Nixongerian design, the United States hoped to take advantage of the Sino-Soviet split by alternately "tilting" to one and then the other of the two Communist giants. The tilting worked for a while. The opening to China in 1972 coerced the Soviets into a détente with the United States. However, the alternate tilting would work only as long as the United States remained even-handed toward both Beijing and Moscow. When Washington lost its even-handedness and opted for a permanent tilt toward China in mid-1979, during the Carter administration—partially because of Brzezinski's personal Polish hatred for the Soviets and partially because of Soviet misdeeds in Angola, etc.—the United States no longer had leverage over Moscow. The stalemate with the Soviet Union in turn also weakened U.S. leverage vis-à-vis the PRC.[25]

By the same token, President Reagan's lopsided anti-Soviet preoccupation merely serves to freeze the U.S. inflexibility (read: lack of leverage) and to reinforce China's bargaining power. Thus, as noted, the Chinese felt secure enough to shunt aside Reagan's exhortations and to tell him point-blank that their intention to normalize relations with the Soviet Union was not to be side-tracked by Washington.

Reagan shares the above premises, but has added two more, which are:

(6) That China could be armed to stand up to the Soviets, to save the United States from bearing the brunt of the conflict; and a showdown between the two Communist giants would weaken both of them to U.S. advantage (the "China pawn" thesis); and

(7) That China under Deng's new economic program has the prospect of being weaned from its Communist system by the U.S. offer of material enticements (the de-Communization thesis).

In view of China's new policy stance and the events since 1969, let us examine the validity of these seven premises.

The assumption about an irreversible split between China and the Soviet Union, which is the most important conceptual pillar of U.S. China policy since 1969, is crumbling, as the relations between the two Communist nations are, to borrow a Reagan phrase from another context, "on the mend."

The second assumption, about a Chinese counterweight, is still valid by itself; but the problem is that China refuses to play as expected. Moreover, China today is strong enough to make waves (such as to force Washington to make concessions on the textiles import issue, on pain of boycotting U.S. soybeans, cotton, and chemical fibers), although it is not strong enough to threaten the security of the United States. Furthermore, China is strong enough to deflect attempts to coax it into any relationship it does not like. That goes for both U.S. and Soviet attempts.

Contrary to what Premise 3 expected, the end of the Vietnam war and the normalization of Sino-U.S. relations did not see Beijing's attention directed undividedly toward its northern adversary, as expected. Instead, with its flanks covered with the United States, the PRC invaded its southern neighbor, Vietnam, in early 1979. It would be naive to believe that Beijing would reverse its present détente course with Moscow if the Taiwan irritant (another "southern" problem for the PRC) is removed from the parameters of Sino-U.S. relations.

Premise 4 above, in blunt language, expected China to become a "technological satellite" of the United States. China has deliberately spread its eggs in different baskets to avoid that trap. In 1982, for example, only 14 percent of China's total foreign trade was with the United States, while 12 percent was with Western Europe, 28 percent with East Asia (including 24 percent with Japan, and 4 percent with Australia); and 25 percent with Hong Kong and Southeast Asia.[26] One month after signing a number of cooperative agreements with President Reagan in Beijing, Chinese Premier Zhao was off to Western Europe, in June 1984, to sign a few more agreements on investments and technology transfers to China. In another instance, the Chinese Defense Minister, Zhang Aiping, stopped over in France to discuss possible imports of French military technology, while on his way to the United States on a much heralded mission for the same purpose commencing June 11, 1984. These are only sample evidences that the PRC is consciously spreading out their vital imports from a variety of sources, in order to avoid becoming irretrievably dependent on any one of them.

Premise 4 also saw a modernizing China dependent on Japanese (besides U.S.) goodwill and technological supplies. True, China is heavily trading with Japan, but it would be difficult to believe that a nuclear power like the PRC would be reduced to a "satellite" of any sort (even the technological variation) to a Japan stigmatized by its own Constitutional restrictions not to have a regular armed forces. In view of the growing U.S. tensions with Japan and the close Sino-Japanese partnership, it would be naive to think that the United States could really use a Japanese leverage on China.

Premise 5 has been frontally rebutted by the professed Chinese "independent" foreign policy, which means that, as we have seen, China would be stooge to no one, Uncle Sam or Uncle Polar Bear. In this respect, the term "independent" has a literal connotation.

The "China pawn" thesis à-la-Reagan, or Premise 6, has already met with Chinese rebuff, as noted.

The last of the seven premises, Reagan's "de-Communization" dream, has also met with rejection, as can be witnessed in the Chinese excision of the visiting President's remarks extolling the virtues of capitalist democracies. Besides, despite some admittedly impressive liberalization of the Chinese economy, there is no sign that the Chinese leaders under Deng will relinquish their so-called "four insists." That means, in the simplest terms, they will never abandon their Communist system. Of course, what is going to happen with future generations is not for us to see, in China as elsewhere. I am often puzzled, nevertheless, by those of our policymakers who are so imaginative in their wild expectations about Beijing renouncing its own communist belief but so unimaginative about the much more real likelihood that Beijing may, for its own sake, choose to reverse its long disputes with Moscow.

There are two basic reasons that these seven premises of our post-1969 China policy have not fared as expected. First, whether the Sino-Soviet split is going to perpetuate is an empirical question. But our policymakers in Washington have made it an article of faith. So, it cannot survive changes in the reality.

Second, our policy architects have neglected one thing: that Premises 2 through 7, if they were to work as expected, would require China being kept completely unaware of what was up our sleeves in our card-playing. If China knew that she was being played as a counterweight against Moscow, egged on to turn "northward," offered technology as a trap, given enticement to debunk her communist system, and so on, she would have reasons to counteract and take circumventing measures. Her independent foreign policy, in fact, can be viewed as such. Underestimating Chinese intelligence is a crucial second reason that the U.S. China-card policy has not worked the way it was intended to.

Our comments above, of course, merely apply to U.S. attempts to build a military partnership with the PRC to combat Soviet influence. It goes without saying that there are other aspects of the Sino-U.S. relationship, normalized since 1969, that are beneficial to both nations and have been advancing on the right track and should continue unabated.

U.S. Policy Response

What should the United States do, if all that has been said about the Chinese independent foreign policy is true? At the conceptual level, we should reexamine the "irreversibility" thesis about the Sino-Soviet split. Equally, we should stop assuming that China would not detect and counteract against our card-playing maneuvers. At the policy level, we should make a number of corresponding adjustments:

(a) We should regain the role of the "pivot" in the triad. As such, the United States should encourage, not deplore, the normalization of Sino-Soviet relations, because a *modus vivendi* between them would give the pivot more room to maneuver. For, if B and C had only conflictual relations, then pivot A would either have to side with one of the two or stay isolated in a delicate center position.[27]

(b) As the pivot, we should return to our previous even-handed policy toward the two communist nations. That requires us to have normal ties with both and avoid a permanent bond with either. The pivot's ability to manipulate the fear of the third player C (Moscow), with the hope of changing its behavior, will diminish once the threat of a permanent AB coalition ("stable marriage") is no longer a threat but a reality. In such an eventuality, the deterrent effect (feeding on C's fear that an AB coalition may happen if C does not behave) will have vanished. As long as the AB "stable marriage" prevails, there is no incentive for C (the Soviet Union) to compete with B (China) for the friendship of A (the United States), as we have witnessed since 1979.[28] By the same token, we will have forfeited our ability to deter undesirable Soviet behavior by the manipulation of the *prospects* of arms sales to China as soon as the prospects are no longer prospects but have become a *fait accompli* or ongoing enterprise.[29]

(c) We should repair our own relations with the Soviets so that we can truly regain our pivot's role. When hostility remains high in the U.S.-Soviet dyad, and when only China has open access to both of the other two triadic members, that gives China an enormous advantage over them. The United States will be like playing the Third Series in the Stryker-Psathas game discussed in Chapter 7. That means we are losing the pivot's role to China. On the other hand, if we maintain a working relationship with Moscow, as the Chinese are attempting to do, there will be no U.S.-Soviet deadlock for anyone to exploit. We will have a dialogue with both wing players, as a pivot should.

If one compares President Reagan's 1984 mission to China with President Nixon's stunning overture to Beijing in 1972, one finds Reagan at a distinct disadvantage. Nixon arrived to find the Chinese militarily worried and grateful for the belatedly bestowed U.S. diplomatic recognition. But Reagan came 12 years later to court a more self-confident China, hoping to build a common coalition. The welcome was enthusiastic but more subdued. While Nixon went to Beijing en route to Moscow, Reagan paid his homage to China because he could not go to Moscow. With Washington at odds with the Soviets, and with Sino-Soviet relations improving, as Hedrick Smith puts it, "the Chinese can afford the luxury of letting President Reagan carry the burden of rhetorical attacks on the Kremlin."[30]

Reagan's diplomacy of abuse in dealing with the Soviet Union, resorting to tough talk and building new weapons systems, did not work. It only boomeranged. The Soviets walked out of the arms control talks in November, 1983, vowing to deploy more seaborne nuclear missiles against the United States and to abrogate a voluntary Soviet moratorium on the deployment of SS-20 missiles in European areas of the Soviet Union. U.S.-Soviet relations reached a chilliest point since the height of the cold war in the 1960s. The Chinese, flinching from the heightened tensions between Washington and Moscow, sought to disentangle itself by pulling away a little bit from the former and moving slightly closer toward the latter. The greatest foreign policy defeat that Reagan could bring to the American people, which no amount of public-relations whitewashing can hide, is to let the United States be completely left out in the cold while a Sino-Soviet détente is deepening. We would lose all our leverage, while they both gain theirs over us.

The moral here is that when the United States has a normal dialogue with the Soviets again, it will regain the leverage it once enjoyed during the early 1970s, when it had a détente with Moscow and an "opening" to China. The United States will once again be able to tilt alternately to China and the Soviet Union and have a leverage over both. Until then, as one commentator puts it, "the Chinese are in the middle, able to play the Russian card against President Reagan as they please."[31]

(d) The United States, by the rules of the game, will gain from maintaining some but not too much tension between China and the Soviet Union. Too much tension would induce each of the two wings to demand excessive loyalty from the pivot and thus trigger polarization, which would be self-defeating.[32] For its own good, therefore, the United States should not attempt to create or abet high tensions between Beijing and Moscow.

(e) Beyond that, over the long haul, we should endeavor to engender ménage à trois. We should do so, not only because we will benefit from the resultant triad-wide stability ourselves, but also because both the other two players will vie for our friendship as the harmony-making pivot. That will in fact give us an unsurpassable leverage in dealing with both. As Berton shows in Chapter 1, pursuing national advantage usually does not contribute to international stability. The fault of the Reagan foreign policy is that it has one single goal in mind, which is to gain advantage over the Soviet foe. Even if that goal were achieved, it would not have brought peace and stability, because it would only have unleashed another round of escalation in the arms race. The time to reverse that course and start on the road to de-escalation and building a ménage à trois is now.

This is not as starry-eyed as it might sound because China, as we have seen, seems to be already trying in that direction. She not only covets good ties with both superpowers, but wants to see normal relations restored between the latter two. Rather than playing on U.S.-Soviet tensions, the Chinese have urged Reagan to end the "sharp confrontation" with Moscow and, specifically, to break the arms control logjam by halting further U.S. missile deployments in Western Europe.[33] This is not altruism, but motivated by self-interest. As U.S.-Soviet tensions are reduced, the acuteness of the arms race will wear off, and the chances of an accidental nuclear war will decrease, which will benefit China as well as other nations.

For a variety of reasons, including mutual suspicion and bureaucratic inertia plus possible incidental costs (such as relaxed defense vigilance among allies), ménage à trois is hard to materialize. But, to show its statesmanship and to maintain its leadership role, the United States has to seize the initiative in its own hands.

To recapitulate, from the standpoint of its long-term strategic interests, the United States would be wise to promote harmony within the triad and, as intermediate steps, to encourage Sino-Soviet amity and to return to an even-handed policy toward both communist nations. The latter also requires that we avoid a "stable marriage" with either and renew our détente with the Soviet Union, while keeping our Chinese connection on track, so that we can be an effective pivot in the triad. That is our answer to the question: What, for the United States, lies beyond China's independent foreign policy?

Notes

1. *Beijing Review*, No. 19 (May 7, 1984), p. 8.
2. The two Congressional measures were a November 15, 1983 Senate resolution on "Taiwan's Future" and a rider to an International Monetary Fund (IMF) appropriations bill passed by both houses on November 17 and 18, respectively, in 1983. The former referred to Taiwan as the "Republic of China" and declared support for its right to determine its own future free of coercion by the mainland Chinese Communists. The rider, for its part, recommended that Taiwan, also identified by its official name, maintain its seat in the Asian Development Bank should Peking be admitted.
3. Cf. address by Walter J. Stoessel, Jr., Under Secretary of State for Political Affairs, before the Los Angeles World Affairs Council in California, on April 24, 1981, in U.S. Department of State, "Foreign Policy Priorities in Asia," *Current Policy* No. 274 (April 24, 1981). Stoessel first described U.S. relations with the PRC as being "governed" by international obligations contracted in the two communiqués, and then declared that U.S. relationship with Taiwan would be, among other things, "consistent with our international obligations." Also Michel Oksenberg, "A Decade of Sino-American Relations," *Foreign Affairs*, Vol. 61, No. 1 (Fall, 1982), p. 191.
4. *The New York Times*, August 8, 1982.
5. *The New York Times*, November 27 and 29, 1983.

6. This was announced during Secretary of Commerce Malcolm Baldridge's visit to China, in the spring of 1983.

7. Reagan's talk to community leaders in Fairbanks, Alaska, May 1, 1984, following his 6-day China visit. See Hedrick Smith, "Reagan in U.S. Says China Trip Advanced Ties," *The New York Times*, May 2, 1984, p. 1.

8. "China View Mixed on Reagan's Trip," *The New York Times*, May 2, 1984.

9. See *The New York Times*, May 2, 1984, n. 7 above.

10. Harry Harding, "U.S.-China Relations Maturing," *The New York Times*, Op. Ed., May 3, 1984, p. A27.

11. *Beijing Review*, No. 21 (May 21, 1984), p. 19.

12. See discussion in Chapter 7, at reference for n. 26.

13. Confirmed to me by Li Shenchi, Director of the Institute of American Studies, Chinese Social Science Academy (Beijing), in a personal interview in New York City, March 17, 1984. On the connection between China's recent domestic shakeups and its new foreign policy, see Carol Hamrin, "Emergence of an 'Independent' Chinese Foreign Policy and Shifts in Sino-U.S. Relations," in *U.S.-Asian Relations: The National Security Paradox*, ed. by James C. Hsiung (New York: Praeger, 1983), pp. 63-84.

14. Premier Zhao Ziyang's administrative report of the 6th National People's Congress, June 6, 1983, *Remin Ribao*, June 24, 1983.

15. See discussion below at reference for nn. 27-28, and 30. Also Michel Oksenberg, "President Reagan's China Trip: A Background Paper" (New York: China Council, The Asia Society, April 1984), makes the same point.

16. Cf. Peter Yu, "A Strategic Model of Chinese Checkers: Power and Exchange in Beijing's Foreign Policy" (Ph.D. Dissertation completed in the Department of Politics, New York University, 1983).

17. International Institute for Strategic Studies, *Strategic Survey 1983-1984* (London: IISS, 1984), pp. 96f.

18. Cf. John Bryan Starr, "U.S.-China Relations in 1980: Looking Beyond the Process of Normalization," briefing packet (New York: China Council, The Asia Society, 1980). See also William G. Hyland, "The Sino-Soviet Conflict," in *The China Factor: Sino-American Relations & the Global Scene* (Englewood Cliffs, N.J.: Prentice-Hall, 1981), ed. by Richard Solomon, p. 147.

19. *The New York Times*, June 12, 1984, p. 3; *China Daily* (Beijing), June 5, 1984.

20. Kishore Mahbubani, "The Kampuchean Problem: A Southeast Asian Perception," *Foreign Affairs*, Vol. 62, No. 2 (Winter, 1983-84), pp. 407-425, esp. pp. 422f; Werner Draguhu, "The Indochina Conflict and the Positions of the Countries Involved," *Contemporary Southeast Asia*, Vol. 5, No. 1 (June, 1983), pp. 95-116.

21. For an elaboration of this thesis, see David Go, "Sino-Soviet Confrontation in Indochina" (Ph.D Dissertation compeleted in the Department of Politics, New York University, 1981).

22. To show his displeasure with the Reagan visit to China, Kim Il-sung took off to Moscow in May, 1984, right after Hu Yaobang, general secretary of the Chinese Communist Party, had come to Pyongyong to brief him on the Reagan visit.

23. See, for example, my "The Conceptual Foundation of U.S.-China Policy," in *Asian and U.S. Foreign Policy*, ed. by James C. Hsiung and Winberg Chai (New York: Praeger, 1981), pp. 121-28.

24. *Ibid*.

25. *Ibid*. Also see Chapter 7 in this volume.

26. *China Business Review*, May-June 1983, p. 58.

27. This is Gerald Segal's first rule for the pivot, discussed in Ch. 7 above. See also Segal, "China and the Great Power Triangle," *China Quarterly*, No. 83 (September 1980), p. 501.

28. Segal's Rules 2 and 3, *ibid*.

29. For an illuminating discussion of this point, see David M. Lampton, "Misreading China," *Foreign Policy*, No. 45 (Winter 1981-82), p. 103; also Andrew J. Pierre, "Arms Sales: The New Diplomacy," *Foreign Affairs*, Vol. 60, No. 2 (Winter 1981-1982), pp. 266ff.

30. Hedrick Smith, "This Time Around Peking Holds Some Cards of Its Own," *The New York Times*, April 29, 1984, p. 1.

31. *Ibid*.

32. Lowell Dittmer, "The Strategic Triangle: An Elementary Game-Theoretic Analysis," *World Politics*, Vol. 33, No. 4 (July 1981), p. 511.

33. Hedrick Smith, n. 30 above.

Bibliography

Documents and Primary Sources

Foreign Broadcast Information Service. Various Issues.

U.S. Congress. Senate. A Staff Report to the Committee on Foreign Relations. *Implementation of the Taiwan Relations Act: The First Year.* Washington, D.C.: U.S. Government Printing Office, 1980.

_____. Senate. Committee on Foreign Relations. Hearings. *East-West Relations: Focus on the Pacific.* 97th Congress, 2nd Session, June 10 and 16, 1982.

_____. Senate and the Congressional Research Service of the Library of Congress. *The Implications of U.S.-China Military*, Washington, D.C.: U.S. Government Printing Office, 1982.

U.S. Department of State. *Current Policy.* Various Issues.

_____. *Department of State Bulletin.* Various Issues.

U.S. Library of Congress. Congressional Research Service. *Chinese Nuclear Weapons and American Interests–Conflicting Policy Choices.* Washington, D.C.: Report No. 83-187F, September 27, 1983.

Articles

Alexandrov, I. "On the Sixtieth Anniversary of the Communist Party of China," *Pravda*, July 1, 1981.

Bialer, S. "The Soviet Union and the West in the 1980s: Detente, Containment, or Confrontation," *Orbis*, Vol. 27, No. 1, Spring 1983.

Bonavia, D. "Weinberger's Bouquet," *Far Eastern Economic Review*, October 13, 1983.

Borisov, O. "The Situation in the PRC and some of the Tasks of Soviet Sinology," *Far Eastern Affairs*, No. 3, 1982.

Brams, S.J. "the Search for Structural Order in the International System: Some Models and Preliminary Results," *International Studies Quarterly*, Vol. 13, No. 2, September 1969.

Campbell, C. "Vietnamese and Thai Officials Meet and Ease Rift on Cambodia," *The New York Times,* June 10, 1983.

Caplow, T. "A Theory of Coalitions in the Triad," *American Sociological Review*, Vol. 21, No. 4, August 1956.

Bibliography

Chalfont, A. "Reluctant Giant," *Guardian Weekly*, October 7, 1972.

Chanda, N. "Seeking the Soft Spots," *Far Eastern Economic Review*, July 21, 1983.

_____ . "United We Stand," *Far Eastern Economic Review*, August 11, 1983.

_____ . "A Glacially Slow Thaw," *Far Eastern Economic Review*, November 3, 1983.

Cheng, J.Y.S. "Normalization of Sino-Japanese Relations: China's Bargaining Position Regarding the Taiwan Question," *Asia Quarterly*, No. 3, 1980.

Dalnev, P. "Peking's Words and Deeds: The Essence of the Difficulties at the Soviet-Chinese Border Negotiations," *International Affairs* (Moscow), No. 11, 1981.

_____ . "Generosity at Someone Else's Expense," *Pravda*, November 30, 1983.

Deng-Ker, L. "Soviet Foreign Policy in Southeast Asia—An Analysis of the Moscow-Hanoi Alliance," *Issues and Studies*, July 1983.

Dittmer, L. "The Strategic Triangle: An Elementary Game Theoretic Analysis," *World Politics*, Vol. 33, No. 4, July 1981.

Downen, R.L. "Reagan, Zhao, and the Taiwan Pawn," *The Asian Wall Street Weekly*, January 2, 1984.

Dragahu, W. "The Indochina Conflict and the Positions of the Countries Involved," *Contemporary Southeast Asia*, Vol. 5, No. 1, June 1983.

Garver, J.W. "The Sino-Soviet Conflict Territorial Dispute in the Pamir Mountains Region," *China Quarterly*, No. 85, March 1981.

Gelman, H. "Soviet Policy Towards China," *Survey*, Vol. 27, No. 118/119, Autumn/Winter 1983.

Gittings, J. "The Great Power Triangle and Chinese Foreign Policy," *China Quarterly*, No. 39, July-September 1969.

Gordon, B.K. "America Redux: East Asian Perspectives on the Superpowers and Asian Security," *Parameters*, Vol. 13, No. 2, June 1983.

Griffith, W.E. "Peking, Moscow and Beyond: The Sino-Soviet-American Triangle," *Washington Papers*, No. 6, 1973.

Hamrin, C.L. "China Reassesses the Superpowers," *Pacific Affairs*, Vol. 52, No. 2, Summer 1983.

Harding, H. "Linkage Between Chinese Domestic and Foreign Policy," Presented at the *Workshop on Chinese Foreign Policy*, Ann Arbor, Mich., August 12-14, 1976.

_____ . "Changes and Continuity in Chinese Foreign Policy," *Problems of Communism*, March-April 1983.

_____ . "U.S.-China Relations Maturing," *The New York Times*, May 3, 1984.

Heaton, W. "China and the Southeast Asian Communist Movements: The Decline of Dual Track Policy," *Asian Survey*, Vol. 22, No. 8, August 1982.

Herbst, K.P. "Railway-Bond Case Threatens U.S.-China Trade," *Asian Wall Street Journal*, June 22, 1983.

Hirschfeld, R.S. "The Reagan Administration and U.S Relations with Taiwan and the People's Republic of China." Paper delivered at the *Conference on U.S. Congressional-Executive Relations and the Taiwan Relations Act*, Taipei, Taiwan, January 9-14, 1984.

Huichan, L. "The Crux of the Sino-Soviet Boundary Question," *Beijing Review*, Vol. 24, No. 30, July 27, 1981 and No. 31, August 3, 1981.

Johnson, C. "East Asia: Living Dangerously," *Foreign Affairs*, Vol. 62, No. 3, 1983.

Keith, R.C. "China and Trilateralism," *International Perspectives*, July/August 1983.

Kim, H.N. "Anti-Hegemonism and the Politics of the Sino-Japanese Peace Treaty," *Asia Quarterly*, No. 2, 1977.

Kim, S.S. "Whither Post-Mao Chinese Global Policy," *International Organization*, Vol. 35, No. 3, Summer 1981.

Kimura, A. "Sino-Soviet Relations: New Developments and Their Limits," *Journal of Northeast Asian Studies*, Vol. 2, No. 1, March 1983.

———. "Sino-Soviet Rapprochement: How Far Will it Go?" *Japan Quarterly*, Vol. 30, No. 3, July-September 1983.

Kimura, H. "The Soviet Proposal on Confidence-Building Measures and the Japanese Response," *Journal of International Affairs*, Vol. 37, No. 1, Summer 1983.

Lampton, D.M. "Misreading China," *Foreign Policy*, No. 45, Winter 1981-1982.

Lee, C. "The Making of the Sino-Japanese Peace and Friendship Treaty," *Pacific Affairs*, Fall 1979.

Lee, E. "Beijing's Balancing Act," *Foreign Policy*, No. 51, Summer 1983.

Legvold, R. "Caging the Bear: Containment without Confrontation," *Foreign Policy*, No. 40, Fall 1980.

Mahbubani, K. "The Kampuchean Problem: A Southeast Asian Perception," *Foreign Affairs*, Vol. 62, No. 2, Winter 1983-1984.

Mancall, M. "The Persistence of Tradition in Chinese Foreign Policy," *The Annals of the American Academy of Political and Social Science*, Vol. 340, September 1963.

Manezhev, S. and L. Novosyolova. "The Role of External Factors in China's Economic Development," *Far Eastern Affairs*, No. 2, 1983.

Manning, R. "Still Up In Arms," *Far Eastern Economic Review*, April 21, 1983.

McBeth, J. "Reach for the Sky," *Far Eastern Economic Review*, December 29, 1983.

Mills, T.M. "Power Relations in Three Person Groups," *American Sociological Review*, Vol. 18, No. 4, August 1953.

Monroe, J.G. "Garver's Pro-Soviet Tilt: Do They Tell the Truth?" *China Quarterly*, No. 88, December 1981.

Nakajima, M. "China May Return to the Soviet Bloc," *Japan Quarterly*, Vol. 30, No. 2, April-June 1983.

Nations, R. "A Tilt Towards Tokyo," *Far Eastern Economic Review*, April 21, 1983.

———. "Raising the Barriers," *Far Eastern Economic Review*, April 21, 1983.

———. "The Wooing of Wu," *Far Eastern Economic Review*, October 13, 1983.

———. "Feeling for a Ceiling," *Far Eastern Economic Review*, November 3, 1983.

Ocampo-Kalfors, S. "Easing Towards Conflict," *Far Eastern Economic Review*, April 28, 1983.

Okita, S. "Japan, China and the United States Economic Relations and Prospects," *Foreign Affairs*, Vol. 57, No. 5, Summer 1979.

Oksenberg, M. "A Decade of Sino-American Relations," *Foreign Affairs*, Vol. 61, No. 1, Fall 1982.

Pao-Min, C. "Beijing versus Hanoi: The Diplomacy Over Kampuchea," *Asian Survey*, Vol. 23, No. 5, May 1983.

Parks, M. "Chinese Leaders Reported Split Over U.S. Ties," *Los Angeles Times*, May 23, 1983.

———. "Stride Seen in U.S.-China Relations," Los Angeles Times Service, *Honolulu Star Bulletin*, August 28, 1983.

Petrov, V. "China Goes It Alone," *Asian Survey*, Vol. 23, No. 5, May 1983.

Pierre, A.J. "Arms Sales: The New Diplomacy," *Foreign Affairs*, Vol. 60, No. 2, Winter 1981-1982.

Pine, A. and A. Bennet. "Textile Pact Might Smooth Sino-U.S. Ties," *Asian Wall Street Journal*, August 1, 1983.

Robinson, T.W. "The Sino-Soviet Border Dispute: Background, Development, and the March 1969 Clashes," *American Political Science Review*, Vol. 66, No. 4, December 1972.

———. "Future Domestic and Foreign Policy Choices for Mainland China," *Journal of International Affairs*, No. 2, 1972.

———. "China's Dynamism in the Strategic Triangle," *Current History*, Vol. 82, No. 485, September 1983.

Schwartz, H. "The Moscow-Peking-Washington Triangle," *Annuals of the American Academy of Political and Social Sciences*, No. 414, July 1974,

Segal, G. "China and the Great Power Triangle," *China Quarterly*, No. 83, September 1980.

──────. "China's Strategic Posture and the Great Power Triangle," *Pacific Affairs*, Vol. 53, No. 4, Winter 1980–1981.

Simon, S. "David's Goliaths: Small-Power Great-Power Security Relations in Southeast Asia," *Asian Survey*, Vol. 23, No. 3, March 1983.

──────. "The Indochina Imbroglio: External Interests," *Australian Outlook*, August 1983.

──────. "The Two Southeast Asias and China: Security Perspectives," *Asian Survey*, Vol. 23, No. 3, May 1984.

Smith, H. "Deepening U.S.-Soviet Chill," *The New York Times*, June 18, 1981.

──────. "This Time Around China Holds Some Cards of Its Own," *The New York Times*, April 29, 1984.

──────. "Reagan in U.S. Says China Trip Advanced Ties," *The New York Times*, May 2, 1984.

Stryker, S. and G. Psathas. "Research on Coalitions in the Triad: Findings, Problems, and Strategies," *Sociometry*, Vol. 23, No. 3, September 1960.

Stuart-Fox, M. "Resolving the Kampuchean Problem: The Case for An Alternative Regional Initiative," *Contemporary Southeast Asia*, Vol. 4, No. 2, September 1982.

Su, C. "U.S.-China Relations: Soviet Views and Policies," *Asian Survey*, Vol. 23, No. 5, May 1983.

Tashjean, J.E. "The Sino-Soviet Split: Borkenau's Predictive Analysis of 1952," *China Quarterly*, No. 94, June 1983.

Tow, W.T. "Sino-Japanese Security Cooperation: Evolution and Prospects," *Pacific Affairs*, Vol. 56, Spring 1983.

Ukraintsev, M. "Entering the Fourth Decade: Notes on the PRC's Foreign Policy," *Far Eastern Affairs*, No. 4, 1981.

──────. "Soviet Chinese Relations: Problems and Prospects," *Far Eastern Affairs*, No. 3, 1982.

Vinacke, W.E. and A. Arkoff. "An Experimental Study of Coalitions in the Triad," *American Sociological Review*, Vol. 22, No. 4, August 1957.

Weisskopf, M. "China Hits Decision on Asylum," *Washington Post*, April 5, 1983.

White, N. "People's Diplomacy: Its Use by China to Influence Japan, 1949–1976," *Contemporary China*, Fall 1979.

Whiting, A.S. "Sino-American Relations: The Decade Ahead," *Orbis*, Vol. 26, No. 3, Fall 1982.

Woodard, K. and A.A. Davenport. "The Security Dimension of China's Offshore Oil Development," *Journal of Northeast Asian Studies*, Vol. 1, No. 3, September 1983.

Wren, C. "China Attacks the Foreign Policy of the U.S.," *The New York Times*, December 28, 1981.

Xiang, H. "Adhere to Independent Foreign Policy," *Beijing Review*, Vol. 25, No. 46, November 15, 1982.

Xiuquan, W. "Memoirs of a Veteran Diplomat: Sino-Soviet Relations in the Early 1950s," *Beijing Review*, Vol. 26, No. 47, November 21, 1983.

Yaobang, H. "Create a New Situation in All Fields of Socialist Modernization," *Beijing Review*, Vol. 25, No. 37, September 13, 1982.

Youlin, M. "Sino-Soviet Relations," *Beijing Review*, Vol. 25, No. 21, May 24, 1982.

Yun, L. "Afghanistan: Soviet Occupation of the Wakhan Area," *Beijing Review*, Vol. 24, No. 7, February 16, 1981.

Zagoria, D.S. "The Moscow-Beijing Detente," *Foreign Affairs*, Vol. 61, No. 4, Spring 1983.

Books and Monographs

Allison, G.T. *Essence of Decision: Explaining the Cuban Missile Crisis*. Boston: Little, Brown. 1971.

Art, R.J. and R. Jervis (eds.). *International Politics: Anarchy, Force, Imperialism*. Boston: Little, Brown, 1973.

Barnds, W.J. (ed.) *Japan and the United States: Challenges and Opportunities*. New York: New York University Press (A CFR book), 1979.

Barnett, D. *China and the Major Powers in East Asia*. Washington, D.C.: Brookings Institution, 1977.

———. *U.S. Arms Sales: The China-Taiwan Tangle*. Washington, D.C.: Brookings Institution, 1982.

Benjamin, R. and R.T. Kudrie. *The Industrial Future of the Pacific Basin*. Boulder: Westview, 1964.

Berton, P. (comp.). *The Chinese-Russian Dialogue*. Los Angeles: University of Southern California Press, 1963.

Blaker, M. (ed.). *Oil and the Atom: Issues in U.S.-Japan Energy Relations*. New York: Columbia University Press, East Asian Institute Project on Japan and the United States in Multilateral Diplomacy, 1980.

Bobrow, D.B., S. Chan, and J.A. Kringen. *Understanding Foreign Policy Decisions: The Chinese Case.* New York: Free Press, 1979.

Borisov, O.B. and B.T. Koloskov. *Sovetsko-kitaikse otnosheniia 1945-1970.* Moscow: Mysl', 1972.

Brams, S.J. *Game Theory and Politics.* New York: Free Press, 1975.

Bromke, A. *The Communist States at the Crossroads Between Moscow and Peking.* New York: Praeger, 1965.

Bunce, V. *Do New Leaders Make a Difference? Executive Succession, Public Policy under Capitalism and Socialism.* Princeton: Princeton University Press, 1981.

Buss, C.A. *The U.S. and the Republic of Korea.* Stanford: Hoover Institution Press, 1982.

Caplow, T. *Two Against One: Coalitions in Triads.* Englewood Cliffs, N.J.: Prentice-Hall, 1968.

Chawla, S. and D.R. Saredesai (eds.). *Changing Patterns of Security and Stability in Asia.* New York: Praeger, 1980.

Chung, C.W. *Pyong-Yang Between Peking and Moscow.* University of Alabama Press, 1976.

Clough, R.N. *East Asia and U.S. Security.* Washington, D.C.: Brookings Institution, 1975.

Clubb, O.E. *China and Russia: The "Great Game".* New York: Columbia University Press, 1971.

Coox, A.D. and H. Conroy (eds.). *China and Japan: The Search for Balance.* Santa Barbara: ABC-Clio Press, 1978.

Dallin, A. (ed.). *Diversity in International Communism: A Documentary Record.* New York: Columbia University Press, 1983.

Destler, I.M. and H. Sato (eds.). *Coping With U.S.-Japanese Relations.* Washington, D.C.: Brookings Institution, 1976.

Doolin, D.J. *Territorial Claims in the Sino-Soviet Conflict.* Stanford: Hoover Institution Press, 1965.

Dutt, A.K. *Southeast Asia: Realm of Contrasts,* 3rd. rev. ed., Boulder: Westview, 1983.

Etcheson, C. *The Rise and Demise of Democratic Kampuchea.* Boulder: Westview, 1984.

Fairbank, J.K. *The United States and China,* 4th ed., Cambridge, Mass.: Harvard University Press, 1979.

Gelman, H. *The Soviet Far East Buildup and Soviet Risk Taking Against China.* Santa Monica: Rand, August 1982, R-2943-AF.

Ginsburg, G. and C.F. Pinkele, *The Sino-Soviet Territorial Dispute, 1949-1964*. New York Praeger, 1978.

Gittins, J. *Survey of the Sino-Soviet Dispute*. London: Oxford University Press, 1968.

Go, D. *Sino-Soviet Confrontation in Indochina*. Ph.D. dissertation completed in the Department of Politics, New York University, 1981.

Gottlieb, T.M. *Chinese Foreign Policy Factionalism and the Origins of the Strategic Triangle*. Santa Monica: Rand, November 1977, R-1902-NA.

Gresham, L.P. *Western Analysis of Sino-Soviet Relations During the 1950's*. Unpublished M.A. thesis, School of International Affairs Relations, University of Southern California, August 1969.

Griffith, W.E. (ed.). *Albania and the Sino-Soviet Rift*. Cambridge, Mass.: M.I.T. Press, 1963.

_____ . (ed.). *The Sino-Soviet Rift*. Cambridge, Mass.: M.I.T. Press, 1964.

_____ . (ed.). *The Sino-Soviet Relations 1964-1965*. Cambridge, Mass.: M.I.T. Press, 1967.

Halperin, M.H. and A. Kanter (eds.). *Readings in American Foreign Policy: A Bureaucratic Perspective*. Boston: Little, Brown, 1973.

Harrison, J.P. *The Endless War: Fifty Years of Struggle in Vietnam*. New York: Free Press, 1983.

Hellman, D.C. (ed.). *China and Japan: A New Balance of Power*. Lexington, Mass.; Lexington Books, 1976.

Hinton, H.C. *Three and a Half Powers: The New Balance in Asia*. Bloomington: Indiana University Press, 1975.

_____ . *The China Sea: The American Stake in its Future*. New York: National Strategy Information Center, 1981.

Hoolerman, L. (ed.). *Japan and the United States: Economic and Political Adversaries*. Boulder: Westview, 1980.

Hsiung, J.C. (ed.). *U.S.-Asian Relations: The National Security Paradox*. New York: Praeger, 1983.

Hsiung, J.C. and W. Chai (eds.). *Asia and U.S. Foreign Policy*. New York: Praeger, 1981.

Hudson, G.F., R. Lowenthal, and R. Macfarquhar (eds.). *The Sino-Soviet Dispute*. New York: Praeger, 1962.

International Institute for Strategic Studies. *Strategic Survey, 1983-1984*. London: IISS, 1984.

Iriye, A. (ed.). *The Chinese and the Japanese: Essays in Political and Cultural Interactions*. Princeton, N.J.: Princeton University Press, 1980.

Jacobsen, C.G. *Sino-Soviet Relations Since Mao: The Chairman's Legacy*. New York: Praeger, 1981.

Jervis, R. *Perception and Misperception in International Politics.* Princeton, N.J.: Princeton University Press, 1976.

Jo, Y.H. and Y. Pi. *Russia versus China and What Next?* Lanham, MD.: University Press of America, 1980.

Knorr, K. (ed.). *The International System.* Princeton, N.J.: Princeton University Press, 1961.

Krause, L.B. *U.S. Economic Policy Towards the Association of Southeast Asian Nations: Meeting the Japanese Challenge.* Washington, D.C.: Brookings Institution, 1982.

Langdon, F.C. *Japan's Foreign Policy.* Vancouver: University of British Columbia Press, 1973.

Larson, J.E. (ed.). *New Foundation for Asian and Pacific Security.* New York: National Strategy Information Center, 1980.

Lee, C. *Japan Faces China.* Baltimore: Johns Hopkins University Press, 1976.

Levin, N. *The Strategic Security Relations in the 1980's.* Santa Monica: Rand (N-1960-FF), March 1983.

Lieberthal, K.G. *Sino-Soviet Conflict in the 1970s: Its Evolution and Implications for the Strategic Triangle.* Sanata Monica: Rand, 1976, R-2342-NA.

Low, A.D. *The Sino-Soviet Dispute: An Analysis of the Polemics.* Rutherford, N.J.: Farleigh Dickinson University Press, 1976.

McClelland, C. *Theory and the International System.* New York: Macmillan, 1966.

Mancall, M. *Russia and China: Their Diplomatic Relations to 1728.* Cambridge, Mass.: Harvard University Press, 1971.

Mehnert, K. *Peking and Moscow.* New York: Mentor Books, 1964.

Mendl, W. *Issues in Japan's China Policy.* London: Macmillan, 1978.

Millar, T.B. (ed.). *International Security in the Southeast Asian and Southwest Pacific Regions.* St. Lucia: The University of Queensland Press, 1983.

Morley, J.W. (ed.). *The Fateful Choice: Japan's Advance into Southeast Asia, 1939–1941.* New York: Columbia University Press, 1980.

Morse, R.A. *The Politics of Japan's Energy Strategy: Resources-Diplomacy-Security.* Berkeley: University of California, Institute of East Asian Studies, 1981.

Mueller, P.G. and D.A. Ross. *China and Japan: Emerging Global Powers.* New York: Praeger, 1975.

Neustadt, R. *Alliance Politics.* New York: Columbia University Press, 1970.

Nisbett, R.E. and L.D. Ross. *Human Inferences: Strategies and Shortcomings of Social Judgement.* Englewood Cliffs, N.J.: Prentice-Hall, 1980.

Oksenberg, M. *President Reagan's China Trip: A Background Paper*. New York: China Council, The Asia Society, April 1984.

Oksenberg, M. and R.B. Oxnam (eds.). *Dragon and Eagle: United States China Relations: Past and Future*. New York: Basic Books, 1978.

Pacific Forum. *The PRC's New Policy Directions: An Assessment*. Honolulu: Pacific Forum, 1983.

Petrov, V. *Soviet-Chinese Relations, 1945–1970*. Bloomington: Indiana University Press, 1975.

Pollack, J.D. *The Sino-Soviet Rivalry and Chinese Security Debate*. Santa Monica: Rand, October 1982, R-2907-AF.

Pye, L. *Chinese Commercial Negotiating Style*. Santa Monica: Rand, 1982, R-2837-AF.

Rapaport, A. *N-Person Game Theory: Concepts and Applications*. Ann Arbor, Mich.: University of Michigan Press, 1970.

Reischauer, E.O. *The United States and Japan*, 3rd ed. Cambridge, Mass.: Harvard University Press, 1965.

Samuels, M.S. *Contest for the South China Sea*. New York: Methuen, 1982.

Scalapino, R.A. *Asia and the Road Ahead: Issues for the Major Powers*. University of California Press, 1975.

Scalapino, R.A. and J. Wanadi, (eds.). *Economic, Political, and Security Issues in Southeast Asia in the 1980s*. Berkeley: Institute of East Asian Studies, University of California, 1982.

Schelling, T. *The Strategy of Conflict*. New York: Oxford University Press (Galaxy Books), 1963.

Segal, G. *The Great Power Triangle*. London: Macmillan, 1982.

Shaw, Y. *ROC-U.S. Relations: A Decade After the Shangai Communique*. Taipei: The Asia and World Institute, 1983.

Sigur, G. and Y.C. Kim, (eds.). *Japanese and U.S. Policy in Asia*. New York: Praeger, 1982.

Simon, S. *The ASEAN States and Regional Security*. Stanford: Hoover Institution Press, 1982.

Smyser, W.R. *The Independent Vietnamese: Vietnamese Communism Between China and Russia, 1956–1969*. Athens, Oh.: Ohio University Press, 1980.

Solomon, R. (ed.). *Asian Security in the 1980s*. Santa Monica: Rand, 1979.

_____. (ed.). *The China Factor: Sino-American Relations and the Global Scene*. Englewood Cliffs, N.J.: Prentice-Hall, 1982.

Starr, J.B. *U.S. China Relations in 1980, Looking Beyond the Process of Normalization*. New York: China Council, The Asia Society, 1980.

Stuart, D.T. and W. Tow, (eds.). *China, the Soviet Union, and the West*. Boulder, CO.: Westview, 1982.

Sutter, R.G. *Chinese Foreign Policy After the Cultural Revolution*. Boulder, CO.: Westview, 1978.

Swearingen, R. *The Soviet Union and Postwar Japan: Escalating Challenge and Response*. Stanford: Hoover Institution Press, 1978.

Tajima, T. *China and Southeast Asia: Strategic Interests and Policy Prospects*. London: International Institute of Strategic Studies, Adelphi Papers, No. 172, Winter 1981.

Tatu, M. *Le Grand Triangle: Washington-Moscou-Pékin*. Paris: Institut Atlantique, 1970.

The Atlantic Council of the United States. *China Policy for the Next Decade: Report of the Atlantic Council's Committee on China Policy*. Washington, D.C.: The Atlantic Council of the United States, October 1983.

The Heritage Foundation. *Asian Studies Center Backgrounder*. Washington, D.C.: The Heritage Foundation, August 23, 1983.

Thomas, R.G.C. (ed.). *The Great Power Triangle and Asian Security*. Lexington, Mass.: Lexington Books, 1983.

Treadgold, D.W. *Soviet and Chinese Communism: Similarities and Differences*. Seattle: University of Washington Press, 1967.

Vasey, L.R. (ed.). *Pacific Asia and U.S. Policies: A Political-Economic-Strategic Assessment*. Pacific Forum, 1976.

Vertzberger, Y. *The Enduring Entente: Sino-Pakistani Relations, 1960-1980*. New York: Praeger, 1983.

Von Neumann, J. and O. Morgenstern. *Theory of Games and Economic Behaviour*. Princeton: Princeton University Press, 1944.

Waltz, K.N. *Theory of International Politics*. Reading, Mass.: Addison-Wesley, 1979.

Watts, W., et al., (eds.). *Japan, Korea and China: American Perceptions and Policies*. Lexington, Mass.: Lexington Books, 1979.

Wich, R. *Sino-Soviet Crisis Politics: A Study of Political Change and Communication*. Cambridge, Mass.: Harvard University Press, 1980.

Wolff, L. and D.L. Simon (eds.). *Legislative History of the Taiwan Relations Act*. New York: American Association for Chinese Studies, 1982.

Yu, P. *A Strategic Model of Chinese Checkers: Power and Exchange in Beijing's Foreign Policy*. Ph.D. dissertation compeleted in the Department of Politics, New York University, 1983.

Zagoria, D. *The Sino-Soviet Conflict, 1956-1961*. Princeton: Princeton University Press, 1962.

──── . (ed.). *Soviet Policy in East Asia*. New Haven, Conn.: Yale University Press, 1982.

Index

Afghanistan (*see also* Soviet-Afghan relations), 2, 11, 12, 17, 27, 31, 35, 36, 38, 39, 47, 67, 80, 81, 82, 86, 121, 123, 125, 173, 177, 180
Albania, 29
Andropov, Yuri; death of, 42; meeting with Huang Hua at Brezhnev's funeral, 40
Association of South East Asian Nations (ASEAN): *See* Sino-ASEAN relations; Soviet-ASEAN relations
Baldridge, Malcolm; visit to Beijing, 5/83, 61, 67
Brezhnev, Leonid; and Asian Collective Security Plan, 31; Brezhnev doctrine, 10; death of, 40, 124; referred to, 3, 33, 57, 126; signing of SALT II, 33; Tashkent speech, 1983, 36-7, 124, 172; Twenty Sixth CPSU speech, 1981, 37; warnings to China if it abrogated 1950 Treaty, 33
Brown, Harold; visit to PRC, 1/80, 35, 177
Brzezinski, Zbigniew; referred to, 177, 182; and US policy toward SU and PRC, 96
Bush, George; visit to PRC, 5/82, 37, 58, 168

Canada, 24, 86
Carter, Jimmy; announcement of normalization of relations with PRC, 75-6; referred to, 57, 123, 182; signing of SALT II, 34
Cuba, 86
Czechoslovakia, 9, 11, 17, 31

Deng Xiaoping; quoted, 5, 166; referred to, 57, 61, 62, 63, 67-8, 74, 81, 84, 103, 123, 124, 150, 158, 176, 182; return to power, 11; and Sino-Japanese Peace Treaty, 74, visit to US, 2/79, 123, 124

Egypt, 24, 26
Ethiopia, 86

France, 17, 112

Game theory, 3-person: US-SU-PRC; coalition formation, 108, 109-10, 112, 127, 128, 181; correlation in shifts within the triad, 116-122, 1969-1971, 117; 1972-1974, 120; 1975-1977, 120; 1978-1980, 120-21; findings, 121-22; directed dyads, 112; gain calculations, 109; menage a trois, 115, 127, 186, 187; n-person game and the triad, 108, 180; perception theory, 109, 112; pivot, 172, 176, 185, 186; romantic triangle, 122, 123, 125, 127-8, 181; and PRC, costs, 124, 125; gains, 124; and SU, costs, 127; gains, 126; and US, costs, 125, 126; gains, 125; stable marriage, 109, 123, 185; Stryker-Psathas experiment, 114-16, 122, 127, 128, 129, 172; compulsory coalitions, 115; findings, 116; power ratio approximation, 114; Sino-American detente, 115; Sino-Soviet alliance, 115; undirected dyads, 112; Vinacke-Arkoff experiment, 109-14; coalition formation, 113; findings, 112, 113; power distribution, 110, 112; triadic power distribution, 112, 113, 114; Sino-Soviet rapprochement,

115; Sino-US coalition, 114; Soviet-American parity, 114

Geng Biao, visit to US, 1980, 35, 177

Haig, Alexander, referred to, 57, 66; visit to PRC, 6/81, 58, 126, 169
Hong Kong, 29
Hua Guofeng; announcement of normalization of relations with the US, 76; referred to, 44, 170; visit to Japan, 1980, 35
Huang Hua; meeting with Andropov at Brezhnev's funeral, 40; visit to Washington, 10/81, 58
Hungary, 11, 28
Hu Yaobang, as head of CCP, 170; quoted, 5; referred to, 65, 138; speech to 12th Party Congress of CCP, 38, 39–40, 138; speech, 5/83, on closer ties with the Soviet bloc, 61; visit to Japan, 1983, 41, 169

India, 26, 27, 29

Jackson, Henry; visit to PRC, 63, 64
Japan—*See also* Japanese-American relations; Sino-Japanese relations; Soviet Japenese relations; domestic political split over recognition of PRC, 73; domestic support for self-defense forces, 74; as fourth actor in East Asia and the Pacific, 17; occupied, after World War II, 8, 71; Soviet occupation of Northern Islands, 73
Japanese-American Relations; Japanese-American resolution to keep Taiwan seat at UN, 1971, 72; Japanese-ROC Peace Treaty, 1951, 72; Japanese recognition of PRC and, 73, 75; Nixon-Tanaka summit, 1972, 71; Partial Nuclear Test Ban Treaty, 1963, Japanese support of, 20; Peace Treaty, 1951, 72, 73; Security Treaty, 1951, 73, 178; revised, 20; Sino-Japanese peace treaty and, 74, 75; Sino-Soviet rapprochement and, 79; Sino-US and Sino-Japanese relations effect on, 77, 78; and Korean peninsula, 77; parallel interests re China, 78; sources of friction, 78, 79; US occupation of, 72; US opening to China and, 71, 75, 178; Vietnam War and, 73

Kapitsa, Mikhail; visit to Beijing, 1983, 67
Khrushchev, Nikita; de-stalinization campaign, 25, 27; referred to, 18, 45, 171; rise to power, 27; and Tito, 27; visit with Eisenhower, 1959, "Spirit of Camp David", 29
Kissinger, Henry; referred to, 96, 182; secret mission to PRC, 10, 95

Lin Biao; fall of, 80; referred to, 24, 26, 44

Macao, 29
Mao Zedong, compared by SU to Hitler, 30; death of, 132; and Khrushchev, rise of, effect on Mao's relations with SU, 27; referred to, 25, 27, 28, 30, 44, 72, 113, 158, 171; and Stalin, signing of Treaty of Friendship, Alliance and Mutual Assistance, 8; Three Worlds Theory, 30, 38, 171
Mondale, Walter, visit to Beijing, 8/79, 34, 120

Nakasone, Yasuhiro, visit to Beijing, 1984, 43, 173
Nixon, Richard, referred to, 158, 181; and Sino-American rapprochement, 45, 95, 185; summit with Tanaka, 1972, 71; visit to PRC, 1972, 10, 55, 71, 181; visit to SU, 1972, 185
Nguyen Co Thach, quoted, 87; visit

with Thai Foreign Minister, 6/83, on Kampuchea's independence, neutrality and nonalignment, 88
Poland, 11
People's Republic of China—*see also* Sino-American relations; Sino—ASEAN relations; Sino-Japanese relations; Sino-Kampuchean relations; Sino-Soviet relations; Sino-Vietnamese relations; aid to Khmer Rouge, 84, 85; Lao resistance, 85; Chinese Communist Party, Twelfth Party Congress, 38, 170, 171, 174; Chinese communist system, 133, 135; centralization of power, 133; closed system, 133-34; deradicalization, 134-35; elites, 133-35; established one party state system, 134, 135; system maintenance v. system development, 134; Civil War, 1949 victory, 8, 26, 72, 95; Deng Xiaoping quoted, 5, 166; referred to, 57, 61, 62, 63, 67-8, 74, 81, 84, 103, 123, 124, 150, 158, 176, 182; return to power, 11; domestic policies; Cultural Revolution, 9, 20, 28, 30; "Dengization," 170, 171; effect on foreign relations, 133, 135, 136; Four Modernizations, 11, 45, 103, 136, 148; Great Leap Forward, 9, 20, 29, 30; market socialism, 132, 135; foreign economic policy; conflicts of jurisdiction, 136, 137; decentralization, 137; diffusion of authority, 136, 137; export oriented industrialization, 139, 141; and foreign businesses, problems faced by, 138, 139, 145; foreign inputs, 136, 138, 139, 140, 144; government v. party involvement, 138; leadership decisions on, 138; Ministry of Foreign Economic Relations and Trade, 137, 138; technocrats v. Maoists, 136; and World Bank, 146; foreign policy, independent, 81, 91, 100, 128, 142, 166, 167, 170-72, 173, 184; codification of, at 12th Party Congress, 1982, 4, 170; definition of, 3; Deng Xiaoping on, 5; domestic policies and, 133; Hu Yaobang on, 5, 38, 39-40, 142; and relations with the Third World, 3, 5, 81, 136, 147, 170; and Three Worlds Theory, 30, 38, 171; and US-PRC relations, 56, 166-67; foreign trade, 183; Hu Yaobang, as head of CCP, 170; speech to 12th Party Congress, 1982, 38, 39-40, 142; speech, 1983, on closer ties with Soviet bloc, 61; and Korean War, 8; leadership group characteristics, 44; Mao Zedong, death of, 132; and foreign policy changes, 132, 135; and Maoists in government, 133, 171; military, 7, 141; political issues, foreign inputs, 142, 146, 147; input linkages, 145-48; Ministry of Foreign Affairs, 142; objectives, 142; Sino-American relations, 142, 143, 144; Soviet Union, 144; Taiwan, 142, 144; zone of influence in South East Asia, 143; public self-image, 156; and Quemoy and Matsu, 9; security issues, domestic inputs, 133; foreign inputs, 140, 146, 147; leadership concern about, 140, 141; and superpower arms race, 4, threat of encirclement, 80, 82, 136, 141, 173; and Soviet Union, alliance with, 2, 8; view of Soviet power, 81; Taiwan Straits Crisis, 28; United Front Policy, 11, 80, 172; United Nations, 1, 7, 10, 38; and US-SU detente, opposition to, 9

Index

Qian Qichen, visit to Moscow, 1984, 44

Reagan, Ronald, meeting with Zhao Ziyang at Cancun, 1981, 58; quoted, 59, 65, 170; referred to, 56, 57, 63, 64, 68, 158, 160, 163, 168, 174, 176, 182, 184, 185–86, 187; visit to PRC, 1984, 1, 43, 68, 144, 166, 169, 176, 185

Regan, Donald, visit to PRC, 1984, 66

Shultz, George, referred to, 63; speech to World Affairs Council, San Francisco 1983, 60; visit to PRC, 1983, 41, 59, 60, 67

Sino-American relations and Afghanistan, 123; and arms control, 176, 187; American credos about China, 153–4, 158, 162, 174; American decision-making processes and, 158–59; American premises in policy toward PRC, 181–84; American view of Chinese restraint in international conflicts, 159, 160; Baldridge, Malcolm, visit to Beijing, 5/82, 37, 58, 168; boycott, Moscow olympics, 35, 161; Brown, Harold, visit to PRC, 1/80, 35, 177; Carter, Jimmy, acceptance of anti-hegemony clause, 123, 166; announcement, with Hua Guofeng, of normalization, 76; and Brzezinski, policy toward PRC, 96, 177; Deng Xiaoping, on Sino-US and Sino-Soviet relations, 62; visit to US, 2/79, 123, 124; distancing of relations and PRC's independent foreign policy, 1, 3, 4, 46, 56, 57, 81, 100, 101, 125, 142, 143, 144, 170, 171, 186; Europe and, 100; Eximbank credits, 123; Geng Biao, visit to US, 1980, 35, 177; Haig, Alexander, visit to PRC, 6/81, 58, 126, 169; Holdridge, John, visit to Beijing, 1/82, 58, 168; Hu Na's defection, 55, 61; Hu Yaobang, speech on closer ties with Soviet bloc, 5/83, 61; speech to 12th CCP Congress, 91; Huang Hua, visit to Washington, 10/81, 58; insurance, Overseas Private Investment Corp., 123; Jackson, Henry, visit to PRC, 8/83, 63, 64; Kissinger, Henry, 10, 95; Korean War, 95, 160; Latin America and, 100, 177; level of relations, 117, 120, 121; Middle East and, 100, 177; modernization, 103, 105; Mondale, Walter, visit to Beijing, 8/79, 34, 120; marks end of US evenhandedness, 120; Most Favoured Nation status for PRC, 123; Nixon, Richard, visit to PRC, 1972, 10, 55, 71, 95, 181, 185; normalization of relations, 1, 11, 12, 33, 55, 75–6, 96, 116, 117, 160, 177, 183; benefits of, 100, 121, 124, 125; costs of, 100, 121, 124, 125, 126; quasi-alliance, period of, 17, 46, 96, 123, 166, 177, 182; strategic partnership, 1, 80; North Korea, 77; PRC application for membership in Asian Development Bank, 55, 62, 65; PRC-Third World relations, 101, 104, 124, 125, 171; Qing Dynasty Huguang Railway bonds case, 55, 58, 63, 169; rapprochement, 10, 13, 81, 95, 182; Reagan Administration, effect on, 14, 17, 55, 56–8, 81, 96, 99, 167, 173; and Reagan's pro-Taiwan stand, 167, 170, 173, 177; Reagan, Ronald, meeting with Zhao Ziyang at Cancun, 10/81, 58; quoted, 59; on US relations with PRC and Taiwan, 56–7; visit to PRC, 1984, 1, 43, 64, 66, 63, 143, 166, 169, 174, 183, 185;

Regan, Donald, visit to PRC, 1984, 66; Sino-American alignment against SU, 15, 81, 96, 115, 171, 176; Sino-Soviet alignment against US, 15, 95, 172; split, 9, 96; rapprochement, 100, 104, 144, 174, 175, 176, 177, 182, 186; Shanghai Communique, 1972, 10, 58, 71; Shultz, George, speech to World Affairs Council, San Francisco 3/83, 60, 61; visit to PRC, 2/83, 59, 60, 67; Soviet-American detente, 9, 117, 120, 173, 176, 186, 187; Soviet military, growth and deployment, 82; presence in East Asia, 10, 125; Europe, 125; Indochina, 101, 171; Taiwan and, as factor in non-recognition of PRC, 95; as leverage in US relations with PRC, 103, 105, 177; Pan-Am flights to, resumed, 62, 159; as problem in US-PRC rapprochement, 96, 104; PRC demands re, 167–68; PRC peaceful reunification with, 62, 100, 104, 105, 168; PRC sovereignty over, 168; PRC-US joint memorandum of Taiwan, 8/82, 37, 55, 58, 59, 61, 66, 68, 96, 98, 144, 168, 169; Taiwan membership in Asian Development Bank, 55, 62, 65, 168; Taiwan Relations Act, 1979, 57, 63, 76, 97, 98, 99, 104, 167, 169; US arms sales to, 37, 57, 58, 59, 61, 64, 77, 97, 98, 99, 104, 142, 157, 168; textile quotas, 55, 59, 63, 65, 158, 161, 169; trade and investment relation, 146, 183; United Nations and, 100, 125; US arms sales to, 58, 64, 79, 88, 100, 126, 169, 183; US Export Administration Act, changes in PRC's status, 65, 169; US technology transfers to, 56, 62, 65, 67, 68, 79, 100, 103, 123, 147, 169; US-PRC agreements and accords cultural exchange, 1984, 66, 169; industrial and technological, 1984, 66; nuclear technology, 1984, 43, 66, 144, 169; science and technology, 1984, 66; Vietnam and, 9, 96, 100, 124, 125, 183; Weinberger, Caspar, visit to PRC, 9/83, 41, 64, 66, 67, 169; Wu Xueqian, visit to Washington, 10/83, 64; Zhang Aiping, visit to US, 6/84, 177, 183; Zhao Ziyang, and Reagan's 1984 visit to PRC, 1, 144, 167, 174; visit to US, 1/84, 64, 66, 77, 99, 100; Zhou Enlai and Mao Zedong, approach to Washington for modus vivendi, 1949, 113

Sino-ASEAN (Association of South East Asian Nations) relations, and arms sales to China, 88, 179; and Chinese threat, fear of, 87, 89, 143, 179; and claims to Spratly Islands, 89–90; improvement of, 80; and Khmer Rouge, 89; and PRC attack on Vietnam, 84; and Sino-American rapprochement, 80; and Sino-Soviet conflict, 87, 179; and Soviet-Vietnamese relations, 83, 180; and Vietnamese occupation of Kampuchea, 143; and ZOPFAN (Zone of Peace, Freedom, and Neutrality), 179

Sino-Japanese relations, Chinese Cultural Revolution, effect of, 20, 72; Chinese economic mission to Japan, 1983, 41; Chinese Leap Forward, failure of and effect on, 20; Chinese support for return to Japan of Soviet occupied northern islands, 30, 73; hostilities, period of, 20; Hua Guofeng, visit to Japan, 1980, 35; Hu Yaobang, speech to 12th

Index

Party Congress of CCP and, 38, 39; visit to Japan, 11/83, 41, 169; Japanese-Soviet development of Siberia, 13; Japanese-US resolution to keep Taiwan seat at UN, 1971, 72; Nakasone, Yasuhiro, visit to Beijing, 1984, 43, 173; Nikaido, Susumu, visit to PRC, 2/83, 41; normalization, 1, 10, 11, 71, 72, 73, 75, 177; peace treaty (1978), 2, 11, 13, 71, 74, 75; and anti-hegemony clause, 74, 75; rapprochement, 11, 80; Sino-Japanese ministerial conference, 41; Sino-Soviet rapprochement and, 78, 175, 178; and Soviet military growth and deployment, 82; Suzuki, Zenko, visit to PRC, 1982, 40; Tanaka, Kakuei, visit to PRC, 1972, 72; trade relations, 72, 145, 183; agreements of 2/78 and 3/79, 75; Liao-Takasaki memorandum, 20, 72; Wu Xueqian, visit to Japan, 1983, 41; Zhao Ziyang, and three principles for development of Sino-Japanese relations, 75; visit to Japan, 1982, 40, 75

Sino-Kampuchean relations, Chinese support of Democratic Kampuchea's seat at UN, 85; insurgents, 85, 179; Khmer Rouge, 84, 85, 178; UN supervised elections after Vietnamese withdrawal, 88; Khmer Rouge and non-communist coalition government, 85; and Sino-Soviet rapprochement, 178; Zhao Ziyang, visit to Thailand, 2/81, and support of Kampuchea's neutralization, 88

Sino-Soviet relations, and Afghanistan, 2, 11, 31, 35, 38, 39, 47, 67, 81, 82, 121, 123, 173, 177, 180; Sino-Soviet negotiations cancelled, 35, 57; Soviet-Afghan border treaty, 35; Soviet troops on Sino-Afghan border, 35; Andropov, Yuri, death of and, 42; Arkhipov, Ivan, postponement of visit to PRC, 1984, 42, 43; arms control, 120; boycott, Moscow olympics, 35; Brezhnev, Leonid, Asian Collective Security Plan, 31; Brezhnev doctrine, 10; death of, 40, 124; on improving Sino-Soviet relations, 3, 33, 57; Tashkent speech, 1982, 36–7, 38, 124, 172; Twenty sixth CPSU Party Congress speech, 1981, 37; Brown, Harold, visit to PRC, 1/80, 35; China, and, Cultural Revolution, 20, 31; competition in International Communist Movement, 30; fear of encirclement, 82, 173, 175; Four Modernizations Program, 38, 43, 45; Great Leap Forward, 29; support of Japan's territorial disputes with SU, 30; view of South East Asia as sphere of influence, 82; Cuban missile crisis and, 29; Czechoslovakia, Soviet invasion of, 9; Detente, efforts toward, 2–4, 12, 33, 67, 125, 127, 141, 142, 144, 147, 166, 167, 170, 171, 172, 180; border talks, 2, 3, 35; Chinese conditions for normalization of relations, 81, 91, 166, 180; on basis of 5 principles of peaceful coexistance, 2, 33, 167, consultations, 31, 42; political negotiations, 29, 31, 33, 40, 41–2, 56, 57, 66–7, 124; river navigation talks, 35; scientific, cultural, technological and sports agreements, 34, 41, 67; Soviet proposal to freeze build-up on border, 67; trade agreements, 3, 34, 40, 43, 67; domestic policies and, 45; Gromyko, Andrei, 33, support for Vietnamese proposal of South East Asian regional conference, 87; Hu Yaobang, speech to 12th Party Congress of CCP and, 39; speech on closer ties with Soviet bloc, 5/83, 61; Kampuchea and, 2, 11, 34, 38, 39, 67, 84, 91, 173, 178, 180; Kapitsa, Mikhail, visit to Beijing, 1983, 42, 67; Korean airliner incident and, 42, 125; levels of relations, 31, 32, 117, 120, 121; Manchuria, Soviet occupation of, 8, 26; Partial Nuclear Test Ban Treaty, 1963, 30; Qian Qichen, visit to Moscow, 1984, 44; Reagan, Ronald, visit to PRC, 1984 and, 43; Sino-American alignment against SU, 15, 46, 80; Sino-American normalization of relations, 11, 33, 81, 122, 123–4, 142; Sino-Indian border dispute and, 30; Sino-Japanese peace treaty and, 11, 31; Sino-Soviet alignment against US, 15, 24, 113, 115, 172; Sino-Soviet conflict and ASEAN, 87, 91, 92; Sino-Soviet rapprochement, consequences of, 175, 178, 179; Sino-Soviet split border war, 2, 9, 10, 11, 30, 31, 34, 121, 172; breaking of relations, 1, 9, 11, 15, 20, 24; causes of dispute, 25, 26, 28–9, 30, 35–6; cold war type period, 46, 172; Indochina and, 2; Krushchev recall of all Soviet technicians, 9, 29; Sino-American relations, effect on 9, 10, 117, 124, 126; Sino-Vietnamese war, 1979, 11, 33; Sino-American relations and, 82, 173; Soviet military presence in Afghanistan-see topic East Asia, 10, 82, 125, 173; Indochina, 121, 126, 144, 166; Mongolia, 35, 36, 38, 44, 144; Sino-Soviet border, 2, 10, 31, 34, 36, 38, 39, 41, 44, 91, 124, 126, 144, 180; Third World, 82, 147, 150; Treaty of Friendship, Alliance and Mutual Assistance, Chinese refusal to renew, 2; Communist Chinese victory, 1949, and, 8; expiration of, 2, 33, 35; financial provisions of, 26; role during Korean war and Taiwan Straits crisis, 33; Vietnam and, 10, 11, 34, 38, 39, 47, 80, 81, 82, 84, 91, 124, 126, 143; Soviet relations with Laos and Kampuchea, 82; Soviet-Vietnamese alliance and Soviet military presence, 82, 83, 84, 86, 87; Zhao Ziyang on normalization of relations, 4, 170

Sino-Vietnamese relations, Chinese conditions for normalization of relations, 85, 143, 178; policy of bleeding Vietnam, 83, 88; and claims to Paracel and Spratly islands, 89–90; and division of the Gulf of Tonkin, 90; and Sino-Kampuchean relations, 85, 89, 178; and Sino-Soviet rapprochement, 175, 178; and Sino-Vietnamese break in diplomatic relations, 84; and Sino-Vietnamese war, 1979, 2, 11, 33, 81, 84, 183; as opposition to Vietnamese hegemonism, 84, 179; and Soviet-Vietnamese alliance, 83, 143; two-front war strategy, 84; withdrawal, 83

Soviet-Afghan relations, border treaty, 35; invasion and occupation, 1979, 11, 31, 35, 39, 47, 81, 82, 120, 123, 177; and Sino-Soviet rapprochement, 67, 82, 183; Soviet troops in Afghanistan, 38; on Sino-Afghan border, 35

Soviet-American relations and Afghanistan, 11, 17, 120, 123, 125, 161, 177; and Angola, 120;

Index

and boycott of Moscow olympics, 35, 161; Brezhnev, Leonid, cancellation of SALT summit in Washington, 126; Brown, Harold, visit to PRC, 1/80, 35; Cold War, 15; effect on, in Asia and the Pacific, 8; resumption of, 46, 120, 125, 186; and Cuban missile crisis, 11; and Czechoslovakia, 11, 17; Deng Xiaoping, visit to US, 2/79, 126; Detente agreements on strategic arms limitations, 17; end of bipolarity, 14; intermediate nuclear forces negotiations, 125, 127, 173, 186, 187; Partial Nuclear Test Ban Treaty, 1963, 9, 17, 20; periods of, 11, 13, 14, 17, 20; SALT II, 35; and Sino-American rapprochement, 10, 120, 121; and Hungary, 11; and Korean airliner incident, 42; level of relations, 117, 120, 121; Nixon, Richard, visit to Moscow, 1972, 185; nuclear parity, 113; and Poland, 11; Reagan Administration, effect on, 14, 185, 186; Reagan, Ronald, visit to PRC, 1984, 43; and Sino-American alignment against SU, 15, 80, 96, 115, 171, 176; and Sino-American rapprochement and normalization, 33, 121–22, 125, 126; and Sino-Soviet split, 126; and Soviet-Vietnamese alliance, 82; construction of new naval base, 86, 87; military presence in Indochina, 82, 83, 121, 126; threat to US Pacific fleet and Asian bases, 82, 84; TU-95 reconnaissance flights, 86; and U-2 incident, effect on, 20; and US embargo of grain and pipeline equipment to, 159, 161

Soviet-ASEAN (Association of South East Asian Nations) relations, and ASEAN zone of peace proposal, 87; and Sino-Soviet conflict, 87, 179; and Soviet threat, fear of, 88; and Soviet-Vietnamese relations, 83, 179; and Vietnamese relations with Thailand, 87

Soviet-Japanese relations, Chinese support of Japanese territorial disputes over Northern Island with SU, 30, 73; hostility, period of, 20; and Japanese-PRC peace treaty, 13, 74–5; Neutrality Pact, 1941, 25; Reagan, Ronald, visit to PRC, 1984, 43; Siberia, joint development of, 13; Sino-Japanese trade relations and, 20; Soviet-Japanese joint declaration on the normalization of relation, 17; US-Japanese security treaty, revised, effect on, 20; US-SU detente, effect on, 20

Soviet Union (*see also* Sino-Soviet relations, Soviet-Afghan relation, Soviet-American relation, Soviet-ASEAN relations, Soviet-Japanese relations and Soviet-Vietnamese relations); Afghanistan, invasion of, 11–12; Andropov, Yuri, death of, 42; referred to, 40; Brezhnev, Leonid Asian Collective Security Plan, 31; Brezhnev doctrine, 10; death of, 40; Cuban missile crisis, 11; Czechoslovakia, invasion of, 9; Hungary, invasion of, 11; Khrushchev, Nikita, 25; and de-stalinization campaign, 25, 27; peaceful coexistence policy, 28; leadership group characteristics, 44–5; military presence, in East Asia, 10, 81, 125, 173; Indochina, 120, 121, 126, 144, 166; Sino-Soviet border, 2, 10, 31, 35, 36, 38, 39, 41, 44, 91, 124, 126, 144, 180; Third World, 82, 147, 150; Vietnam, bases in, 82, 83; Pacific fleet, use of Vietnamese ports, 2, 82; Poland, 11; Soviet aid to, Afghanistan, 86; Cuba, 86; China, 26; Eastern Europe, 86; Egypt, 26; Ethopia, 86; India, 26; Kampuchea, 86; Vietnam, 2, 81, 85, 86, 126, 179; Sputnik, 28; Stalin, Joseph, neutrality pact with Japan, 1941, 25; Treaty with Chiang Kai-shek, 1945, 25; referred to, 26; World War II, Pacific phase, 8; occupation of Manchuria, 8, 26

Soviet-Vietnamese relations alliance, 1978, 2, 11, 33, 47, 143; China and, 82, 83, 124, Council of Mutual Economic Assistance, Vietnamese admission to, 1978, 11, 33, 86; Gromyko, Andrei support of Vietnam's proposal for SEA regional Conference, 87; as main threat to regional peace, 88; Nguyen Co Thach, on Soviet-Vietnamese relations and Vietnamese independence, 87; and Sino-American relations, 126; and Sino-Japanese rapprochement, 32; and Sino-Soviet relations, 101, 175, 178, 179; and Soviet aid to, 2, 82, 85, 86, 126, 179; and Soviet-ASEAN relations, 83; and Soviet military increase in naval capability, 82; presence in Indochina, 101, 126; use of Vietnamese bases and ports, 2, 82, 83, 84, 86; and Soviet support for Vietnamese invasion of Kampuchea, 2, 83; Vietnamese laborers in Soviet bloc countries, 86; Vietnamese move into Soviet camp, causes, 85, 126

Stalin, Joseph, death of, 27; neutrality pact with Japan, 1941, 25; referred to, 26, 27, 30, 45; treaty with Chiang Kai-shek, 1945, 25

Suzuki, Zenko, visit to PRC, 1982, 40

Tanaka, Kakuei, normalization of relations with PRC, 72–3; summit with Nixon, 1972, 71; visit to PRC, 1972, 72

United States (see also Japanese-American relations, Sino-American relations, Soviet-American relations, Taiwan), and Asia, position in communist takeover of South Vietnam, 8, 10; containment of communist threat, 96; defense of South Korea and Taiwan, 8; disengagement from Indochina, 10; and reduction of fores in East Asia, 10; effect of European Cold War on US-SU relations, 8; post-World War II Pax Americana, 8; and Vietnam war, 11, 71, 113; and escalation, 30; and non-recognition of Hanoi, 126; and relations with Western Europe, 17; domestic factors against recognition of PRC, 95; domestic views of foreign policy formulation: credos actors and reactors, 160; linkage politics, 160, 161; long-term visions v. short-term concerns, 162, 163; and other's foreign policy evolving view of international relations, 161, 162; monolithic and centralized policy processes, 158; motivational factors, 156, 157, 158, 174; rational actor model, 157, 158, 164; presidential leadership in foreign affairs, 158–59; stimulus-response approach to events interpretation, 159, 160, 174; and US foreign policy bureaucratic politics and organizational-processes model, 157, 174; diffused policy processes, 158, 159; environmental factors, 156, 157, 174; static view of international relations, 161; Marshall plan, 26; Military presence, Asia, 82; bases in

Philippines and Guam, 82; maritime supremacy, 82; and World War II, Pacific phase, 8

Taiwan (Nationalist China) (see also Sino-American relations) Chiang Kai-shek, treaty with Stalin, 1945, 25; Chinese policy of peaceful reunification with, 58; Civil war, 8; and claims to Spratly island, 89, 90; derecognition of, by Japan, 71, 75; by US, 96; economic growth, 101, 102, 136, 139; Japanese-American resolution to keep Taiwan seat at UN, 1971, 72; Japanese peace treaty with, 1951, 73, 74-5; Joint US-PRC Memorandum on, 8/82, 37, 55, 58, 60, 61, 66, 68, 96, 98, 144, 168; membership in Asian Development Bank, 62, 65, 168; membership in UN and Security Council seat, 8; nationalist government retreat to Taiwan, 1950, 95; Pan American flights resumed, 6/83, 62, 159; PRC-Taiwan reunification, 73-4, 104, 105, 168; Reagan, Ronald on US-Taiwan relations, 56, 59, 167; as reason for US non-recognition of PRC, 95; and role in US containment of communist threat in Asia, 96; Sino-American relations effect on US-Taiwan relations, 95, 103; strategic value of, 101; as counterweight to PRC and SU, 102, 103, 105; to US global interest, 101, 102, 104; Taiwan Relations Act, 97; arms sales, 98, 99, 105; definition of US policy toward, 97; effect on US-Taiwan trade, 98; implementation of, 98; provisions of, 98; Taiwan Straits crisis, 28; military balance in, 104, 105; trade with Japan, 75; with US, 101, 104; united front with SU against Chinese communists, 25; United States arms sales to, 37, 57, 58, 60, 61, 64, 77, 96, 104, 105, 168; coproduction of F-5E in Taiwan, 58; grant of diplomatic immunity to Coordination Council of North America Affairs, 57, 63, 168; normalization of relations with PRC and, 57, 76, 96; support of Chiang Kai-shek during Civil War, 160

Vietnamese-Kampuchean relations, and Chinese attack on Vietnam, 84; coalition government for Kampuchea, 178, 179; neutralization of Kampuchea as end to Chinese threat to Vietnam, 88; and Sino-Soviet rapprochement, 178; and Soviet-Vietnamese relations alliance, 11, 33, 47; support of Vietnam's invasion of 2, 83; Vietnamese membership in COMECON, 11, 33; and Vietnamese-ASEAN relations, 84; Vietnamese conditions for troop withdrawal, 85; invasion of, timing, 33; war, 2

Weinberger, Caspar, visit to PRC, 9/83, 41, 64, 66, 67, 169

Wu Xueqian, visit to Japan, 1983, 41; to Washington, 10/83, 64

Yugoslavia, 29, 30, 32

Zhang Aiping, on Chinese purchases of arms abroad, 77; rehabilitation of, 45; visit to France, 1984, 183; to US, 6/84, 117, 183

Zhao Ziyang, on PRC and US detente with SU, 1; quoted, 4, 99, 170; and Reagan's 1984 visit, 1, 143, 167, 174, 176, 183; referred to, 37, 138, 144, 166, 173; visit to Japan, 1982, 40, 75; and three principles for the development of Sino-Japanese relations, 75; visit to Thailand, 2/81 and support for Kampuchea's neutralization,

88; visit to US, 1/84, 43, 64, 65, 66, 77, 99, 100, 169; Western Europe tour, 1984, 1, 176, 183

Zhou En-lai, meeting with Kosygin, 1969, 31; with Nixon, 1972, referred to, 44, 113

About the Editor
and Contributors

James C Hsiung (Ph.D., Columbia University) is Professor of Politics at New York University. He is author of many books including *Ideology and Practice: The Evolution of Chinese Communism; Law and Policy in China's Foreign Relations;* etc. His latest work is: *U.S.-Asian Relations: The National Security Paradox* (ed.). Among his other works are *China in the Global Community* (coedited with Samuel S. Kim), and *Asia and U.S. Foreign Policy* (coedited with Winberg Chai). He is an Executive Editor for *Asian Affairs,* a consulting editor for *World Affairs* and for *Asian Thought and Society,* and President of the Contemporary U.S.-Asia Research Institute, Inc. He is working on a book on the Sino-U.S.-Soviet triad as a 3-person game.

Peter Berton is Professor of International Relations and Coordinator of the East Asian Regional Studies Program at the School of International Relations, University of Southern California. He received his M.A. and Ph.D. degrees from Columbia University (East Asian and Russian institutes). Editor Emeritus of *Studies in Comparative Communism,* Professor Berton is the author of among other works, "Direction and Analysis of U.S. Foreign Policy," in *Asia and U.S. Foreign Policy* (J.C. Hsiung & W. Chai, eds.) (Praeger), contributor and translator, *The Fateful Choice: Japan's Advance into Southeast Asia, 1939-1941* (Columbia University Press), and coeditor (with Paul Langer and George Totten) of *The Russian Impact on Japan* (University of Southern California Press).

Gavin Boyd is a professor of Political Science at Saint Mary's University, Halifax, Nova Scotia, Canada. He is editor of *Regional Building in the Pacific*; co-editor (with James N. Rosenau and Kenneth W. Thompson) of *World Politics: An Introduction*; co-editor (with Werner J. Feld) of *Comparative Regional Systems*; and author of many other works. Among his current research interests is the feasibility of a Pacific market-economy community.

Winberg Chai (Ph.D., New York University) is former Vice-President for Academic Affairs, and a professor of Political Science, University of South Dakota. He is author and co-author of many books on Chinese culture, history, and politics, including *The Search for a New China*. He coedited (with James V. Hsiung) *Asia and U.S. Foreign Policy*. A past president of the American Association for Chinese Studies, he is a member of the National Committee on U.S.-China Relations. He is currently a special adviser to the Kingdom of Saudi Arabia, and listed in *Who's Who in the World*.

Steve Chan (Ph.D., Minnesota) is Professor of Political Science, University of Colorado (Boulder). His research interests include foreign policy decision making, international conflict resolution, political economy, and China. He has authored or coauthored articles in a dozen scholarly journals, including the *American Political Science Review, Comparative Political Studies, International Studies Quarterly, Journal of Conflict Resolution, Journal of Peace Research,* and *World Politics*. Among his published books are: *Understanding Foreign Policy: The Chinese Case* (with Davis B. Bobrow and John A. Kringen); *International Relations in Perspective*; and *Foreign Policy Decision-making*.

Shao-chuan Leng (Ph.D., University of Pennsylvania) is Doherty Foundation Professor of Government and Foreign Affairs, and chairman of the Asian Studies Committee, at the University of Virginia. His publications include: *Japan and Communist China,* and *Justice in Communist China*. He is coauthor of *Sun Yat-sen and Communism*; coeditor of *Law in Chinese Foreign Policy*; and editor of *Post-Mao China and U.S.-China Trade*. His latest work is *Criminal Justice in Post-Mao China* (coedited with Hungdah Chiu).

Sheldon Simon (Ph.D., Minnesota) is Professor of Political Science, and Director of the Center for Asian Studies, at Arizona State University. He has taught at George Washington University, the Universities of Kentucky, Hawaii, and British Columbia, as well as Carleton University. He has lectured and conducted research on Asian security matters regularly throughout the Asian-Pacific. He is author or editor of five books and at least 50 articles and book chapters in scholarly volumes. His most recent book is: *The ASEAN States and Regional Security*.

George Oakley Totten, III (Ph.D., Yale) chairs the Department of Political Science at the University of Southern California. He was the first Director of the USC-UCLA Joint East Asian Language and Area Studies Center. He studied Chinese at Columbia, and Japanese at Michigan. He served as an Army Military Intelligence Japanese Language officer during and after World War II. He has authored, edited, and translated, sometimes with others, 8 books, and contributed to 12 others in addition to writing numerous articles on the politics, history, and culture of East Asia. The books include: *The Social Democratic Movement in Prewar Japan*;

Developing Nations: Quest for a Model; *The Whaling Issue in U.S.-Japan Relations*; and *Traditional Government in Imperial China*.

Stephen Uhalley, Jr. (Ph.D., University of California) is Professor of History, Director of the Asian Studies Program, and Acting Director of the Center for Asian and Pacific Studies, at the University of Hawaii. He is a Marine Corps veteran of the Korean War, and a former officer of the Asia Foundation. He was a Senior Fellow at the East-West Center, a Faculty Associate of the American Universities Field Staff, and Scholar in Residence at the Asia Society, in New York. He has written numerous articles on Asia, was editor of the *Journal of the Hong Kong Branch of the Royal Asiatic Society,* is the author of a biography of Mao Zedong, and has contributed the China profile in the *Yearbook on International Communist Affairs* each year for the past 12 years. He has traveled widely, including several visits to China and the Soviet Union.